THE LIBRARY OF HOLOCAUST TESTIMONIES

By a Twist of History

By a Twist of History

The Three Lives of a Polish Jew

MIETEK SIERADZKI

Introduction by Antony Polonsky

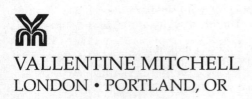

VALLENTINE MITCHELL
LONDON • PORTLAND, OR

First Published in 2002 in Great Britain by
VALLENTINE MITCHELL
Crown House, 47 Chase Side
Southgate, London N14 5BP

and in the United States of America by
VALLENTINE MITCHELL
c/o ISBS, 5824 N. E. Hassalo Street
Portland, Oregon 97213-3644

Website: http://www.vmbooks.com

British Library Cataloguing in Publication Data

Sieradzki, Mietek
By a twist of history: the three lives of a Polish Jew. – (The library of
Holocaust testimonies)
1. Sieradzki, Mietek 2. Jews – Poland – Biography
3. Holocaust, Jewish (1939–1945) – Personal narratives 4. Jews –
Cultural assimilation – Poland 5. Poland – Politics and government –
1945 –
I.Title
940.5'318'092

ISBN 0-85303-426-5
ISSN 1363-3759

Library of Congress Cataloging-in-Publication Data

Sieradzki, Mietek, 1921–
By a twist of fate: the three lives of a Polish Jew / Mietek Sieradzki;
introduction by Antony Polonsky.
p. cm. – (The Library of Holocaust testimonies, ISSN 1363-3759)
ISBN 0-85303-426-5 (pbk)
1. Sieradzki, Mietek, 1921– 2. Jews–Poland–Biography.
3. Diplomats–Poland–Biography. 4. Jews, Polish–Gr5eat
Britain–Biography. 5. Refugees, Jewish–Soviet Union–Biography.
6. Poland–Ethnic relations. I. Title. II. Series.

DS135.P63 S477557 2001
372.438'092–dc21
[B]

2001044569

Typeset in Great Britain by FiSH Books, London.
Printed in Great Britain by MPG Books Ltd., Bodmin, Cornwall

I dedicate this book to the memory,
ever green, of my mother and father.

Contents

Illustrations

The Library of Holocaust Testimonies

It is greatly to the credit of Frank Cass that this series of survivors' testimonies is being published in Britain. The need for such a series has long been apparent here, where many survivors made their homes.

Since the end of the war in 1945 the terrible events of the Nazi destruction of European Jewry have cast a pall over our time. Six million Jews were murdered within a short period; the few survivors have had to carry in their memories whatever remains of the knowledge of Jewish life in more than a dozen countries, in several thousand towns, in tens of thousands of villages and in innumerable families. The precious gift of recollection has been the sole memorial for millions of people whose lives were suddenly and brutally cut off.

For many years, individual survivors have published their testimonies. But many more have been reluctant to do so, often because they could not believe that they would find a publisher for their efforts.

In my own work over the past two decades, I have been approached by many survivors who had set down their memories in writing, but who did not know how to have them published. I realized what a considerable emotional strain the writing down of such hellish memories had been. I also realized, as I read many dozens of such accounts, how important each account was, in its own way, in recounting aspects of the story that had not been told before, and adding to our understanding of the wide range of human suffering, struggle and aspiration.

With so many people and so many places involved, including many hundreds of camps, it was inevitable that the historians and students of the Holocaust should find it difficult at times to grasp the scale and range of the events.

By a Twist of History

The publication of memoirs is therefore an indispensable part of the extension of knowledge, and of public awareness of the crimes that had been committed against a whole people.

Martin Gilbert
Merton College, Oxford

Biographical Note

Mietek Sieradzki was born in Kalisz, Poland, in 1921, where he attended secondary school. Following the German invasion of Poland, he fled to the Soviet Union where he did odd manual jobs – until 1941 in confinement. In 1945–46 he joined the staff of the Polish embassy and in 1946 he was sent via Warsaw to work at the Polish embassy in London as attaché. From 1950–53 he worked at the British Section of the Ministry of Foreign Affairs in Warsaw. The following year he was Secretary of the Polish Delegation to the Neutral Nations Repatriation Commission in Korea and from 1954–55 was acting head of the British Section at the Ministry of Foreign Affairs in Warsaw. He also worked from 1950–53 and 1954–55 as Polish–English interpreter at top government talks and conferences and as a guide to foreign VIPs. In 1956 he was Polish member of the International Commission for Control and Supervision in Cambodia with the rank of Minister Plenipotentiary and in 1957–61 Polish chargé d'affaires to Canada. From 1961–68 he took the post of Deputy Director of Department III at the Ministry of Foreign Affairs in Warsaw (dealing with English-speaking and Nordic countries).

In 1968 he left the foreign service and began teaching in Warsaw and doing odd translations into English. He emigrated to and settled in Britain in 1969 and the following year worked in the Overseas Branch of the National Westminster Bank in London. He finally settled at the BBC's External Services (later known as the World Service), first as Russian and Polish monitor at Caversham (near Reading) but for most of that period at the Polish Section in London, in later years as its deputy head. Retired in 1992, he wrote his memoirs in 1993–95.

Introduction

Mieczysław Sieradzki, the author of this fascinating memoir, is a great survivor. He was born into a poor and observant Jewish family in the town of Kalisz on the western border of the former Congress Kingdom in 1921 and at the age of three his parents moved to the small town of Zagórów, 60 kilometres. north of Kalisz, where his father's family lived. His father, a hard-working shoe-top maker (*cholewkarz*), was the second of seven children and came from a family who were followers of the Gerer rebbe, one of the most important hasidic leaders in central Poland. His mother, who came from a similar background and was the twelfth of 13 children, was much more secular and acculturated than her husband and exercised an enormous influence on the young Mietek. As he writes:

> Mother was a beautiful, vivacious woman...[Her] behaviour was generally untypical for a Jewish small-town woman of the time. She liked to read novels and listen to records played on our hand-cranked gramophone. I must have heard some of the records so many times that I would find myself singing or humming tunes from *Carmen*, *Rigoletto*, *Pagliacci*, *Aida*, Gounod's *Faust* and especially from operettas such as Lehar's *Merry Widow* and Kalman's *The Gypsy Princess* and *Maritza*.

It was due to her that Mietek attended not only a *heder* but a Polish government primary school in Zagórów, where he obtained a good general education. In order to ensure that he had a proper secondary education, his family sent him to a Jewish private secondary school in Kalisz (a considerable financial burden), where in addition to the general curriculum, which was taught in Polish, he studied three subjects in Hebrew: the Hebrew language, the history of the Jews and the Bible.

When the war broke out, it was his mother who persuaded him to flee eastwards, where she eventually was able to join him and they survived the war together in the USSR. His father remained in Kalisz and was eventually sent to the Warsaw Ghetto. He did not survive the war.

As the war came to an end Sieradzki, on the urging of his mother, moved to Moscow, where he made contact with the Union of Polish Patriots, the communist-dominated group which was to form the core of the post-war Polish government. Although he did not have strong political views and seems to have had little sympathy for communism, being motivated rather by a hope that the new Poland would be more just and prosperous than the pre-war country, his intelligence and linguistic skills (above all, his knowledge of Russian and English) gained him a position in the foreign service of the new government, which was then being established.

A great deal has been written on the involvement of Jews in Poland with communism and their role in the government after 1944. Certainly, post-war developments greatly stengthened the popular Polish identification of Jews with communism. In the civil war conditions of post-war Poland the Jewish community could only expect protection from the new communist-dominated authorities. More important, communists of Jewish origin played a significant, though not dominant role in the new regime. In the political apparatus, one could mention Jakub Berman, who was responsible for ideological and security questions on the Politburo of the Polish Workers' Party (PPR) and Roman Zambrowski, who had been one of the principal creators of the communist-dominated Polish army in the USSR.

Jews also played a key role in the cultural policy of the new regime. Writers of Jewish origin were prominent in *Kuźnica* (The Forge), a group of writers who hoped to restructure Polish cultural life in the new political conditions, drawing on the traditions of the Polish Enlightenment and avoiding as much as possible the extreme versions of Marxism and social realism. Among the principal Jewish members of the *Kuźnica* group were the literary critic Jan Kott, Adam Ważyk, Kazimierz Brandys, Paweł Hertz, Seweryn Pollak, Mieczysław Jastrun and Adolf Rudnicki. The most significant figure in the group was probably Adam Ważyk (1905–82). For close to ten years, to use the words of the critic Artur Sandauer, 'He was the official artistic authority. He wrote dramas which were immediately produced and inevitably failed; film scripts that were immediately shot and met with a similar fate; he excoriated Norwid for his petty-noble ideology and the producers of Coca-Cola for serving atomic death. He delivered a programmatic lecture at the Fifth Conference of the Association of Polish Writers and carried over Stalin's linguistic theses to the methodology of literary studies.'[1] Although he was later to repent his Stalinist past and make an important contribution to the thaw in Poland prior to 1956, he was seen by many in the Stalinist period as the official face of communist culture.

Jews were also widely held to play a key role in the security apparatus of the new regime. In his *Europe: A History*, Norman Davies writes that, in Poland, 'Popular knowledge...has always insisted that the notorious communist Security Office (UB) contained a disproportionate number of Jews (or rather ex-Jews) and that their crimes were heinous'. He goes on to concede that 'few hard facts were ever published', but claims that this point of view has become 'all the more convincing' because recent 'disclosures' have 'broken the taboo' and are particularly credible, since 'they were made by a Jewish investigator on evidence supplied by Jewish participants ...The study deals with the district of Upper Silesia, and, in particular, with the town of Gliwice (Gleiwitz).' Following its author, John Sacks, Davies claims that 'in 1945 every single commander and three-quarters of the local agents of the UB were of Jewish origin; that ex-Nazi camps and prisons were refilled with totally innocent civilians, especially Germans; and that torture, starvation, sadistic beatings, and murder were routine' (*Europe: A History*, pp. 10–22). However, Sacks' book *An Eye for an Eye: The Untold Story of Jewish Revenge Against Germans in 1945* is quite irresponsible and is little more than an

---

[1]Artur Sandauer, *O sytuacji pisarza polskiego pochodzenia żydowskiego w XX wieku (Rzecz którą nie ja powinienem byłt napisać)*, Warsaw, 1982, p. 50.

extended interview with Lola Potok, one of the Jews in the UB. In it, he produces no documentary evidence to justify his claims, which have been used to argue, in Davies' words, that 'in this light, it is difficult to justify the widespread practice whereby the murderers, the victims, and the bystanders of wartime Poland were each neatly identified with specific ethnic groups'.

Andrzej Paczkowski in Warsaw is doing pioneer research on this subject. He and Lech Głuchowski have made an assessment of the nationality of UB functionaries, making use of a confidential study prepared by the Ministry of Internal Affairs in 1978. According to this study, between 1944 and 1945, there was a total of 287 functionaries who held leadership positions in the UB. The number of those listed as having 'Jewish nationality' totalled 75. This meant that Jews made up 26.3 per cent of the UB leadership, while the figure for Poles was 66.9 per cent. The remaining 6.9 per cent were Russians, Belorussians and Ukrainians. The proportion of Jews at lower levels of the organization was considerably less. In another document Stanisław Radkiewicz informed Bolesław Bierut that the Security Office in November 1945 employed 25,600 personnel and that 438 (or 1.7 per cent) of them were Jews. Furthermore, the rapid increase in the number of UB functionaries that took place in 1945 occurred in a political framework which placed the political orientation and class origins of the candidate above almost all other considerations. To quote Paczkowski and Głuchowski:

The great majority of candidates actually consisted of young – and very young – political transients, with no professional experience and mixed reasons, if not questionable motives, for joining the UB. There was a constant movement of lower-level cadres in and out of the UB between and 1945 and 1946. At this time, approximately 25,000 employees left the UB: about the same number that were employed by the UB at the end of 1946. The majority had been released from the UB for drunkenness, theft, abuse, or for a lack of discipline.[2]

---

[2] Letter to the *Times Literary Supplement* around January 1997.

Sieradzki's memoir illuminates a somewhat neglected aspect of this problem, the situation of Jews in the Polish Foreign Ministry. He demonstrates convincingly that even during the Stalinist years from 1949 to 1955, professional criteria were largely observed in its functioning. He himself held a number of important positions and because of his excellent English was entrusted with taking the Indian Prime Minister Pandit Nehru around Poland. He was also a member of the Neutral Nations Repatriation Commission established at the end of the Korean War and after holding the position of head of the Polish mission in Canada, he returned to Poland where he served in the section of the Foreign Ministry which dealt with English-speaking countries. His career in the Polish Foreign Ministry came to an end as a result of the 'anti-Zionist' campaign in 1968, in which a group of younger party functionaries, led by Mieczysław Moczar exploited the alleged sympathy for Israel of the small number of Jews who had remained in Poland to purge them from official positions and make an unsuccessful bid for power. The account of 1968 in the memoir also adds to our understanding of what it meant for acculturated Polish Jews and their non-Jewish spouses.

Moving to England he obtained a position in the Polish Service of the BBC. While the broadcasts of the Polish Section of Radio Free Europe in Munich might have had a greater audience in Poland, what distinguished the BBC Polish Service, part of the BBC World Service – 'the Rolls-Royce of radio broadcasting' – was their accuracy and reliability. Here, his vast knowledge of Polish affairs and of the situation in the communist bloc was greatly appreciated. When he retired after 22 years in the BBC World Service in 1992, his expertise was recognized when he was asked to write and broadcast a weekly political commentary. Characteristically, as he put it, 'On reflection, I decided it was time to call it a day and gratefully declined'.

Throughout his two lives, in Poland and in England, he has been supported by his beloved wife Krystyna, for many years one of the mainstays of *Soviet Jewish Affairs*. We are delighted that this memoir will now appear as a tribute to both of them.

Antony Polonsky, *Brandeis University, 2001*

Foreword

Since I settled in Britain in 1969 I have on a number of occasions been urged to write my memoirs by people who knew something of my past or to whom I happened to relate some episodes of my life. I have always been reluctant to do so. Not just because while still professionally active, I could not spare the time or, to quote Sophocles, believed that 'one must wait until the evening to see how splendid the day has been'. Whatever the day, in my case, may have been, it was not so much the thought that it was not splendid enough that inhibited me. What I, a private person and an introvert by nature, recoiled from was the prospect of the ego trip and baring of one's soul I would have to indulge in while piecing together the story of my life for that story to be of any value. Moreover, I had doubts as to how faithfully I would be able to recount events by relying chiefly on my memory and whether what I still remembered of my experiences was worth sharing with others.

When I retired in 1992 other considerations prevailed. My son, who had in the past expressed the wish to read my reminiscences, now tried to persuade me to write them and even provided me with a word processor for the purpose. Moreover, having declined to write and broadcast regular political commentaries, which my employer urged me to do when I retired, and thus with time no longer being a problem, I had to find something less demanding to occupy my mind. What I set out to do was to write a family chronicle, or as much as I remembered of it, to reminisce on how a poor Jewish boy was transposed by a twist of history and misguided beliefs into an exciting career in the Polish foreign service but who in the process became painfully disillusioned and returned to his spiritual roots, and to give an illustration of the role Jews played in that service at a critical juncture of history. This latter strand I regard as unique because, to the best of my knowledge, nobody else has written about it and, considering how few of us are still around, nobody is likely to.

When I finally sat down to writing I found that reconstructing the story of my life, *inter alia*, through letters, photographs, press cuttings, amateur films and the like, though, regrettably, not official files (except for some British Foreign Office records), was emotionally and intellectually gratifying. However, facing up unreservedly and openly to my political and emotional past proved a trying experience. In fact, the entire exercise turned out to be more demanding than I had anticipated. And in the course of writing I often became acutely aware of what Churchill had in mind when saying about writing a book: 'In the beginning it's a toy, then a mistress, a master, a tyrant, at the end you [want to] kill it.' As for me, I very nearly shelved my manuscript when thinking of the prospect that both what I have written and what I may have left out or failed to elaborate upon might be misinterpreted or even distorted. But having made the effort, I put aside those misgivings.

I am greatly indebted to my wife for her invaluable advice, I am grateful to my brother Naftali, his wife Philippa and my close friend Janek Gelbart for reading the manuscript and offering valuable suggestions.

I also highly valued the appreciation, encouragement and suggestions of the late writer, Chaim Bermant, who read the first version of my manuscript, as well as the candidly critical, but very helpful remarks of my last BBC boss, Eugeniusz Smolar.

Part One

1 • *Childhood in Poland*

Kalisz

Kalisz, where I was born into a Jewish family in 1921, is a fair and most ancient Polish city – the most ancient in the sense that it has the oldest historical record, having been mentioned in the middle of the second century AD by Claudius Ptolemy in his *Guide to Geography* under the name of Calisia. It was one of the key points on the old amber route linking the Roman Empire with the Baltic coast. Results of archaeological research have confirmed the information handed down by the Alexandrian scholar.

Kalisz was (and probably still is) a beautiful city with numerous parks and profuse greenery covering about 60 per cent of its area. It also boasts many old churches and a fine theatre in a park extending on the banks of the River Prosna where boat races took place. Up to the Second World War the Prosna flowed in several arms through the city which was sometimes referred to as the 'Venice of the North'. The German occupiers filled up the river bed running along Babina Street where my maternal grandparents, some of my uncles and aunts and my closest school friend lived.

In the middle of the thirteenth century Kalisz received city privileges from King Bolesław the Pious who also granted a charter of rights to the local Jewish community, which was a model for the privileges later granted to Jewish communities in other Polish cities.[1] (That was about the time when Jews were being expelled from, among other places, England.) In fact Kalisz is reputed to have had the most ancient Jewish

3

community in Poland, the first Jews having arrived there in the twelfth century. A large group came to Kalisz from the Rhineland and other parts of Germany by way of Silesia in the middle of the thirteenth century. It is likely that my mother's ancestors were among them, since her maiden name was Berliner and her mother's maiden name was Luksemburg. (I still remember my great-grandmother of that name sitting on a bamboo chair at the ripe age of 94. She died at that age in about 1934.)

Before the First World War Kalisz (about halfway between Warsaw and Berlin) was the westernmost city of the Russian-occupied part of Poland and was the first to be taken by the Germans in 1914. The Russians withdrew without a fight. On the night of 3 August shooting broke out, allegedly provoked by the Poles. The German command under Major Preusker took 20 hostages and demanded a ransom of 50,000 roubles. Although the demand was met, those and other hostages were shot. Among them were my uncle and my grandfather, Mayer Berliner. My grandfather was the sole survivor and escaped by feigning death. He was, however, as a result, disabled for the rest of his life. At the command of Major Preusker, Kalisz was almost totally destroyed. Out of a population of 70,000 only about 5,000 remained. When I was born, three years after the war ended, the city was still largely in ruins. When I was three we moved to my father's little home town, Zagórów, about 60 kilometres north of Kalisz, where I spent my boyhood.

Zagórów

One of my earliest recollections is a day in June 1928, when I was exactly six-and-a-half years old. Heavy rain had been pouring all morning, but it had stopped by the time I was returning from *cheder* (Jewish religious elementary school). Somebody helped me over a wide overflowing gutter. As I was passing the water pump on the market square from which I used to fetch water, I noticed my father standing in front of the house in which we occupied a first-floor one-room flat. When, surprised, I asked him why he was outside he explained, in words I cannot now remember, that the doctor (there was only one in town) – or was it a midwife – was attending to Mother who was giving birth to a baby. That was when my brother Naftali – Ninek in Polish – was born.

Soon after that event we moved to a two-room flat nearly opposite the new fire station which my father and uncle, among other volunteers, had helped to build. In time we became friendly enough with our landlady, widow Majewska, and her two daughters to be invited to their Christmas Eve dinners. I remember my mother and myself joining in the carol singing. This was very untypical in a place where the Jewish community was socially completely separated.

I received my primary Jewish education in *cheder* (I still remember *shnayim ochzim b'talis...*[2] and the teacher who had the unseemly habit of plucking hairs from his ginger beard and sticking them under the desk), but I imbibed the Jewish traditions primarily in the home of my grandparents Sieradzki (the name derives from the town of Sieradz some 70 kilometres south-east of Zagórów). I visited them very often and especially for Friday evening Sabbath dinners when I would join Grandfather Abraham in singing joyous chasidic tunes, one of which I still remember. I also remember the delicious Sabbath *chulent*, *kugel* and other delicacies. And the Jewish holidays. It was at my paternal grandparents' home that I experienced the solemnity of *Rosh Hashana* and *Yom Kippur*, the fun of *Succot*, the joys of *Purim* and *Chanukah* (with the *Chanukah geld*), the mysteries of *Pesach* (at *Seder* it was I who asked the Four Questions of the *Hagadah*). To me it was a home of warmth and tenderness especially on the part of my father's younger sister, Aunt Bronka. I also remember with great affection the youngest sister, Genia, whom I had some difficulty in regarding as an aunt as she was just a few years older than me. (Many years later I was happy to see both sisters again in Israel.) Grandmother was also warm-hearted and kind, though she did not show it so much because of the diabetes she suffered from, which affected her greatly. Whenever Grandfather travelled to Warsaw to buy sole leather for his shop catering for the local cobblers, he would bring her a rare treat, grapefruit, which was believed to be good for diabetics. It was only in my grandparents' home that I saw this 'exotic' fruit until I came to the West.

I thought Grandfather was very orthodox and 'pious'. But this image paled in comparison with his son Lipman who lived with his family in the nearby district town of Słupca. He was so devout that he spent all his time on religious study. His poor wife not only had to manage an understandably run-down household (I once saw it) and look after five small children, but also to run their small leather shop. In time he became so learned that the local community offered him the position of rabbi. He declined, arguing that he could not accept remuneration for providing a religious service. Incidentally, the family on my paternal grandmother's side – her maiden name was Levi – had great rabbinic forebears, but, I never had the inclination or opportunity to investigate the genealogy.

To come back to Grandpa Abraham. He alone would not call me Mietek as everybody else did but Menachem-Mendel – my Jewish name preceded by its Hebrew equivalent. In his presence only Yiddish would be spoken at home, although when I heard him speaking to his invariably Christian, or strictly speaking Catholic, cobbler clients I thought his Polish was very good indeed. I was convinced his contacts with them were strictly of a business nature. Generally he seemed to me somewhat reserved and narrow minded. Yet many years later, when I revisited Zagórów after the war, I found out from one of those clients, Mr Łakomiak, the kind of conversations they engaged in. They talked not only about their own family lives (Łakomiak knew things about my parents that I had not known), but also about their respective religions. Łakomiak recalled Grandfather telling him: 'Your God and our God are really the same one God.' But then Łakomiak was not typical, he was not at all anti-Semitic.

The rather stern image I had of my grandfather was also softened years later when I visited Israel and Aunt Bronka showed me the letters of poetic tenderness he had written to his bride-to-be in a most elegant Hebrew handwriting.

Obviously as a child I could not have known the real man. What was certain though was that his was a strictly observant Jewish home. And it was from this home that the 19-year-old Shloyme (Szlamek) – my father-to-be who was the second of seven children – was married (through a matchmaker, how else?) to the 21-year-old Perla (Pola) Berliner, who was the twelfth of 13 children). One of the first things Pola did was to get rid of Szlamek's chasidic garb, even though she came from an equally strictly observant home and her father was also a Gerer (Góra Kalwaria) chasid. She even boasted of a family relationship with the Gerer Rebbe's Alter family – the Gerer Rebbe was the most revered chasidic sage at the time.

Father became a shoe-top maker (*cholewkarz* in Polish). His workshop was set up in the kitchen. For some time he even had an apprentice. I would often lend a hand in delivering the shoe-tops to his cobbler clients. Only once did I lose one shoe-top, but I can still remember the grief I felt. Most of Father's cobbler clients, including Łakomiak, were the same as Grandfather's. When, some 27 years later, I (and my wife) unexpectedly called on Mr Łakomiak I first asked him whether he knew who I was. A broad smile appeared on his face and he called excitedly his wife from the kitchen. 'Do you recognize him, old girl?', he asked. She did not. Then he said slowly: 'I know who you are all right, what I am not sure about is whether you are the older or the younger one' (meaning my brother). It was a very emotional encounter for both of us.

My recollection of Father at work is a very sad one. He seemed to work non-stop. When I woke up in the morning he was already at his bench and he was still there when I went to bed. He obviously did not work on the Sabbath or any of the Jewish holidays, but I can hardly remember him taking a vacation of any sort. He earned about 200 złotys a month which was hardly enough for a family of four. In order to tide him over the time between making his purchases and collecting the money from his clients he often had to borrow. The Polish words for promissory note and endorsement were in frequent use in our home. Overworked though he was, Father still found time for his two boys. He would help me with some of my homework, especially with drawing at which I was hopeless and he was good. But he was more strict in our upbringing than Mother, applying the occasional slap on the bottom.

He taught himself some accounting and acquired some other skills. By nature an introvert, he would not show his feelings. Respected as a very upright, unassuming and straightforward man (maybe too straightforward for his own good and that of his descendants who may have inherited the trait) he was chosen for a time as representative of the American Joint Distribution Committee in the local community. More importantly, he was elected and re-elected for several terms as one of the two aldermen representing the Jewish community in the 11-member town council. The other one was for a time Mr Kronman, an amateur artist and our family friend, whom I remember for the hurt he caused me, when upon my brother's birth he very unwisely teased me that Mummy would now love my brother rather than me.

Mother was a beautiful, vivacious woman. She was not happy with the arranged marriage. She did not love Father, as she admitted to me in later years, and stayed with him only because of us, her sons. She tried to enrich her drab life. For a time she worked as a manicurist and another time as a librarian. Occasionally an out-of-town theatre director by the name of Henryk Zylberberg would stage in Zagórów an amateurs' show in Yiddish. Mother would play the lead female part. I still vividly remember a scene from a show in which the heroine, a queen, played by my mother was about to be burnt at the stake. My brother and I, who were in the audience, started crying and my brother (or was it both of us) yelled out in terror, 'Don't burn my mummy!'.

Mother's behaviour was generally untypical for a Jewish small-town woman of the time. She liked to read novels and listen to records played on our hand-cranked gramophone. I must have heard some of the records so many times that I would find myself singing or humming tunes from *Carmen*, *Rigoletto*, *Pagliacci*, *Aida*, Gounod's *Faust* and especially from operettas such as Lehar's *Merry Widow* and Kalman's *The Gypsy Princess* and *Maritza*.

Other attractions were visits by family friends – the afore-mentioned Mr Kronman, and Mr Kiwała who used to play the principal male parts opposite Mother in the amateur theatre shows. From time to time Mother would go to Kalisz, Poznań or elsewhere to visit family or friends and to see an opera or a play.

I myself would go for my summer vacations, by dilapidated coach, to my maternal grandparents in Kalisz. I remember being woken in the early hours every morning by Grandpa Mayer studying Talmud or Tanach in monotonous *sotto voce*. Once or twice Grandma Trana would buy me a chasidic coat and cap, which on my return home mother would get rid of.

Mother's lifestyle was very hard on Father both financially and emotionally, although that latter aspect was not evident to me at the time. But as a child I never felt neglected by her. She loved and cared for us; she managed the household, such as it was; she cooked, washed and scrubbed. She had high hopes and ambitions for her sons. She wanted to develop my musical abilities and planned to provide violin lessons for me. But either the violin was too expensive or the lessons could not be afforded, so it ended with my taking a mandolin course at school. But first she had decided that *cheder* would not be a sufficient basis for my future education. The standard of its general knowledge tuition was very poor. So I was to be transferred to the local state school – in fact, the only school in town and in the area – to become the only Jewish child among several hundred Catholic pupils. As in all state-run schools in Poland there was Catholic religious instruction (a one-hour lesson per week) from which of course children of other denominations like myself were excused. There was no religious assembly nor prayers said in class before the start of lessons. Yet the decision to transfer me there could not have been an easy one for my mother.

About 20 per cent of Zagórów's 4,000 inhabitants were Jews. Many of them were small shopkeepers. In general, they were not better off than the Gentile population, but they were different, and they kept themselves to themselves.

Anti-Semitism was prevalent, apparently inspired or encouraged by the Catholic clergy. For the most part it was not violent although Zagórów had its pogrom in 1936 or 1937, when hundreds of peasants from the surrounding villages descended on the town centre. There were no fatalities, but a number of Jews were injured, and windows and shops were smashed. As my brother told me (I was in Kalisz at the time), one peasant climbed over the fence to the backyard of our grandparents' home. Our father and his elder brother, Mendel, who were strong men, threw him bodily back to where he had come from. This deterred others from scaling the fence.

9

How did anti-Semitism affect me as a child? Apart from the occasional stones thrown by Christian children when we were returning from *cheder*, for instance, what I remember most is fear. When I had to venture to the outskirts of town or beyond and I saw boys, especially if they had a dog, I would almost instinctively whisper (or just think of) the *Goymel* benediction, although even as a boy I was somewhat sceptical about the value of religious practices. I used the benediction to avert danger, although, in fact, it is used to give thanks for having been saved from danger or having recovered from illness. I also remember the fear of being attacked, especially on Catholic holidays like Good Friday (Jews being held collectively responsible for the death of Jesus), and Corpus Christi when the big Catholic procession through the town would keep us indoors and out of possible harm's way.

My transfer to the local state school has to be seen against this background. And yet I do not recall any special fear associated with that change in my life. What is more, I did not experience any open hostility on the part of my new class mates. Maybe this was partly due to the fact that I tried hard to fit in and get along with my peers. What I do remember, however, is that the singing teacher, Wróblewski, who was reputed to be anti-Semitic, would always call me Shmul, which I took to be an expression of anti-Semitism. When I finally plucked up courage to remind him in front of the class that my name was Mietek, he explained that he had once had a Jewish pupil of that name whom he liked and that was why he called me Shmul. Despite my objection he continued to call me by that name. Also, although I did not attend Catholic religion classes, strangely enough the catechist seemed to take a liking to me and would sometimes talk to me during break time. I recall him playing a mathematical game with me several times until I got the knack of it and knew how to win. I remember the game to this day.

I think it was in 1935, when I was in the seventh and last grade of primary school, that the school organized a trip to several cities in Poland. My parents had to contribute 22 złotys to the cost, the rest being covered by the school. It was my first chance to see what I considered a big city like Poznań. We were promised that first we would visit the city's zoo, so when we were led downstairs into a beautiful, clean, tiled place I assumed that that was the zoo. It turned out to be a public lavatory! Strangely enough, I have no recollection of the zoo itself.

What I do remember is our visit to the opera. However, my only recollection of that occasion is an incident during an interval. Our seats were high up in the balcony, and I was sitting at the end of our group. Next to me in the other direction sat a priest and another group of schoolchildren he was evidently in charge of. When the curtain went down the priest struck up a conversation with me and referred to the Jewish character who had apparently appeared in the scene we had just seen on stage. What followed was a fierce diatribe against Jews: how dirty, repugnant, greedy and much else they were. I was too upset and angry to utter a word. My friends sitting next to me could hardly contain their laughter. The priest, somewhat nonplussed, asked them why they were chuckling. One of them plucked up courage and said: 'Mietek *is* a Jew.' Greatly embarassed, the priest completely changed his tune – what he had said before was true only of the few really bad Jews, but he respected and even liked Jews like me. Some fake compliments followed. The priest's behaviour was not entirely uncommon, but I was disgusted. No wonder I was oblivious to much of what went on on the stage.

The next leg of our excursion was Częstochowa with its monastery of Jasna Góra, the holy of holies of Catholic Poland, which was visited by thousands of pilgrims every year. We were put up in a pilgrims' hostel and slept on mattresses on the floor. Early in the morning I was woken by a burning sensation on my face. When I touched it I realized my face had been smeared with black shoe polish. I was the only one to have been treated in this way but I do not remember complaining about it. It would not have done any good anyway. I just assumed that the religious fervour of the place prompted someone to play that prank on the Jew.

The big occasion was to be, of course, a visit to the monastery. I was a bit nervous, but what I did not expect was that mass would be in progress on our arrival. When my group joined the congregation in kneeling down I was awe-stricken. On the one hand, I was terribly afraid to stick out as

11

the only one standing, but on the other, my Jewish upbringing held me firmly back from going down on my knees. The school headmaster leading our group must have noticed my predicament and told me over the heads of the group: 'Mietek, you may remain standing.' That was a tremendous and unexpected relief. Ironically, after war broke out it transpired that the headmaster, an ethnic German, had been a spy for Nazi Germany.

My going to the 'Polish' school and Mother's secularist and assimilationist tendencies did not mean that I was alienated from Jewish traditions and causes. I continued to visit my grandparents, and I do not recall any overt negative reactions on their part to what they must have regarded as one more of my mother's assimilationist 'antics'. I went to synagogue with Father. I remember being prepared for my *bar-mitzvah*. It was with some trepidation that I mounted the synagogue *bimah* (raised dais) to read or rather intone the relevant portion of the Torah. If there was any *bar-mitzvah* party, it must have been a very modest one. I also remember being taught how to put on *tefillin* (phylacteries). I took an interest in Zionism and briefly joined the *Hashomer Hatzair* (The Young Guard).

I think it was in 1935 that Father received a tragic message and told Mother to go to Kalisz, because her mother was very ill. In fact she had already died, but he was trying to soften the blow. Grandmother was killed in a ghastly accident. She was crossing the road over a bridge near her home, when an approaching taxi struck her. She had tried to stop it by raising her hand but was hit, thrown up and smashed her head against the kerb, her brain splattering on the pavement. It turned out the taxi was carrying a newly wed couple from their wedding reception and the driver was drunk. Mother, who loved her mother deeply, was inconsolable. As she told us, there had been a huge crowd at the funeral, including Christians. Apparently Grandma had been very popular.

Back in Kalisz

Mother was determined that I should continue my education after completing primary school. As there was no secondary school in Zagórów she made arrangements with those of her brothers and sisters who lived in Kalisz and who could afford it to take turns in putting me up until we as a family could move there. For the two years 1935–37 I changed lodgings monthly from one uncle or aunt to another. It was difficult but quite bearable. It was only in 1937 that my parents were able to move to Kalisz. We lived in a poor two-room flat with an outside rat-infested lavatory in Szopena Street opposite the well-known Fibiger piano factory. In fact, it was a bedroom-cum-dining room and a kitchen which served also as a bathroom of sorts and Father's workshop.

I attended the Jewish secondary school for four years until the war. Apart from the general curriculum, including Latin which was taught in Polish, we had three Judaic subjects in Hebrew: the Hebrew language, the history of Jews and the Bible. I was one of the best pupils in class, but I had an aversion to learning anything by heart, poetry in particular, whether it be Adam Mickiewicz or Chaim Nahman Bialik. Maybe my poor memory is the price I have paid for it. I remember, however, Mother telling me one morning that I had sat up in bed in the middle of the night and recited while still asleep: '*Quo usque tandem abutere Catilina patientia nostra...*' (from Cicero's denunciation in the Roman Senate).

In order to earn some pocket money I used to coach the children of better-off families. I recall one podgy father who would come in during the coaching of his boy, make some condescending comments and jingle the coins in his pocket. It was at that time that I took a dislike to the rich and ostentatious. Some of the money earned in this way I lost playing poker with my best classmates Janek (Jakub) Gelbart and Jumek Madowicz, and with Janek's brother-in-law, who was usually the winner.

Despite our poverty these were happy years for me. But the ominous clouds of war were gathering. We were generally aware that war was imminent but had no idea what was in store for us. I, as a 17-year-old and not at all politically inclined, had only a hazy notion of what was going on in the world. However, I was aware of the German-Jewish refugees crossing the border into Poland, I heard all sorts of amateurish speculation and I was also under the influence of Mother's instinctive fears.

Notes

1   The first item in the Statutes of Kalisz was a guarantee of the Jews'
    security – anyone accused of killing a Jew had to pay with his own life.
    This was the first time in the Middle Ages that the death penalty for
    killing a Jew was introduced in Europe. A second vital clause in the
    Statutes was the punishment for stealing Jewish children and pressing
    them into Christianity. This, too, was a novel guarantee and protection
    which the Jews elsewhere did not enjoy.
2   First words of a legal case in Talmudic studies relating to two men
    'getting hold of a prayer shawl' they had found.

2 • The Trials of War and Exile

Go East Young Man

On 1 September 1939 Nazi Germany attacked Poland and the Second World War began. As a result of the 23 August Ribbentrop–Molotov Pact the eastern part of Poland was invaded by the Soviets on 17 September. A new partition of Poland had thus been brought about.

A few days after the outbreak of war and before the Germans overran Kalisz, my father and I headed east in an attempt to reach Łódź where my mother and brother were to join us later. There was practically no civilian public transport at the time, so for the most part we travelled on foot. We would sleep in the open fields and wake up shivering. German planes flew above us apparently to raid Warsaw and on the way they strafed the fleeing civilians. Some people right next to us were hit, and human corpses and dead horses lay along the roadside. We also came across some dejected troops from Polish army units retreating in some disarray. When asked why they were retreating they would say that they were regrouping to engage the Germans at a more convenient place.

As history records, Poland was the first victim of Hitler's aggression to put up a resolute resistance. However, it had to wage that desperate September campaign alone. Britain and France, though they declared war on Hitler in accordance with their treaty obligations, were unprepared for it. The Soviet 'stab in the back' invasion made Polish resistance hopeless. And Hitler employed his air force in the most savage way by indiscriminately bombarding towns and villages,

15

peasants working in the fields and us – the wretched refugees on the roads – terrorizing the entire population.

Eventually, German troops caught up with us near the town of Opatówek. We were detained by the Todt military labour organization and made to work on a road. On one occasion when I stopped for a rest from digging a trench, the soldier guarding us did not react until he saw his sergeant coming. Pointing to the sergeant he urged me to resume digging straight away. We were not given any food and it was only at the end of the day, when we were taken to a big barn, that there was black *ersatz* coffee from a bucket for us. In the barn a couple of officers would taunt us by saying it was the Jews who had provoked the war. I alone was silly and naïve enough to try and argue with them. (I had learnt German in school.) I had never read anything to suggest that, I told them. One of the officers got angry and threatened to kill me in the morning. When I started crying, he took out his revolver, put it to my temple and said: 'If you don't stop crying I'll shoot you now.' Looking slightly sideways I saw a red-haired soldier standing behind a pillar indicating to me with his finger on his mouth to keep quiet. Eventually, they let everyone go except me. They would not let Father stay with me, and he waited outside. When finally they did let me go it was already curfew time and Father and I were scared. We were walking briskly when we heard quick footsteps behind us which naturally increased our fear. A soldier caught up with us. It was the red-haired one from the barn. He walked with us and, greatly agitated, told us that this madness – meaning the Nazi-imposed war and the atrocities – could not last. He was an Austrian communist and said emphatically that the six million people who had voted for the communists in Germany would not allow it to continue.

When we reported for work the next morning, the officer with whom I had argued the previous evening was in charge. Before we set out for the road construction, he ordered that I, '*der Student*', should carry the heavy wooden stamper. He would not permit Father to carry it for me and I had to cope with the heavy load as best I could.

It was on the third or fourth day that they released us. We eventually reached Łódź and got in touch with Mother's youngest sister Sara (Sala) who lived there. There were food shortages in the city. Queues formed in front of bakeries, one for Christians and a much longer one for Jews. As I did not look Jewish I would join, with pounding heart, the much shorter 'Christian' queue. So at least we had bread. We stayed in Łódź only briefly. There seemed to be no point in fleeing further as the Germans had caught up with us, so we returned to Kalisz.

We did not yet know what the Germans had in store for us, but Mother was restless and intuitively very apprehensive. She was determined that we should all move east and before anything was finally decided, resolved that I should go first, preferably with some of my classmates. She went to Janek's parents to persuade them to let him go too. They were very reluctant; she apparently had to bang on the table to make her point before they eventually agreed. She thus saved his life. Father deftly sewed a 50-złoty banknote, which was a lot to us, into my belt and I, having said my good-byes and hoping we would all somehow be reunited, was on my way. I had no premonition that this would be the last time I saw my father. He has since always been in my thoughts and my heart. Nor did I realize the gravity of the step I was taking towards an unknown future.

By then the trains were running again. Janek and I set out on our perilous journey on 14 November 1939. We were joined by the third of our threesome, Jumek. The train was dirty and we caught lice. Jumek, coming from a better-off home, could not bear it and was also very homesick, so he returned to his family in the town of Błaszki. He did not survive the war.

Janek and I reached Warsaw where we stayed for a while at his uncle's house. We then continued eastwards towards what was then called the 'green line' between German-occupied and Soviet-occupied Poland, assuming the Soviets would allow refugees to cross the 'line'. We travelled part of the way by horse-cart. It was then that we saw German soldiers setting their dogs on some unfortunate people who were trying to scramble up a fence in an attempt to escape them. The dogs were tearing at their clothes and biting them. We considered ourselves lucky to be able to proceed unharassed. We were heading for the border village of Małkinia, in the region of Białystok.

While walking towards the 'green line' we found ourselves

at the edge of a forest. At a little distance there was a single hut, in front of which stood a German soldier. When he saw us he ordered us to approach him, which we did. He led us into the hut and we were told to stand at the end of a line of about half a dozen men being inspected by another German soldier. He ordered everybody to hand over any money or valuables they had; otherwise, he warned us, there would be dire consequences. Janek and I gave him some coins saying we had nothing more. I had no intention of parting with the 50-złoty banknote sewn in my belt. Then he led us into a second room. What we saw there was quite unexpected and frightening. More than a dozen men were standing in circles round the middle of the room. The men in the inner circle were stripped of their clothes which were being minutely inspected by three seated soldiers. Even heels were torn from their shoes to see if anything was hidden there. As the last arrivals, Janek and I were placed in the outer circle close to the wall. While we were contemplating the seriousness of our situation, a girl whispered in my ear: 'Come with me.' I half suspected a trap, but we had nothing to lose so we followed her. The teenager led us out of the room and down what seemed to be a tunnel or just a cellar with an exit into the wood. We were saved and happy. But then Janek realized that in the confusion he had left his rucksack behind containing everything he possessed. Courageously, or foolishly, he decided to return for it and I waited for him with bated breath. Finally he returned safely with his rucksack. We could not believe our good luck. We never had a chance to discover the identity of the girl who saved us, but she was probably the daughter of the Polish owner of the hut.

We were now able to reach the 'green line'. We found ourselves in an open field amidst a crowd of other refugees pressing forward towards the 'line', while Soviet soldiers, trying to keep us away, shouted: '*Davay nazad! Davay nazad!*' (Move back! Move back!) – the first Russian words I ever heard. The Soviets were letting the refugees in only at certain times. Eventually we were allowed to cross into Soviet-occupied territory, and we had the Germans behind us for good.

We went first to Białystok where Janek met up with his brother and stayed there for a while. I headed on towards the city of Lvov where Janek and his brother eventually joined me. These journeys took us some time. Often we had nothing to eat for a day or two except maybe onions on one occasion, or sugar on another, which put us off eating either for a long time. In Lvov I had an address of a family who had given shelter to a cousin of mine from Kalisz, Beniek Berliner. I arrived there just after midnight to find that Beniek was no longer there. However, the host couple got out of their bed and offered it to me. I never forgot their great kindness.

I managed to enrol in a local school, even though our intention was to go south in order to cross the border to Romania. We eventually went to Kosov, where we waited for a guide and the right time to be smuggled across the mountain frontier. While there we paid a visit to the Kosover Rebbe, Chaim Hager, who made us most welcome. (The rebbe was later murdered by the Germans, but his rabbinical family is well known in Bnei Brak in Israel.) As time was dragging on I decided to go back to school in Lvov, and we agreed that Janek would summon me to Kosov as soon as the crossing of the frontier became possible. However, the opportunity to do so came so suddenly that Janek could not miss it by waiting for me and went to Romania where he survived the war.

In the meantime my mother and brother had arrived in Lvov. My father had stayed behind because, as my mother maintained, he wanted to dispose of our meagre possessions before joining us. However, after the war, I was told by his youngest brother, Yitzhak, an Auschwitz survivor, that my father had taken this opportunity to detach himself from my mother. Whatever the reason, it cost him his life and left us, his sons, without a much-loved and needed father. (Incidentally, in the few weeks that Polish troops had managed, patchily, to fight the German invader, Yitzhak was a non-commissioned officer in the Uhlans (cavalry). It was rare for a Jew to be in that formation.)

My brother remembers things slightly differently. According to him Father's staying behind may have been the result of an unfortunate accident. Mother had taken my brother to a tailor somewhere in our neighbourhood, where they were to pick up two suits she had ordered for him – a great occasion for him considering our family's very modest resources. As they were leaving, someone came running in great panic, telling them that the area where we lived had been cordoned off by the Germans and that some special forces were searching for Jews. Mother instantly decided not to go back home and with what little money she had on her to proceed forthwith to Warsaw where she had some relatives. They managed to get to the capital by train and reach the flat of Mother's cousin. Other refugees were there and my brother remembers that they slept some ten to a bed. Mother was restless and resolved to leave Warsaw and travel east to join up with me. When they reached the River Bug, separating the part of Poland occupied by the Germans from that occupied by the Soviets, on a very dark and frightening night, Mother somehow found a farmer with a boat, who was willing to risk ferrying them across the river in return for payment. As they were crossing the river they were spotted by German soldiers who started shooting at them. Soon shots were coming also from the Soviet side. Miraculously they escaped unharmed and reached the other side from where they proceeded to Lvov. Throughout this ordeal my brother recalls that on a number of occasions Mother's courage, initiative and resourcefulness saved their lives, just as he remembers with great affection Father's calm courage and reassuring presence during numerous brushes with the Germans at home.

My mother and brother found accommodation in one place, and I lived elsewhere with my cousin from Kalisz, Natek Kempiński, who had also arrived in Lvov. The two of us made a modest living as street vendors selling cigarettes and headache-powder. We would stand on a corner and shout: *'Prapory! Kogutki!'* (a cigarette brand and a headache-powder). On one occasion a 'wholesaler' was to sell us a batch of merchandise, and we were to strike the deal at the Mikolasza pedestrian passageway. Once there, with no one else around, one of the two so-called 'wholesalers' pulled out a very long knife and demanded that we hand over both the money and the merchandise, which in the circumstances we did.

Exile

In June 1940 the Soviets decided to remove all those they considered unreliable elements, including the refugees, from the areas adjacent to the German-occupied territories. A mass exile followed, mostly to Siberia. In the small hours of one morning Natek and I were woken up, ordered to dress and to follow the soldiers (presumably of the NKVD, later KGB) into trucks. A brief interrogation followed and our particulars were taken down. We were asked, *inter alia*, whether we had any close family in Lvov. This turned out to be important. Having declared that I had my mother and brother there, I was to be taken to a *posyolok* – a settlement for families – and was promised to be reunited with them. Natek, on the other hand, who had no close family in Lvov, was taken to a much harsher labour camp, which he fortunately survived. I had no idea what was happening to my mother and brother, but I later learned they had been taken to another *posyolok*.

The journey by train in atrocious conditions in cattle trucks took a very long time and we never knew where we were being taken. I was alone and miserable. One family (Lubelski) travelling in the same truck tried to console me. Eventually we were transferred from the train to a creaky river-boat, where we slept on the floor pestered by mice, lice and other vermin. All this was extremely hard to bear and it was a great relief when at long last we disembarked on the riverbank near a forest. But little did we know what awaited us.

We were told to build shacks for ourselves. The situation was very chaotic and there was much misery. On one occasion, for instance, when we were short of nails for the shacks, we were ordered to remove them from a fence we had just built. We were admonished and repeatedly reminded: *priviknyesh, priviknyesh, nye priviknyesh zdohnyesh* (you will get used to it, if you don't, you will die). And we did get used to it, in order to survive, all the hardships notwithstanding. One problem was the mosquitoes. In the open we suffered greatly from them. We could not imagine a harsher punishment for Hitler and his henchmen than tying them naked to the trees there and leaving them for the deadly insects to finish them off slowly.

Eventually we found out where we were: the place was called Zimnyi (meaning wintry), *nomen omen*. Situated amid marshes and forests, it was close to the rivers Sos'va and Loz'va, about a hundred kilometres east of Serov, in the region of the Northern Urals.

Once we had settled in somehow, my first job was to chop rough pieces of wood into wedges for joining logs into rafts. Masses of logs were floated from the region. The normal daily output was 150 wedges per person. On the first day I produced 30 and in the process I inadvertently hit my left thumb with the axe, from which I still have a small scar. When told that some Stakhanovites produced three times the normal daily output, that is 450 wedges, I was utterly incredulous. And yet after a couple of months or so I managed to produce up to 300 a day, and thus earned the privilege of getting *blinis* (pancakes) with my evening meal. They tasted delicious.

In the autumn I was moved to the more demanding job of lumberjack. We had to learn the skill of felling trees and soon became adept at choosing the right tree and the right spot where the tree would have room to fall. The way to do it was, first, to partially cut the tree from the side it inclined to – the direction it would fall – with saw and axe. The next step was to saw it from the opposite side starting slightly higher than the front cut until the weight of the trunk would break the tree away from the stump. Quite often, however, there was not enough room for the tree to fall, and it would lean on the branches of another tree. Then, of course, we would cut that other tree and the two would fall to the ground. Sometimes the two trees would fall on a third and the third on a fourth, and so on, until eventually the last tree would fall and bring all the other trees down too. The difficulty, however, grew with the number of trees that would not fall down, because it became increasingly perilous to be felling the last tree and finding a safe spot between the falling trees to avoid getting crushed by them.

On one occasion we had cut down 13 trees which had not fallen and which were all leaning on a fourteenth. We were told it was too risky for us to cut the fourteenth tree ourselves. An 'expert' lumberjack was summoned from a neighbouring labour camp to do it. He was an ethnic German 'political' prisoner with two or three university degrees, who was serving a 25-year sentence. It was fascinating to watch how he coped with this tricky task. The last bit of sawing of the fourteenth tree he did by himself, though it was a long saw for two, in order not to expose anybody else to danger. However, the major problem was to find a safe place to hide when all the 14 trees would come crushing down. When a tree comes down, especially under such a heavy weight, it breaks sooner and it 'kicks back' somewhat, the cut-off end of the trunk coming to rest on the stump. So the safest position he evidently planned for himself and used, as soon as the tree began breaking, was to lie down under and along the end of the trunk next to the stump. The rest of us watched with apprehension from a safe distance, then with admiration we congratulated him as he clambered out from among the welter of felled trees.

I forget what was the daily norm for tree felling, but what I do remember is what my red-haired work mate, Heniek, said when we started; that if we ever fulfilled the norm I might call him Hans (a hated German name). As it happened we soon did fulfil and even over-fulfil the norm and from that time onwards we called him Hans, so that now I am no longer quite sure whether his real name was indeed Heniek.

Our path to work was another ordeal. It was winter, and we rose in the dark. First we collected our daily one-kilogram ration of brown bread, which I usually put under my quilted jacket in an attempt to prevent it from freezing. It then took us about an hour-and-a-half to walk the distance of some seven kilometres to work, but when we arrived it was still dark. We would light a fire and rest around it for a while. The bread was meant to be for lunch, but I could never wait that long. I would sharpen the end of a branch, stick the bread on it, hold it near the flames and start to eat around the defrosted edges, leaving half of it or less for lunch.

The coniferous wood certainly had a great pristine beauty. However, our circumstances, the hard work and the bitterly cold weather put us in no mood to admire the surroundings. The temperatures were so low that on the way to work some of my workmates suffered frost-bitten noses, ear lobes or toes. The statutory temperature limit for working outdoors was −46°C, but I remember that on one occasion we worked at −52°C, which, had I not experienced it myself, I would now find difficult to believe. We did not feel the cold so much because there was no wind at all in the forest and while working we sweated even in those temperatures.

When eventually I had worn my felt boots (*valonki*) into holes my big toes became frost-bitten, which probably caused the pain I developed in my knees. I went to see the settlement NKVD doctor, who was a young, very pretty, if somewhat plump, dark-haired woman, probably also exiled. I thought she took a liking to me. Anyway, having examined my knees she took me off the tree-felling work. I was transferred to lighter work, though not for long.

Next I was assigned to the building of a canal between the rivers Sos'va and Loz'va. The work was supervised by a Chinese civil engineer, an inmate of a neighbouring labour camp. It was late winter or early spring 1941. First we hacked grooves in the ground, which was frozen up to a depth of about half a metre, to form squares of about 60 by 60 centimetres. We then prised out the frozen cubes of earth with crowbars, and the digging could begin. We dug through various layers of earth; first hard, then softer clay that was difficult to dig through, and eventually mud. Halfway down the V-shaped canal ditch, we placed platforms made of several boards. Those digging up the mud below would throw it on to the platform, so those standing on the platform could throw the mud out of the ditch.

The 'free' Russians living in the area were not much better off than we were. I recall one family where the father was a highly skilled engineer in a nearby defence factory. He earned a pittance even though he was in the highest grade. Anyway, there was not much for him to spend it on. In fact the family lived on what they grew themselves in the small plot they had at the back of their ramshackle cottage.

Family Reunited

As soon as I found out where we were I wrote to my erstwhile hosts in Lvov. My mother did the same. And thus through that family in Lvov we found out about each other's whereabouts. Mother at her end and I at mine petitioned the NKVD to have us reunited. Mother was particularly insistent and pestered her local authorities. Over seven months later, escorted by an armed NKVD soldier, I travelled by train to join my mother and brother. On the way through Sverdlovsk I remember seeing posters announcing performances by the best-known of the pre-war Jewish comedians in Poland, Dzhigan and Shumacher.

I finally arrived at Suslonger Desyatyi Kilometr (Tenth Kilometre), in the province of Yoshkar Ola of the Maryiskaya Autonomous Republic (over 600 kilometres east of Moscow). It was an NKVD settlement like the one I had been in, but conditions were somewhat better. The first employment of my mother, who knew Russian (her home town , Kalisz, had been in the Russian part of Poland prior to the First World War), was to deliver mail. Later she worked as a telephone operator. My brother was sent to work in the forest where he was chopping wooden blocks to feed the local generator. His later job was building railway tracks. This region was also densely forested and produced plenty of logs. I had to join the menfolk in rolling the logs on to railway platforms. Despite the tough and isolated conditions in the settlement, the Jews there managed to develop some social and cultural life. My brother participated in the children's artistic group. There were a few girls in the settlement but practically no boys of my age, so I was soon initiated into manhood.

It was there that the alarming news of our father being in the Warsaw Ghetto reached us through our cousins, the Albersteins who had fled from Kalisz to Vilno. We also found out Father's address and wrote to him. Father apparently wrote back several times, but only one postcard ever reached us. The postcard, which I have kept as a sacred memento, was addressed in Russian; Father's address in Warsaw was given as Nowolipki 7/14, the Warsaw post-office stamp in German was dated 19.IV.41. Father first addressed me and then apologized to my mother and brother for doing so and explained that this was because he had been deeply touched by my postcard to him. In that postcard I had written, among other things, that his somewhat strict way of bringing me up had helped me to survive the hardships I had to endure. He expressed joy at my reunion with my mother and brother, and wrote: 'I would give up much of my life to be able to see you all.' He asked me to write to him at least once a week. This was the last message we ever received from him.

'Freedom'

Following the German attack on the Soviet Union, the Polish government-in-exile concluded an agreement with Moscow in July 1941, signed in London by Prime Minister Sikorski and Soviet Ambassador Ivan Maisky. Under this agreement all Polish detainees were to be released and given freedom to choose where they wanted to live within the Soviet Union, with the exception of restricted areas. Our family's prime desire was to go somewhere south where it was warm. We thought of moving to the historic and exotic city of Samarkand, but we never reached it. However, we did travel south, first to Saratov, and eventually we settled in the city of Astrakhan at the mouth of the Caspian Sea. The smell of fish was overwhelming, but they were delicious and came in many different varieties. Other Polish Jews had also come to Astrakhan.

Some of us soon got work in the port. My first job was in a workshop producing huge boilers. This entailed hammering large metal sheets inch by inch to make them curve. I and another worker, standing opposite each other, would alternately swing big, heavy sledgehammers and strike the sheet, the hammers passing only inches away from the other's head. Good for the growth of biceps the job may have been, but it was a high-risk one for the skull especially as both of us were beginners.

Fortunately we soon managed to become dockers and organized ourselves into a 12-man Polish brigade (working gang) with our own foreman. I was its secretary. After some months we came second in a 'socialist competition' with 13 other brigades. The work was very hard; there were very few conveyer belts, and for the most part we had to carry loads into or out of the ships on our shoulders or backs. Flour came in sacks of 60 kilograms, sugar and rice in sacks of 90 and 100 kilograms, cotton in square hard bales of more than 100 kilograms which were wheeled on trolleys, and wool came in huge softer oblong bales carried on the back and held with a hook from the front. They weighed anything from 100 to over 200 kilograms. I could carry bales of up to 150 kilograms, but we were told of some stout and experienced dockers who could carry bales of up to 300 kilograms. On one rare occasion we were offered a privately paid job of transferring boxes of glass from one ship to another. They were carried on special supports strapped on the back from the shoulders. The gangway between the two ships was somewhat slippery, due to frost or water. I remember carrying a particularly heavy box of thick glass, which apparently weighed 150 kilograms, and being held by two of my workmates so I did not slip.

Eventually we decided collectively to hire ourselves out for work on a ship going to the southern Caspian port of Krasnovodsk. Our intention was to join the Polish Army of General Anders which was stationed there at the time prior to leaving the Soviet Union for Iran. We naturally wanted to take our families with us. This made our intention pretty obvious, and it took some hard pleading. Three of us, including the foreman and myself, went to see the rear-admiral, who was head of *Kaspflot*, our employer, to plead with him to let us go. He must have been a very tense and irascible man for when a telephone call interrupted our visit he smashed the receiver to pieces because it would not work. But he promised to consider our request.

We were all finally allowed, together with our families, to board a ship, also named *Astrakhan*. When we set out on our 90-kilometre journey on the Volga canal towards the open sea, it was still sunny and warm but after we had covered about one-third of that distance a sudden wave of extremely cold weather swept in. Almost overnight the river froze and we were stuck. Days of great misery followed. The greatest problem was to procure food. Not surprisingly local fishermen would not accept payment in money because of the wartime conditions; we had to barter our soap and tea and whatever else we had for fish. It was with great reluctance that I eventually agreed to part with my most cherished possession – the Kalisz school uniform. We even stole some bales of cloth from the ship's hold to trade them for fish. However, all that was not enough and we, the menfolk, had to walk back on the frozen river to Astrakhan to stock ourselves up with bread. On top of everything else our foreman's infant son died and we had to go ashore to bury him. The primitive burial in desolate surroundings was a distressing event which I have never forgotten.

The authorities in Astrakhan did not know what had

happened to the ship and had sent out a plane to search for it. Eventually they sent an icebreaker to tow us back to Astrakhan. That dashed our hopes of joining the Anders Army and leaving the Soviet Union.

Djambul

As we no longer had anything to do in Astrakhan, we all went in different directions. Our family travelled east to the central Asian Soviet Republic of Kazakhstan. We finally settled in Djambul, close to the Kirgiz and Uzbek republics. (Incidentally, there are at least three places and one mountain called Djambul in Kazakhstan, named after the Kazakh national poet who was illiterate most of his life and handed down his poems and folk ballads orally. He died in 1945 at the age of 99.) I obtained a job as an assistant driver of a one-and-a-half-ton lorry with *Kazsovkhoztrans*. First, I had to learn to drive, smashing some barrels in the process. But even when I received my 'third class' driver's licence I was not actually given much of a chance to drive. We carried mainly grain, so I spent most of the time loading and unloading it. Sometimes the driver would pinch some of the grain, and occasionally I was encouraged to join in. Apparently most people stole from their places of work to supplement their pittance of a pay, the cynical excuse being that since everything was state – that is, common – property, it belonged to everybody and we could just help ourselves to whatever we wanted.

At one time, during a trip to Tashkent I ate some unwashed fruit from a stall and came down with typhus on my return. I was so gravely ill that several weeks later one of our acquaintances on meeting my mother in the street asked her when my funeral was to take place. Mother, panic-stricken, rushed to the hospital only to find out that I had just come through the crisis and was on the way to recovery.

My next job was as driver for the chairman of a nearby *kolkhoz* (collective farm). I drove a little pick-up vehicle. On one occasion when I ran out of petrol which had to be fetched from some distance, some *kolkhoz* hands put me on a horse, gave me a bucket and told me to go and fetch petrol. They soon realized I did not know how to ride a horse, and evidently thought they might have a bit of fun at my expense. One of them slapped the beast on the backside so that it bolted and, naturally, I fell off. Fortunately I suffered only bruises. That was my first and last experience at horse riding.

On another occasion I was sent by the chairman to fetch a sack of grain from a farmer, which I gathered was some kind of bribe. On my way back I was suddenly caught by torrential rain and sleet. The truck got stuck in the mud in the middle of a steppe. I left the vehicle, covered my head and shoulders with a sack and went to look for help. I must have covered at least 15 kilometres before I arrived soaked and frozen at a Kazakh village. The people there took great pity on me, dried, warmed and fed me, and sent a tractor to pull the pick-up from the mud. By that time the sack of grain had disappeared. Back in the *kolkhoz* I expected a serious dressing down by the chairman and feared much worse. It was wartime and I could easily have been accused of sabotage, because in the dropping temperature the water in the engine might have frozen and burst it. Instead, whether out of the goodness of his heart or because the missing sack of grain was most probably a bribe, the chairman behaved like an understanding father. He concluded that I was obviously not cut out for the job of a driver and that I would be much better off if I left the post. Greatly relieved, I was only too happy to oblige. Anyway, my career as a manual worker had come to an end.

Soon after I contracted amoebic dysentery – a serious disease endemic in this part of Asia. I was taken to hospital where a different treatment was applied every week but after six weeks I was as ill as I had been when first admitted. Completely emaciated, and my life hanging by a thread, I suffered a nervous breakdown. I was determined to get out of hospital. This was well nigh impossible without recourse to some stratagem, amoebic dysentery being a highly contagious disease. I got in touch with a Russian patient who had somehow been cured but luckily for me preferred to stay in hospital, presumably to continue to be fed there. We managed to trick the nurse by showing her his faeces as mine and mine as his. Thus we both got what we wanted: he stayed and I was discharged. It was then that I found out from my Polish doctor that, according to him, the only effective cure for the disease was Rivanol, which in time of war a civilian hospital would not have. An acquaintance of ours, a Mr Forster who worked in a pharmacy in Djambul, went to great lengths to procure it for me. For two weeks nothing changed but on the fifteenth day the distressing symptoms completely disappeared. It was like a miracle cure.

In 1944 I worked as a teacher for nine months at a primary school for mainly Ukrainian refugee children in the Djambul region and I still have the certificate confirming my appointment.

From the beginning of our stay in Djambul I had an almost obsessive desire to learn English. I had no inkling at the time that this ambition would to a large extent determine the course of my future life. Before the war I had had a few lessons in the language at an extra-curricular course at school in Kalisz. In Djambul I somehow managed to get hold of an English grammar textbook and a dictionary, and subsequently a copy of Henry Fielding's *Tom Jones*. I would lie on the hay on our cement floor and study the grammar in my spare time and later I would read and re-read *Tom Jones*. In time I knew enough to help out other refugees who were coming to the local post office to send telegrams in English to their relatives in America asking them for food parcels. I was paid a small fee for this service and soon assumed a semi-official role as a translator at the entrance to the post office.

I also enrolled for an English correspondence course run by *In-Yaz* (*Inostrannyie Yazyki* – Foreign Languages) from Moscow. They sent me scripts for study and test papers, which I completed and sent back. In due course I obtained an intermediate and subsequently a final certificate testifying that I had completed an English, *In-Yaz*, three-year central (that is, national) course and achieved a university-level knowledge of the language. Before long the certificate proved helpful also in a non-academic context. But as I was later to find out, my self-taught English suffered from some notable mistakes, especially in pronunciation.

The arrival of a food parcel, which our family, like many others, received from time to time, was a great event in our lives and a godsend for us. They came from Uncle Mendel, Father's eldest brother who lived in Tel Aviv. Mendel had married Latsa, the daughter of the Kalisz rabbi Mozes, whose family had settled in Palestine. Latsa's brother, Yehuda Mozes, founded and owned *Yediyot Aharonot*, later the biggest Israeli daily newspaper, and Mendel, after he emigrated in about 1934 to Palestine from Kalisz, where he had had a small printing-house, worked with the paper which he helped to found for the next 50-odd years. (Incidentally, it was Mendel who before the war brought over from Poland to Palestine his two sisters, Bronka and Genia, thus saving them from the Holocaust. Bronka married Mordechai Silberstein but remained childless; Genia married Azriel Azrielant, they had two sons, Avi and Ofer, who became successful businessmen.)

Occasionally there was time for sport and leisure. For a brief period I captained a Polish football team in Djambul. Once we played against a Russian team. When I scored a goal, a Russian deliberately kicked me hard on the shin but my team did not dare to retaliate.

I had a girlfriend, Marysia, in Djambul. She was being wooed by a somewhat older but relatively better-off maths teacher whom she despised. (After I left Djambul, however, they got together and later married. After the war they settled in Melbourne, Australia and did well in the clothing business. Years later she sought me out during a visit to Warsaw.) Marysia and I used to go to a dance-hall where mostly Western music was played. The dance-hall was frequented by youngsters from other refugee or exiled communities. The Chechens were particularly rowdy and aggressive and drew knives on anybody who got in their way; they therefore had a fearsome, even sinister, reputation. The Chechen population had been deported by Stalin from their homeland in the Caucasus to Kazakhstan for allegedly collaborating with the Nazis.

With Sheep to Moscow

When the war ended, I did not want to wait until mass repatriation became possible. I became restless and was eager to leave Djambul where the atmosphere seemed stifling. A few local ZPP (Union of Polish Patriots) activists had already left. Among them my acquaintance, Felicja Kozub and her husband, a well-known pre-war Cracow trade union leader.

As I later realized the Union of Polish Patriots had been set up by the Soviets in 1943 as one political nucleus of the future Soviet-dominated regime in Poland, the other being the small communist underground in Poland also directed from Moscow. The Union's leaders were a group of pre-war Polish communists who survived the purges and the war in the Soviet Union, including Poland's future presidents Aleksander Zawadzki and Edward Ochab, Prime Minister Piotr Jaroszewicz, powerful ministers Jakub Berman, Hilary Minc and Stefan Jędrychowski, and my future boss in the Ministry of Foreign Affairs, Marian Naszkowski. The Union also organized Polish military units in the Soviet Union with a large proportion of Soviet officers, which became the backbone of communist Poland's armed forces.

So with Mother's blessing I decided to go to Moscow. Under conditions of the then still prevailing war regime and with Moscow being a restricted area, this was by no means easy. To accomplish such a feat I had, for the first and only time in my life, to resort to bribery, a practice that was widely used in the USSR. It took a hefty bribe to get the job as one of the sheep-minders who were to take a herd from Djambul to a place outside Moscow by train. The journey took about three weeks. There were about 20 sheep in my cattle truck, which was getting smellier and dirtier by the hour. I slept on a bundle of straw and waited impatiently for a chance to wash at the stations *en route*. When at one of them my piece of soap – a commodity then at a premium – was stolen, my mood sank.

Having delivered my charges just to the west of Moscow, I boarded a suburban train to the city. On these trains there was no control of permits to enter the restricted area of Moscow, as distinct from stringent checks on long-distance trains. When, soon after my arrival in Moscow, I was questioned by a militiaman about the reason for my being there, I produced my *In-Yaz* certificate dated 17 May 1945 and told him I had come to the city to take my examination. That put me in the clear.

Moscow was in jubilant mood. The joy and great relief, which obviously I shared, that the horrible nightmare of the war was at long last over was the first manifestation of people's unmistakably genuine feelings I experienced in the Soviet Union. Throughout the war, we – exiles or refugees – had little or no contact with local people. When I was in the two forced-labour settlements, we were isolated from the local population, had little or no access to any newspapers or radio and our only preoccupation was survival. We knew of the hardships and deprivations ascribed to the war effort, but not much else. When living under the freer conditions in Djambul, our contact with the local, mainly Kazakh, people was very limited and any adverse reactions to the war, to the suffering, to the number of casualties, to personal bereavements were not visibly manifested in the atmosphere of fear and suspicion and the official propaganda of optimism.

My starting point in Moscow was the ZPP headquarters where, somewhat unexpectedly I found Felicja Kozub. I was delighted to see her. I asked her whether she could help me find some suitable employment before repatriation. I suggested that my knowledge of English could perhaps be of use at the Polish embassy. Obviously, I was by then fluent in Russian. She made some enquiries and I was invited to the Polish Press Agency (PAP) office to have my English tested by a lady correspondent. She found my command of the language satisfactory and I was employed by the embassy for a three-month probationary period. Thus began a new stage in my life as a member of the Polish foreign service.

3 • Early Days at the Polish Embassy

I was assigned to the science section run by Professor Jan Dembowski, an eminent biologist and specialist in zoo-psychology and experimental zoology, who later became the first president of the post-war Polish Academy of Sciences. In the embassy I worked in a very large room stacked ceiling high with sacks of books. Our work at the time consisted almost exclusively in searching for, buying, collecting, packing and dispatching by rail, books, mainly Polish, for the heavily depleted Polish universities. The professor and I would rummage in libraries, antique book shops and any other places where we might find books, in Moscow and occasionally in Leningrad. We received the books as gifts from some institutions.

The professor and his wife, also a biologist, were very kind to me. They encouraged me to study biology. On our trips to Leningrad the professor would take me to the theatre. Once in the foyer during an interval he asked me to observe that people were instinctively always walking anticlockwise and then explained that this was because the left side of the body being the weaker, was making the smaller circle. He would also tell me interesting stories relating to his scientific work. For instance, before the war he had cooperated with an American female colleague who was bringing up her child and rearing a monkey of the same age. They found that in the first year or so the monkey showed greater intelligence than the human baby.

The three-month probationary period having passed, I was employed by the embassy on a permanent basis, evidently on the professor's recommendation. Soon after I was discreetly summoned by the NKVD. I was seen by a bald and rather short man. He took out a file from his desk and read to me the particulars I had given in Lvov in June 1940 before I was deported beyond the Urals. I was dumbfounded. Here we were at the end of 1945, and in those intervening five years there had been the most terrible and destructive war in the course of which much of the European part of the Soviet Union had been overrun and devastated by the German army, I had covered great distances, yet through all these turbulent times an NKVD file had been updated and followed me, and had now landed up in Moscow. I was amazed at the NKVD's efficiency. The official pointed out that in Lvov I had given my (birth certificate) name as Mendel and Father's as Szlama but now, I was Mieczysław and Father's name was Stefan. I mumbled some explanation about having given the Polish equivalents of the first names and that I had always been called Mietek, a diminutive of Mieczysław. He did not seem to be very interested and it soon became obvious that he was simply using the discrepancy as a kind of blackmail. What he really wanted was for me to 'observe' and report to him on the Polish ambassador, no less. The ambassador at the time was Professor Henryk Raabe, a zoologist. I told the NKVD man that I, a junior employee, had no possibility of 'observing' the ambassador, which was both true and less provocative than saying: 'I won't spy on my ambassador.' He still tried to persuade me but was not too insistent. Anyway, I never reported to him, nor – surprising as it may seem – did I ever hear from him again.

Soon after I became an embassy staff member I tried to enrol at the Institute of Foreign Relations, a university-level training school for future diplomats. But I quickly discovered I had no chance of being admitted to that élite establishment, so I tried the next best thing – the Institute of Foreign Languages. They were ready to accept me but required my secondary school certificate which, unfortunately, I had left behind in Kalisz. Very upset, I wrote to my mother in Djambul about it. She confided in Hela, a young friend of ours. Hela, who had a crush on me, was eager to help me out. Smart, resourceful and relatively well-off, she procured and sent me a secondary school certificate in which somebody's name had rather clumsily been scratched out and mine inserted instead. I was in a dilemma about whether I should use it, but in the end my strong determination to enter the institute prevailed. The institute's authorities did not detect the forgery until a year later when they summoned me. This prompted me to leave Moscow for Warsaw forthwith.

Meanwhile, however, while continuing to work at the embassy, I studied English at the institute and enjoyed and profited from it. One rather young woman professor seemed particularly good, though she had never been outside the Soviet Union. It was at the institute that I discovered some of the mistakes of my self-tuition – when, for instance, I pronounced 'battle' as 'bottle' to the amusement of my fellow students. Apart from English grammar and pronunciation I studied English and Russian literature. I was examined on *Othello*, and, of course, the obligatory Marxism-Leninism. At the exam the bearded professor told me: 'You deserve a five [the top mark], but since you will be living in other countries you must be extra good and study more, so I will mark you only four.' I worked hard and managed to do two institute years in one.

Early on a beautiful, dark-haired fellow student, Tatyana, took a fancy to me and under the pretext of my bringing her an exercise book invited me to her flat. This was the beginning of a passionate love affair. What I did not know was that she was married. At the time her husband, a well-educated high-ranking official at the Ministry of Light Industry and about 15 years' her senior, was abroad on official business. By the time I found out, we were too involved to break off the relationship. They may both have been Jewish, but I never asked her about it. They were, apparently, friends of the Maiskys (Ivan Maisky was the Soviet ambassador in London in 1932–43). For obvious reasons, I was not keen to and never did meet her husband nor did I ever meet any of their friends. But her background and connections combined with my being a foreigner and as such suspect by definition, my hailing from a Soviet-dominated country notwithstanding, meant that we laid ourselves open to risks much greater than we realized at the time.

Sometimes we would meet at my tiny basement room, on

other occasions she would arrange with her friends, a Spanish couple, to let us have their room for an afternoon. We often went to the theatre, especially the Bolshoy. For an embassy employee it was easier to get tickets. We both loved the ballet, and I saw *Giselle, Swan Lake, Romeo and Juliet, Fountain of Bakhchisaray* and other major ballets several times. I admired the impressive skill and artistry of the great Ulanova, of Lepeshinskaya, Plisetskaya and other prima ballerinas, and the near-acrobatic performances of the male dancers. I also liked the Moyseyev ensemble's folk dancing.

After some time Tatyana, greatly alarmed, told me that she had been warned by the NKVD to stop seeing me and threatened with exile if she did not. To drive it home they showed her photographs of our very intimate encounters. We still continued to see each other, though less frequently, until my departure for Warsaw. Tatyana wrote me a passionate farewell letter. A few years later, when I was in Moscow on business, we saw each other again.

At one point, my brother who had left Djambul soon after me, visited me in Moscow. After the privation of the past and the cold and hunger he endured on his long and perilous journey to Moscow, he found the experience of standing, thanks to my diplomatic card, in the queue to the Moscow circus, which was reserved for VIPs, verging on the surreal and the contrast between the misery of Djambul and the rich cultural life in Moscow overwhelming. Less pleasant was the experience he encountered in a Moscow hotel restaurant, where, together with Tatyana, we went for an evening meal and where he invited a girl to dance. He was soon dragged from the dance-floor by two NKVD plain-clothes officers into the hotel kitchen where they seized his wallet from his back pocket. Evidently, the bulge must have aroused their suspicion and they thought it was a revolver. Tatyana and I came running to his rescue, however, and all was well.

With what feelings was I leaving the Soviet Union? I had come to like the ordinary, long-suffering, warm-hearted Russian people, I had come to love their beautiful language, their marvellous music, melodious songs and much else. Politically, however, I was pretty ignorant. I had had no chance to read or otherwise learn about the criminal past of the Soviet regime, though I could often see sadness and fear in people's eyes and the few local acquaintances I had showed a distinct reticence in respect of anything to do with the Soviet past. As for the things we had witnessed ourselves, we were under the powerful influence of the official media – there being no other – and other propaganda, and even people with greater minds and much better knowledge and experience than I had fallen for it. As for the rest, we used to rationalize it. Thus, our exile in 1940 was explained by the fact that in view of the imminent Nazi–Soviet war the authorities had had to remove from what was the frontier zone all those they considered unreliable elements and, however difficult the conditions, our exile had saved our lives. (The overwhelming majority of Polish Jews who escaped the Holocaust were saved by that exile.) The hardships and sometimes chaos we experienced on a par with the local population were explained, at least partly, by the total war that was being waged. And everybody was aware of the decisive part the Soviet Union had played, at tremendous sacrifice, in defeating the Nazi scourge.

As for the NKVD attempt to recruit me as an informer at the embassy, I saw this as a routine method probably used by intelligence and counter-intelligence organizations elsewhere in the world.

Sceptical by nature, I was doubtful and suspicious about much I was being told and taught at the Marxism-Leninism course in the Institute of Foreign Languages in Moscow. Nonetheless, the general ideology had some appeal for me in as much as I imagined it could bring about a more just society in which people like me would no longer feel and be treated like underdogs both on account of poverty and Jewishness. Moreover, I believed that a new, 'socialist' Poland would open the doors to those who had been socially disadvantaged before the war, without suffering the rough edges of the Soviet system. In that frame of mind I was returning to my native country.

And yet I drifted into Poland's communist service rather than taking a conscious decision to join it. Like thousands of others, I was swept along by events and circumstances. The choice, as it were, was made for me.

Warsaw

I was glad finally to have left the Soviet Union. On coming back to Poland my thoughts focussed on what had happened there, on the ghastly fact that all my large family and, in particular my father, had in all probability perished in that most monstrous genocidal extermination.

My first concern was to find out what had happened to my father, though I had little hope that he was still alive. I went to Kalisz where I found Father's youngest brother, Itzhak, the only member of our extended – several score – family on Father's side who had survived the Holocaust in Poland. On Mother's side the only ones, of the even larger family, to survive in Poland were her younger sister, Sala and her son, Leon. All three had been inmates in Auschwitz. (They eventually settled in Israel.) Itzhak was in touch with Henryk Zylberberg – whose name had by then changed to Maliński – Mother's erstwhile theatre director in Zagórów. Zylberberg had been commander of the Jewish Fighting Organization unit, in which Father fought in the Warsaw Ghetto Uprising. A certificate to this effect issued by Zylberberg-Maliński also testifies that he had been with Father in the Warsaw Ghetto from the beginning of 1941 and that Father died a hero's death on 28 May 1943.

Naturally I wished to see Zylberberg myself to talk to him about Father, but Itzhak strongly discouraged me from meeting him. (It was only years later that he told me he had wanted to spare me finding out the gruesome details of Father's death. Father had fought in the Uprising to the very end, but had died in the street, his body swollen from hunger. I have never been able to forgive myself for not insisting then or later on seeing Zylberberg.) Father's tragic death epitomized for me the incomprehensible horror of what the Nazis had done to my family, relatives, friends, and to my people. It is difficult for me to describe the traumatic feelings brought about by the full realization that my past had been annihilated. In any case, I felt a painful rage against the Nazis which, in essence, has been with me ever since.

But I could not go on living with that rage alone. Dramatic general and personal developments kept me preoccupied. Around me was the euphoria of liberation from the Nazi scourge and the enthusiasm of reconstruction of the country which seemed to affect everybody. With hindsight, however, I must admit I was not fully aware of the political and human costs the introduction of the new political and economic system entailed.

In the meantime my mother and brother separately returned to Poland. By then Mother was with her future second husband, Dr Jakub Zineman, to whom I had introduced her in Djambul. It was primarily this liaison that prompted my brother to leave Djambul on his own. His deep love for and memory of Father was very much alive in him and, as he later realized, he had not been mature enough to accept the new relationship.

My stepfather-to-be was a teacher. He had taught in my Kalisz secondary school, although this was before my time. He was also a writer. His books include biographies and biographical novels, among others on Emile Zola, Disraeli, Max Nordau, Karl Marx and Theodor Herzl, but he is best known for his pre-war *History of Zionism* which was a standard text-book and used in my Kalisz school. As a Zionist activist and writer, he cooperated before the war with the Zionist leader and Sejm (parliament) deputy, Itzhak Grynbaum, who later became the first Minister of the Interior in Israel.

Having married, my mother and Zineman headed for Paris where they settled. My brother, whom I had no chance to see in Poland, stayed for a short while with Uncle Yitzhak and his wife Franka in Kalisz before joining Aunt Sara and her son Leoś in Łódź. With Leoś, he joined the Zionist youth movement *Ha-Oved Ha-Tsioni*, organized by Aliya Bet activists from Palestine, and before long they set off (by train) with a group of youngsters and some of their parents, Aunt Sara among them, across Czechoslovakia and Austria. From Austria they sneaked, in a very tough mountain trek, across the border to Italy where they were taken to a Zionist camp in Rivoli. At one point, my brother and a friend of his contemplated the idea of trying to go to America rather than Palestine. With this purpose in mind, they managed to get themselves across the border to Menton on the French Riviera. However, they were caught there by the police in the early hours of the morning while trying to board a bus to Paris, and sent to prison in Nice where they were rather roughly treated as they were taken for Romanian spies. After about a month they were brought to court (Joint provided them with a defence lawyer) and sentenced to a year's imprisonment. Released on parole for a visit to Mother in Paris, he never returned and still owes the French 11 months. In Paris he had a change of heart about America and resolved that the only way for him was to follow his Zionist instincts. He went to Marseilles where with 600 other immigrants he boarded a yacht designed for 30 people. What followed were six weeks of misery in cramped and horrible conditions on rough seas. When they eventually came close to Palestine shores they were surrounded by the British Navy and escorted to Haifa from where they were taken in barges to Cyprus. After 14 months in the Winter Camp there, he was released in one of the quotas allowed to go to Palestine in April 1948 and was brought to Tel Aviv just before the establishment of the State of Israel.

Why did our family thus disperse again? Had we been together at the time our future was being decided, maybe the outcome would have been different. Mother had always had a fascination for Paris and this may have been her decisive motive for settling there. For my brother, who did not share my beliefs and illusions, it was natural to follow his Zionist inclinations. We were not exceptional in this respect. In pre-war Poland it was not unusual for Jewish families to be divided by their different political allegiances. In my friend's family, where the parents were Chasidic Jews, their seven grown-up children represented a political spectrum from Jabotinsky revisionists to near-communists and had heated political discussions. The sons of the leader of the General Zionists in pre-war Poland, the above-mentioned Itzhak Grynbaum, were communists.

London

Just a few days after my arrival in Warsaw I reported, as instructed by the embassy in Moscow, to the Ministry of Foreign Affairs in Aleja Szucha, virtually the only street in

Warsaw which had buildings left standing. It was an eery feeling to be entering the building of the ministry as the Gestapo had had its headquarters in the adjacent building.

While waiting in the secretary's room of the Head of Cadres (personnel) Department, Stefan Wilski, to be seen by him, I overheard part of his conversation with the then second secretary at the Polish embassy in London (bearing an aristocratic, hyphenated name; he later defected in Sweden). The man was saying that unless the embassy got five people with a knowledge of English, it would have to close down. Wilski replied: 'I can't give you five people, but one such man is waiting to see me in the next room.' That is how my rather speedy dispatch to London came about. It took just a couple of months or so, and I barely had time to find my bearings in Poland before I departed.

When I disembarked in London from the Polish ship, I asked a policeman how to get a taxi to take me to 47 Portland Place (the Polish embassy's address). My English was good enough to be understood, but when the bobby kindly waved down a taxi for me and told the cabby the address in near cockney, I was dismayed. I had a similar difficulty in understanding the British on the telephone, but after a few weeks I had overcome this problem, which was fortunate because I talked a lot on the phone as I was dealing with administrative matters. I was soon appointed to the most junior diplomatic rank of attaché. My job, though at times exciting, was fairly routine and unremarkable.

Most problems the embassy was dealing with through the Foreign Office arose out of the July 1945 withdrawal of recognition by the British government of the Polish government-in-exile in London and the recognition of the government in Warsaw, and of the demobilization of the Polish armed forces under British command. A great number of very complicated and difficult questions arose, the disposal of assets, property, archives, civilian and military repatriation, resettlement and the like. My participation in those dealings was at first incidental and minimal.

It was only in 1949 that I became more involved by taking a minor part in the discussions at the Treasury of the Anglo-Polish Ad Hoc Committee on Non-Political Matters (unofficially referred to as the Mixed Committee) and in some arrangements following from these discussions. The Polish delegation to the committee was led by the embassy Number Two, Counsellor Albert Morski, a grim-faced, rather dogmatic communist, an expatriate from Canada, and, at times, by the First Secretary, Andrzej Szemiński. I attended all but one of the twenty-odd meetings of the committee where I had a chance to make some limited use of my knowledge of international law which I was studying at the time. In spite of the committee's name, politics dictated the contents of the discussions and their outcome was meagre as on a majority of contentious questions no agreement was reached. Nor was it realistically possible considering the nature of the Polish side's claims which had remained unresolved since the Anglo-Polish Financial Agreement of June 1946.

Those claims were part of the efforts of Poland's communist authorities to extract, through the British government, as much as possible of the financial and other assets which they regarded as state assets, from the former Polish government-in-exile in London, its various agencies and the former Polish armed forces under British command. At the same time the Warsaw government sought to weaken, by substantially reducing its financial and other resources, the position and influence of the strongly anti-communist Polish government-in-exile which was still recognized at the time by many governments and continued to hold sway over the sizeable post-war Polish community not only in Britain but in the world at large, not excluding Poland itself. It was not only the émigré political élite but also the majority of the members of the former Polish armed forces that had refused to return to a communist Poland.

The main claim of the Polish side at the 1949 Mixed Committee was that assets of the Polish government in London had been illegally disposed of and alienated between 28 June 1945, the date the (communist dominated) Polish Provisional Government of National Unity was formed, and 6 July of that year when the British government recognized it. The Polish side argued that those assets, estimated by Warsaw at about three million pounds, had not been returned to Poland in spite of assurances to safeguard and promise to recover them if alienated, given by the British government at Potsdam and in the Financial Agreement of 1946. It further claimed that all such property alienated by third parties should be traced and returned. Morski privately intimated to the British that the Polish negotiators in the compensation talks proceeding at the same time in London proposed to say that while the Polish government in Warsaw was prepared to compensate British holders of assets in Poland the British government had negligently allowed some three million pounds' worth of Polish assets to disappear in Britain. In other words, they intended to use this argument as a bargaining counter.

The British side argued that its government could not accept any responsibility for any assets acquired and disposed of prior to 6 July 1945, the date it recognized the Polish government in Warsaw. All transfers of titles by the Polish government in London prior to that date were legal and the British government could not interfere or be in any way responsible for acts of the former Polish government or its officials. The British government had made every effort to safeguard Polish government property on withdrawal of recognition from the London Polish government on 6 July 1945 by the establishment of the Interim Treasury Committee which took over all such property, and could not be responsible for assets which did not come into its hands after that date. In other words, the British side deemed the Polish claim wholly without foundation. However, the Polish government, if it so wished, could take legal proceedings for the recovery of alienated property.

The Mixed Committee did agree that the remaining property held on behalf of the Polish government by the Interim Treasury Committee under the 1946 Financial Agreement should be transferred to the Polish government by 30 September 1949 and, where this was impracticable, an agreed equivalent should be paid. It was also agreed to wind up the Social Insurance Committee of the Polish merchant navy. On Polish estates, though there was no agreement in principle, a practical compromise was found. On the remaining questions of civil and military assets, military funds, state archives and so on, no agreement was reached. On military archives the British side maintained that operational records remained with the War Office as propery left by a disowned and demobilized army (at this the Polish side protested), of those deposited with the Interim Treasury Committee the majority had been or were being handed over. However, certain documents had been retained under the Financial Agreement until no longer required; as large numbers of Poles had remained in the United Kingdom the British government needed the archives dealing with their rights and services in the UK.[1]

Apart from work I took a great interest in the United Kingdom and especially its political system and democratic traditions. On a number of occasions I was asked by my superiors to attend House of Commons debates and to report on them. Listening in the diplomatic gallery I often marvelled at the powers of oratory of some of the speakers, at the open yet civilized controversies, including some sharp interjections by the two communist MPs at the time, Gallacher and Piratin, and at the sense of humour often displayed even in heated debates. I found similar qualities of oratory and repartee, sometimes in cruder form than in the House of Commons, on Sunday afternoons in Hyde Park where speakers standing on chairs or wooden boxes spoke without restraint on a wide variety of political, religious, racial and other, often quite eccentric, topics – some of the speakers attracting crowds; others, just a handful of people or even none. I would wander from one gathering to another and relished the unique phenomenon.

At the end of 1946, the then chargé d'affaires, Karol Lapter, persuaded me to join the communist Polish Workers' Party. I was still naïve enough not to realize the significance of that step, the more so since membership did not involve me at the time in any party activity except for attending meetings of the embassy party organization. It was a very passive membership. I remember, later on, some of us at the embassy were dubbed 'pink' rather than 'red', which was, indeed, an apt description of our views.

Once or twice during my stint in London I was asked to act as an interpreter. On one occasion I was accompanying a Polish miners' delegation to a British miners' conference at Llandudno in north Wales. On the train one of the delegates wanted a beer so I took him to the restaurant car. By the time we were ready to rejoin the other members of the delegation I discovered, to my horror, that the rest of the train had vanished. Apparently, it had been detached at Crewe and headed for Llandudno while the engine with the restaurant car was going further north. I was worried about my charges who were left in the train on their own without knowing any English, or even their exact destination and without any money. At the next stop I and my beer-loving miner took a taxi to Llandudno. Luckily we arrived at the railway station there just as the train with the rest of the delegation was coming in. The 'abandoned' miners were angry, thinking we had played a trick on them, but everything ended happily.

At the conference itself my confidence in my English pronunciation was boosted when a conference stenographer asked me for the meaning of the word 'złoty' (Poland's currency unit). I was pleasantly surprised that this was the only word he did not understand in the translation of the Polish delegation's address which I had read out, while he had to query 13 words in the Scottish delegate's address.

In September 1948 the British Institute of Bankers organized an International Summer School at Christ Church College, Oxford, to which Polish bankers had been invited. However, because of some visa difficulties the bankers failed to arrive on time, so in their stead the London embassy sent three of its young diplomats of whom one was a Glasgow University graduate in economics and two, including myself, were studying economics at the time. The summer school was very instructive and enjoyable. My colleague and I spent some evenings on the town and a couple of times had to climb over the fence back into the college when we returned late and found the gates had been locked.

From that period I remember the then Polish Consul-General, Marcel Reich-Ranicki whom I suspected of cooperating with or acting for Warsaw's 'civilian' intelligence. He returned to Poland in 1949 and left it for good in 1958 for West Germany where he became the leading literary critic, 'the man who has made and broken the reputations of generations of authors'. It was only in 1994, when the Polish Ministry of Internal Affairs released the relevant documents, that his five-year-long work for the Polish communist security service was confirmed. Until then Ranicki had denied his past association with that service.

Ranicki, of Jewish origin, had lived in Germany until 1938 when he was deported to Poland. In and outside the Warsaw Ghetto he survived the war hiding in cellars and backrooms. Out of gratitude to the Poles who hid him and the Soviet army which eventually liberated him, he agreed to cooperate with the communist security services. After a stint at the Polish military mission in Berlin he was appointed vice-consul (and later promoted to consul) in London in 1948. Only in 1994 did he admit all this and confess in *Der Spiegel* that he had been a professional spy with the nominal rank of captain and the brief to watch the Polish exile community in Britain. 'I personally did not gather the information – my mission was to evaluate the reports delivered by informants and then pass them on to Warsaw. To call me a top agent would be flattery indeed', he was reported to have said. He denied he had had anything to do with the Polish officers in Britain who were persuaded to return to Warsaw after the war, and who were then tortured and put on trial. That, he said, had probably been the work of the military attaché in the Polish embassy in London.

One of the main tasks of the consul and his staff, especially those working for the security service, and, for that matter, also of the Polish Cultural and Social Association – and the other bodies sponsored by the Polish embassy – was to influence the émigré Poles in favour of the Warsaw government. With rare exceptions they did not appear to have been very successful. Like some other members of the embassy proper, I had no connection or contacts with any émigré Poles.

From the very start I was determined to combine work at the embassy with studies at London University. In 1947 I joined University College as an external student in economics, but I also attended lectures (and tutorials) there and at the London School of Economics. In addition to the obligatory economic subjects I had chosen a line of studies corresponding to a foreign service school: international law, international relations, political history and the like. I was allowed by Ambassador Jerzy Michałowski, who must have cleared it with Warsaw, to enrol at the university and was given time off to attend lectures. This was considered a worthy investment since there were virtually no trained diplomats in the nascent post-war Polish foreign service.

I read international law at the LSE under Professor Schwarzenberger, a Jewish refugee from Nazi Germany. He pronounced English in a most peculiar way: his 'vee Brrritish' sounded highly amusing. Schwarzenberger represented the London school of international law as opposed to the better known Cambridge school represented by Professor Lauterpacht, a Jewish immigrant from Poland. At one of his lectures which touched on the nationality issue, Schwarzenberger turned to me as coming from the Polish embassy asking how come Poland had a defence minister who was a Soviet citizen. He had in mind Marshal Rokossowski. Rokossowski as a young man had left Poland and became a famous Soviet general in the Second World War. From 1949 to 1956 he was Poland's defence minister. Schwarzenberger evidently wanted to embarrass me, which angered me. I stood up and said that I was attending his lectures not as a representative of the embassy but as a student. However, if he was so interested in the dual citizenship of Poland's defence minister I could meet him privately and explain that that was not at all so unusual; that, for instance, Poland's pre-war President Mościcki had held both Swiss and Polish citizenship. The comparison was not quite appropriate, but my fellow students applauded me enthusiastically, presumably because there were many left-wingers at the LSE and also because they seemed to have enjoyed my repartee. Schwarzenberger never addressed me in that way again.

I had no language difficulties at all except at first with the English pronunciation of Latin words, which is completely different from that which I had been taught in Poland. When at a lecture by another professor on the law of the sea, I heard 'the high seas are *reeznalyes*', I was baffled and it took me a while to realize that this was *res nullius* (meaning 'beyond the law').

I took my final examination in 1950. During an interval after the exam in economics I compared notes with an embassy friend of mine, who was also taking the exam. To the question whether an 'economic law' could be suspended by government action, I had answered in the negative, arguing that since it was a 'law' nobody's action could suspend it. My friend, an otherwise very bright man, had answered in the affirmative, probably under the subconscious influence of communist practice that a government could do almost anything. This must have had a decisive effect on his exam results.

I did not wait for the results so as not to spoil my holiday in Paris in case they were bad. On my return I took a taxi straight to Senate House, the university building, in front of which the results were by then displayed on a board. I looked through the list of passes and could not find my name, then I looked through the list of those who had failed and could not find my name either, although unfortunately my friend's name was on it. Perplexed and apprehensive, I moved to the left side of the long board and almost by chance spotted my name, looked at the heading and saw 'Honours'. I was delighted. There was only one first class honours result and 12 upper-second class, among whom there were four other Poles besides myself. There were well over a hundred lower-second class and a somewhat greater number of ordinary passes. Among the latter, I saw the name of Daniel Zynger, the son of pre-war Poland's best-known Jewish journalist, and later a *Jewish Chronicle* editor in London, whose pen-name was Regnis (Singer backwards). Daniel himself became a very distinguished journalist working, among others, for *The New Statesman* and later *The Economist*.

In January 1951 the émigré *Polish Daily*, a paper which, not surprisingly, was very hostile to the communist regime in Poland, wrote about the recall to Warsaw of the embassy's First Secretary, Kazimierz Dorosz and added that I was to take his place 'as a reward...for passing with honours his examination at the London School of Economics'. In fact, I was already back in Poland by then.

My time in London was, of course, not all work and study. I enjoyed seeing plays and musicals in the West End and frequented dance-halls. As a great fan of Fred Astaire I even took a few tap-dancing lessons, but soon realized that my memory was not good enough to remember the steps, so I gave it up. Around November 1947 I met Denise at the Lyceum dance-hall. She became my girlfriend for the remaining three years of my stay in London. We saw each other frequently and used to go dancing regularly. At a dinner-dance at the Café de Paris we were once asked whether we were professional dancers. My involvement with an English girl could not have escaped the watchful eyes of the security people and Warsaw must have become concerned that I might defect, the more so since a number of defections from the embassy had occurred in the preceding months. So as soon as I had finished my university studies my superiors thought of a way of luring me gently back to Poland without arousing my suspicion that they no longer trusted me. Towards the end of 1950 the opportunity occurred and I was asked to act as interpreter at the 'World Peace Congress' in Warsaw. (Incidentally, the congress was scheduled to be held in Sheffield, but after several hundred foreign delegates had been refused visas for Britain or otherwise prevented from coming to Sheffield, it was transferred to Warsaw.[2]) The request was not couched in words implying that I was being recalled but rather that I was being asked to fulfil a temporary and important assignment. Yet I could smell a rat and knew that this was the end of my stay in London and I would not be permitted to return.

Notes

1   Cf. Public Record Office, Ref. FO 371/77497.
2   Among the 'respectable but misguided' people who, as communists or 'fellow-travellers', were refused visas to enter Britain were Professor Joliot-Curie, former head of the French Atomic Energy Commission and president of the World Peace Committee; Louis Aragon, the French poet; Pietro Nenni, leader of the Italian left-wing socialists; and Dmitri Shostakovitch, the Soviet composer. Pablo Picasso was among those who were allowed to enter Britain.

4 • *International Commissions*

Although I did not believe the story I had been fed by my superiors, I went along with the pretence. However, I did not pack all my belongings, but asked Krysia, a trusted embassy friend of mine at the time and, as it turned out, my future wife, to pack for me what I had left behind should I not come back. Until Krysia was recalled from London at the end of 1952 we met in Warsaw while she was on holiday, enjoying theatre outings and visiting friends together, and kept in frequent touch by correspondence. We did not realize then that our friendship and mutual attraction would develop into a loving relationship leading to marriage.

I travelled via Paris where Mother and Zineman lived in a tiny, fourth-floor flatlet in a shabby house with no lift at rue Crozatier in 12th *arrondissement*. I spent a painful evening with them, as they were trying to dissuade me from returning to Poland, followed by a sleepless night during which I hesitated, agonized, but eventually decided to return. There were a number of considerations I weighed up, the important one being a basic sense of loyalty: my superiors had trusted me and invested in my university education which I had just successfully completed, and I should not now betray them. But there was much more to it than that. Had I defected, many people, and not just in Poland, would have said: as long as he had the cosy position in London and his university studies were in effect financed by the Polish government he was loyal, but as soon as he was recalled and about to face uncertainty and a much harsher life he 'chose freedom'. Many would also have added: of course, you can't trust a Jew to be a loyal citizen of Poland let alone the country's representative. And that meant that defection would have caused harm to my Jewish and non-Jewish friends in Poland.

Obviously, by then my erstwhile beliefs, hopes and illusions about a socialist Poland had taken some knocking. But, though the balance between belief, doubt and rejection had been imperceptibly shifting all the time, there had been no sudden seeing of the light on my part. I was only vaguely aware of the atrocities that had been committed by the Warsaw regime on its opponents, such as the members of the former Home Army. I had not been in Poland for long enough, I had no contacts with Polish émigrés and what little I had heard or read about I was inclined, in my then frame of mind, to attribute to exaggerated anti-communist propaganda. As for anti-Semitism, whatever had been going on in the Soviet Union – and I did not know the real facts about that either – and despite the Kielce pogrom, Poland still seemed different in as much as there was no official anti-Semitism at the time. In fact, people who then dared express such views were severely reprimanded and/or expelled from the party. It was only later that my rather naïve hope that the Polish regime would suppress pre-war nationalism and anti-Semitism was completely dashed.

Somehow my cousin, Natek's sister, Eda Kempińska became privy to or perhaps just suspected what was going on that night. Before the war Eda studied French in Paris and she returned to France from a vacation in Poland in the last train the Germans let through in 1939. Having leaned towards the communists during the war, or perhaps even become a member of the party, she subsequently worked in the culture section of the Polish embassy in Paris. Eda evidently regarded it her duty to report my hesitations to the then chargé d'affaires, Ogrodziński, who promptly summoned me the next day and gently probed my intentions to make sure that I was returning. I could not forgive Eda for informing on me.

Back in Warsaw, contrary to my expectations, I did not experience any tangible consequences. Evidently, the fact of my return was regarded as proof of my loyalty. Nonetheless, in time I realized that some suspicion lingered on.

Having done my duty at the Peace Congress I was assigned

to the British Section at the Ministry of Foreign Affairs. But my most exciting job in those early 1950s was Polish–English interpreting at conferences, for foreign delegations and VIPs, for Polish dignitaries, including the president, and on state occasions.

At one international trades union conference, when the Greek delegate was delivering his address, his colleague who knew some English was sitting beside me in my English translator's tiny cubicle helping me to keep pace with the speaker in reading the English translation of the speach by pointing with his finger on the text. As the proceedings were being translated into four languages, the three other translators had to switch to my English translation to be able to keep pace with the speaker as none of us knew any Greek, while the Greeks had nobody who knew any of the three remaining languages. The speech was rather long. Cramped in the tiny cubicle with not enough air for the two of us, we were perspiring profusely. But there was no other way. However, as it turned out, we suffered the discomfort to no purpose. When we finished reading the translations to our microphones and the delegates were acknowledging the end of the speech by loud clapping, the astonished speaker was still speaking. My Greek companion had evidently lost his bearings and made me finish the translation before time.

I experienced a potentially more serious misfortune at the state banquet for the visiting Chinese premier, Chou En-Lai. Standing just behind him I was to translate his speech into Polish from an English text I was given beforehand paragraph by paragraph; that is Chou En-Lai would stop after each paragraph he delivered in Chinese to give me time to translate that paragraph from the English text into Polish. To my utter horror, however, he went on speaking after I had translated the last paragraph. He was evidently adding to his planned speech, completely oblivious of the fact that I, his translator, knew no Chinese. Here I was faced by hundreds of people including the highest state dignitaries, the diplomatic corps and other VIPs expecting me to translate the concluding part of the Chinese prime minister's speech, which I would be unable to do. Fortunately, a member of his staff standing just behind me started whispering into my ear a translation of what Chou

En-Lai was saying – in Russian. Evidently he did not know English and took it for granted that I knew Russian. Luckily, I did, but I might not have. However, I thus was able to translate the last sentences of the speech, and felt greatly relieved.

An even more serious incident, with nearly disastrous consequences for me, occurred at a reception given by the British ambassador on the occasion of the coronation of Elizabeth the Second. I was translating the rather longish toast of Prime Minister Cyrankiewicz. I easily remembered six or seven things he was toasting but momentarily hesitated to remember the last. It was enough for the applause to break out which cut me off. From the Polish government's point of view that last element was by far the most important, in fact the only politically important one, because it concerned the hallowed word 'peace'. The commotion among those who knew both languages was plainly visible. Prime Minister Cyrankiewicz, when told about it, was furious and dispatched someone to the British ambassador to explain that an important omission had occurred. I was obviously very upset, and later learned that some generals were insisting I be prosecuted for 'a deliberate provocation', which sounded pretty ominous. Apparently reason prevailed and, spared any serious repercussions, I continued to do my job. However, on a subsequent occasion Cyrankiewicz was unhappy to see me act as interpreter at a government function but Foreign Minister Skrzeszewski soon persuaded him not to object and later I continued to act as interpreter on state occasions also to Cyrankiewicz himself and his wife, the well-known actress Nina Andrycz.

In the early 1960s I had one more rather unpleasant experience: I was interpreting for the party boss, Gomułka (a few of his Politburo members being present) and the leader of the Indonesian Communist Party, Aidit, whose English, particularly his pronunciation, was not always very clear. So a couple of times, before translating, I had to clarify with him what he meant. Gomułka got very impatient and rather rudely interjected: 'Don't talk to him, just translate!' He would not hear any explanation on my part. Politburo member, Zambrowski, who evidently realized my predicament, spoke up to defend me.

During the Burmese Prime Minister U Nu's one-day visit to Warsaw on 11 November 1955, it was agreed to exchange diplomatic missions between the two countries.

While performing these functions, I was able to meet and get to know many important and interesting people, although not all important people were interesting. I met heads of state, premiers, government ministers, American senators and other politicians and businessmen, including the likes of Henry Ford, parliamentarians, including British MPs, British trade union delegates, writers like Stefan Heym, not to mention ambassadors presenting their letters of credence to the Polish president. I was also able to visit many places I would not, otherwise have had a chance to see, and in the course of it all I learnt a lot.

One of the most interesting weeks I spent was with Indian Prime Minister Nehru and his daughter, Indira Gandhi, on their visit to Poland, 23–25 June 1955. He appeared to me wise and courteous, though his staff were literally terrified of him and when wanting something from him, would ask for the mediation of his daughter or, on a couple of occasions, of mine. Nehru slept only four or five hours a night and was full of vigour in the morning. I was particularly impressed by his daughter: she was perceptive and discerning. Often she would know what was said in Polish before I had a chance to translate it.

Most of the time Nehru spent on sight-seeing in Warsaw, Cracow and Silesia and visiting the site of the former German extermination camp in Auschwitz. There he seemed so greatly moved by what he saw – the crematoria, the inmates' barracks, the heaps of human hair, suitcases, spectacles, children's toys, etc. – that the questions he asked the guide, through me as the interpreter, for additional explanations were asked in visible anger.

Nehru's visit to Poland was primarily a courtesy, symbolic one underlining his support for Moscow's 'ally'. Although as the originator of nonalignment Nehru was equidistant from Soviet communism and Western capitalism, he (and his daughter after him) pursued a model of development based on centralized economic planning which was similar to the Soviet one. In fact, Nehru arrived in Warsaw from Moscow where he had just completed a very friendly 15-day visit to the

Soviet Union. Consequently, his conversations with Polish leaders did not contain any memorable political overtones. As their joint communiqué stated, there were 'no problems or controversies between the two countries'. His conversations and those of the ministers accompanying him focussed mainly on bilateral economic and cultural relations. With Prime Minister Cyrankiewicz Nehru additionally discussed the problems of Indo-China, 'where both Poland and India have been associated in the International Commission as they had previously been associated in the International Commission in Korea'.

As for the political contents of other conversations I interpreted, one that stuck in my mind was that between the powerful Politburo member Jakub Berman, who was responsible, *inter alia*, for the security services, and the influential American senator Hubert Humphrey, later the Vice-President and subsequently failed presidential candidate. When the senator enquired about the then imprisoned Gomułka, Berman argued in defence of the regime intimating, among other things, that – unlike some other East European countries – Poland was not 'spilling the blood' of its former leaders – an obvious reference to the executions that had occurred in Czechoslovakia, Hungary and Bulgaria. Indeed, Poland was the only East European country where no major communist leader was put on public trial and executed. According to the Polish communist leader Edward Ochab, it was Bierut (the Polish Stalinist leader at the time) who saved Gomułka and hence also his co-defendants in spite of strong pressure from Beria and Stalin.[1]

Moscow Again

My interpreting phase was interrupted by two assignments. In April 1952 I was included in Poland's delegation, headed by the well-known economist Professor Lange (a pre-war socialist who spent the wartime years in the United States), to the International Economic Conference in Moscow. (In view of my experience there in 1946 I was somewhat apprehensive to go, but decided to risk it.) The conference took place in the glittering Hall of Columns of the House of Trade Unions and among the delegations there were some exotic looking people from the Third World. There was, however, nothing exotic or captivating in the speeches delivered there.

This time I managed to see some of the famous sights of Moscow I had not seen before. My colleagues and I were taken, among other places, to the Kremlin to visit the churches and museums there. We saw some exquisite exhibits, including jewellery and works of art made of silver and especially ivory, some of which must have taken a lifetime to produce. Places like Lenin's mausoleum with its glass and black marble crypt and the waxy-looking corpse of Vladimir Ilyich I had seen before.

I stayed at the hotel with two other members of the delegation: Michał Hoffman, who later for many years, headed the Polish Press Agency (PAP), and Aleksander Wołyński. Wołyński, a laryngologist by training, had been an officer in the Soviet army during the war. He became an international trade specialist in post-war Poland, a high-ranking official. Wołyński entertained us by his seemingly inexhaustible store of anecdotes and jokes, some of Jewish provenance, which in later years helped him greatly in overcoming many an impasse in his negotiations. (Following the 1968 'anti-Zionist' campaign in Poland the Wołyńskis emigrated to Britain and my wife and I kept in touch with them in London.)

During my stay in Moscow I saw Tatyana a couple of times, though she was still afraid to meet me. On the eve of our return to Poland I got a nasty infection as a result of a visit to the barber. One side of my head was swollen and I was taken to the Botkinskaya hospital (Lenin was treated there in 1918 after being shot at by Fanny Kaplan of the Socialist-Revolutionaries). I stayed there for nine days, the infection was spreading near to the brain, and it was touch and go. Tatyana visited me several times, and when I got better she sketched my face on a couple of occasions to entertain me – she was very good at drawing. During the few days I spent in the hotel after I was discharged from hospital and before returning to Warsaw I noticed a marked deterioration in the standard of service and meals in comparison with those during the conference.

In Warsaw I discovered and met for the first time two cousins of my father from Lublin. They were the sisters Tosia Feder and Bronka Sawicka. Tosia, who had been imprisoned as a communist in pre-war Poland, was exchanged for a Polish prisoner in the Soviet Union around 1933. She married a Soviet-Armenian diplomat, Mandalian, who, I believe, was Soviet ambassador in pre-Franco Spain. He was executed in the purges of the late 1930s and Tosia herself was exiled. At the end of the war she was brought back to Moscow and sent to Warsaw to play a part in the new communist administration. She was first offered the post of Polish ambassador to China which she declined. Eventually she became deputy head of the Foreign Department of the party's Central Committee, which post she held for a number of years. Her elder sister, who I believe was a teacher, remained in Moscow. The younger sister, Bronka, survived the war in Poland, helped by Christian Poles, under the assumed name of Sawicka which she retained. She worked in the president's office.

Tosia's son, Andrzej Mandalian, a poet writing in Russian, knew no Polish when he came to Poland but learnt it soon well enough to write in his acquired tongue. At first his poems were of a rather Stalinist nature, but eventually he became disillusioned and changed to a somewhat dissident vein. He married his cousin, Bronka's daughter Jadwiga, a student of Polish philology and literature. She wrote a book on the language of the greatest Polish-Jewish poet, Julian Tuwim: *Filozofia 'słowa' Juliana Tuwima* (*Julian Tuwim's Philosophy of 'Word'*). The marriage failed, they divorced and Andrzej later married, Foreign Minister Rapacki's daughter, also a divorcée.

Despite her bitter experiences and all the later political developments and revelations Tosia, to my knowledge, never admitted that the whole ideology was flawed let alone condemned the communist system and practice. I only saw her a few times over the years but I suppose her life-long commitment and the fear I still detected in her eyes turned her secretive and made it impossible to admit defeat. Bronka on the other hand, whom I and my wife met more frequently when we were in Warsaw, was a very warm-hearted and caring person. She reminded me very much of the other

Bronka in the family, my aunt in Zagórów. She took great interest in the history of the family on my paternal side and would recount fascinating stories about past generations, including our great rabbinical forebears. I very much regret that at the time it did not occur to me to take notes. In effect, much invaluable information has been lost. She remembered my father with affection. The last time I saw her was in hospital where she was dying from cancer. Surprisingly composed and dignified, she asked me to dispatch a letter to her friends in London, the Jewish journalist Joel Cang and his wife, in which she asked them to take care of her daughter who was to visit them later in the year. Parting with the dying Bronka was an extremely painful experience.

Korea

At the end of the Korean War in 1953 two international commissions were set up to deal with its aftermath, one handling military affairs, the so-called Neutral Nations Supervisory Commission (NNSC) and the other organizing the repatriation of prisoners, the so-called Neutral Nations Repatriation Commission (NNRC). Both were composed of representatives of the same five countries: India (as chairman), Sweden, Switzerland, Czechoslovakia and Poland. There was a great demand for people with a good knowledge of English and my ministry wanted to assign me as secretary of the Polish delegation to the NNRC. But the security authorities were still hesitant to approve my going to a place from which I could defect. Presumably the London experience still lingered on. I was 'invited' by the security people for a couple of long 'private' conversations, out of office, in the course of which in a subtle, roundabout way, my potential loyalty was being probed. Although I had been rather cocky during these interviews I evidently passed the test. However, as my inclusion in the delegation was delayed and I joined it only at the last minute, I unfortunately missed its preparatory course. While Krysia, who was one of two Foreign Ministry employees among the five female members of our delegation and who had attended the preparatory course, filled me in on some of its details, when, like all other members of the delegation before me, I was given a revolver, I had not the foggiest idea how to use it. This turned out to be inconsequential since even before we arrived at our destination we had to hand over the revolvers to our military officer and never saw them again.

The train journey to Korea was very long, so on the way I taught some members of the delegation English. (We stopped in Moscow for a day but this time I could not meet Tatyana.) We crossed the immense breadth of the Soviet Union on the trans-Siberian railway but were disappointed to miss most of the really beautiful sights across the Urals and later along Lake Baikal (the deepest in the world) as we happened to be passing them in the night, though for a few early hours we caught some of the majestic beauty of the Baikal landscape. The cities on the way we saw only from the train windows as the stops were mostly brief.

When we crossed into China we were given a very warm welcome. In Manchuria we met a Chinese and Korean youth group who had just returned from a festival in Bucharest. We were genuinely moved when they sang Polish songs for us. From Manchuria we travelled in very comfortable conditions. We spent a couple of days in Pekin where we were invited to the Ministry of Foreign Affairs for a traditional meal. There were about 36 courses, of which you took just a little from each, and our hosts had thoughtfully provided forks and spoons as well as chopsticks, which I did not then know how to use. However, I could not bring myself to eat the 12-year-old black eggs, although most of my colleagues braved it, if only to be able to boast later that they had eaten them. When it came to shark's fins I again recoiled from touching them, but the Chinese hosts flanking me tried very politely to encourage me to eat. By conversing with them I vainly hoped to distract them but eventually, fearful of offending my hosts, I had to taste the jelly-like dish. However, by then it had turned cold and hard as rock, so I had to hold my knife vertically to break off a piece before swallowing it. At least then my hosts let me off the hook. Nevertheless some of the other dishes were very tasty, and we enjoyed ourselves tremendously. In the evening we were treated to a dance party and enjoyed folk songs performed by a Chinese choir, and the next day we went sightseeing in the capital.

On the way to Korea we stopped for a few hours in Mukden – (Shenyang since 1955) where we saw the old town, which included palaces, pagodas, old imperial tombs decorated with bas-reliefs representing elephants, lions and tigers. The next stop-over was in Harbin which had just suffered some devastating floods, and was thus a depressing sight. We visited the local museum and a well-stocked superstore. We saw the first sight of the havoc wreaked on Korea by the prolonged war when crossing the River Yalu – the border between China and Korea. The train moved very slowly on a makeshift bridge from which we saw spans of the destroyed bridge sticking out of the river. Further on we came across many a bomb crater, which we found very dispiriting. But we also saw captivating mountainous scenery of primaeval beauty. The train went through many tunnels, and between them the mountains and hills were bare, save for just some shrubbery here and there. Every inch of soil between the hills and on some slopes too, was under cultivation, for sorghum, rice and other local plants.

When we arrived in the capital of North Korea, Pyongyang – or Phenian – we were shocked by the devastation. I remember seeing people living in dug-outs covered by flat-lying windows to let in the light.

Next on our way, at Kaesong station we were warmly greeted with bunches of flowers by Korean girl-soldiers. Our final destination was the village of Panmunjom in the demilitarized zone between the two Koreas, where the NNRC operated. It was a bleak place with not a tree or shrub in sight. We were first billeted in Kaesong in vacated Korean houses, with the typical paper partitions and sliding doors, and later in fairly simple wooden huts specially built for us in Panmunjom itself. It was comfortable enough though the water was reddish from the clay soil unlike the soft clear water in Kaesong. Three times a week we drove to the baths. When we arrived in Panmunjom in September it was still very warm. On Sundays we would climb the nearest hill or make a trip by truck on a bumpy, winding and very dusty road to a waterfall, some ten miles away, where we had an invigorating bath.

The commission had been set up under the Armistice Agreement of July 1953. At its head was the Indian

Lieutenant-General Thimayya, the future chief of the General Staff of India, and in the last two months or so of the commission's work, the Indian diplomat, Chakravarti, took over. He was later Indian high commissioner in London. Poland's representative in the commission was Stanisław Gajewski, a former socialist, one of the most able diplomats of communist Poland, whose next posting was ambassador in France, where he had a close rapport with the then President de Gaulle.

One of my tasks as secretary to the Polish delegation was to attend the regular meetings of the commission taking place, first in the so-called Peace Pagoda and later in the Indian village in the middle of the demilitarized zone, and take detailed minutes of the proceedings. Krysia was assigned to assist me and we spent long evenings together preparing the minutes from our respective notes taken at the meetings.

The commission with its Indian custodial force was to retain custody of the prisoners who refused voluntary repatriation in the first two months' post-armistice period which was completed by the beginning of September. By that time the United Nations command had returned to communist control over 70,000 North Koreans and over 5,000 Chinese, while the communist side returned a total of over 12,700 UN prisoners, including nearly 8,000 South Koreans, about 3,500 Americans, nearly 1,000 Britons, and others. The total number of communist soldiers who refused repatriation was 22,600 (nearly 8,000 North Koreans, the remainder Chinese). The number of people on the UN side refusing repatriation was 359 (335 South Koreans, 23 Americans and one Briton).

The Armistice Agreement provided that political representatives of the prisoners' home countries could interview them, in the presence of representatives of the NNRC, to persuade them to return to their homelands. First we had to inspect the ground where special tents for the interviews were to be built. Although the terrain had been cleared of mines we still came across some grenades, blind shells and suspicious-looking coils of wire. The NNRC formed about 30 five-man teams (one from each member country of the commission), so-called 'subordinate bodies', to conduct interviews with POWs, mostly individually (rarely in groups) in as many 'explaining' booths. I was a member of one of the teams dealing with 'southern' prisoners. Each enclosure for the interviews had two exits, one for those prisoners who had chosen to be repatriated and the other for those who continued to refuse repatriation.

The process of 'explanations' encountered the greatest difficulties from the outset and met with negligible response from the prisoners. Explaining sessions were frequently cancelled or postponed. Some prisoners refused to be interviewed at all, others who were interviewed chanted anti-communist slogans or screamed insults at the explainers and, in some instances, even attempted to attack them. Many looked simply frightened during the interviews and, by and large, declared that they did not want to be repatriated. This was particularly the case with the more numerous prisoners held in South Korea. Apparently, the interviews of those, far fewer, held by North Korea were usually more orderly though some sang communist songs and others attempted to make propaganda speeches. But they, too, refused repatriation.

In time we realized that there was intimidation and even a reign of terror in the prisoner-of-war camps. Anyone suspected of wishing to return to the other side was, apparently, terrorized, mutilated or even killed. We were shown pieces of flesh, allegedly human liver or heart of those killed, which other suspected would-be returnees were made to eat as a warning and a deterrence. This, apparently, was particularly the case in the 'southern' camps controlled by Taiwanese Chinese. We, the commission members, were horrified.

The Chinese Prime Minister, Chou En-Lai, alleged in a message to the United Nations General Assembly that 'special agents' of South Korea and of the Chinese nationalists in POW compounds had been instructed to disrupt explanations and prevent prisoners from requesting repatriation, and that they were 'using force and such terrorist tactics as murder' against the prisoners. What we saw and heard suggested that there may have been some truth to Chou En-Lai's allegations. Probably most prisoners genuinely did not want to be repatriated anyway and those who did had already been repatriated voluntarily, so why were such methods used, if indeed they were?

Consequently, only a tiny number of prisoners interviewed agreed to be repatriated. The commission's work was marred by some disagreements between its members. The Swiss and Swedish representatives accused communist 'explainers' of harassing prisoners, while the Polish and Czechoslovak commissioners insisted that prisoners be made to attend interviews even by force. In all this the Indian chairman tried to mediate for compromise.

Early on there were some serious disturbances when NNRC members entered a compound to inspect a hospital in an enclosure. Some prisoners, apparently resenting the presence of the Polish and Czechoslovak delegates stoned Indian guards, attempted to climb the barbed-wire barricades and attack the neutral team. This forced the Indian guards to open fire to restore order, leading to the death of three POWs. There followed threats by the South Korean government to 'expel' Indian troops from Korea, which led to strong NNRC protests and a determined Note of the Indian government to the United States and the United Nations. As a result the US 'urged' the South Korean government to desist.

Throughout the existence of the commission it was apparent that it was the Chinese who were not only closely following its work but also supervising the position taken by the Polish and Czechoslovak delegates. Probably, like most of the delegation, I did not know how this was being done. It was only many years later that I read about it in a transcript of the hearing before the Committee of Un-American Activities of the House of Representatives, in April 1966, of Władysław Tykociński, who had defected to the West from his last post as head of Poland's military mission in Berlin. In 1953–54 Tykociński had been deputy chief of the Polish delegation to the NNRC. Tykociński told the committee in Washington that a leading Chinese group stationed in Kaesong had not only supervised the work of the two communist delegations to the commission but had given orders to them, almost daily or nightly, as the Chinese liked to work at night, at briefings attended by Stanisław Gajewski, Tykociński himself and the military adviser, Colonel (later General) Marian Graniewski.

The Chinese standing adviser to the Poles was Ma Mu-min.

Eventually, the NNRC was dissolved in February 1954, although this was opposed by the Polish and Czechoslovak delegates. The Indian chairman agreed that the commission's terms of reference under the Armistice Agreement had not been completely carried out, but he declared that the mandatory 90-day period for explanations had passed and could not be extended without agreement between the UN and the communist commands, and such agreement had not been forthcoming.

Around 80 Korean and Chinese prisoners who had refused repatriation insisted on being sent to a neutral country, so they accompanied the custodial force back to India. Most wanted to go to Mexico.

In view of the situation, the NNRC prior to its dissolution did not have much to do and, for that matter, neither did the military supervisory commission. They came to call us, the NNRC – the Neutral Nations *Recreational* Commission, while we retaliated by calling them, the NNSC – the Neutral Nations *Superfluous* Commission. We were, indeed, occasionally entertained by Chinese opera artists and dancers, North Korean choirs, or taken to Kaesong for a musical show. Some groups, such as that from the Chinese People's Army on a so-called comfort mission, would even sing Polish songs and dance Polish folk dances for us – all excellently performed. The food prepared by Chinese cooks was very good, and I still remember the delicious taste of the pheasants prepared by them and served by Chinese waiters. The officers' mess at the Indian headquarters was a good place for those who liked a drink, and occasionally General Thimayya would invite us there for a 'sherry party'.

Members of the delegations spoke English, but sometimes my fellow Slav, the Czech colleague would address me in Czech and expect to understand my answer in Polish. Once, while standing in front of my hut, he asked me where was *zachod*, which in Polish means 'west' or 'sunset'. Though somewhat surprised at the question as it was about six o'clock and the sunset was clearly to be seen, I pointed in that direction. He strained his eyes and said he could not see it. No wonder, for the word *zachod* means 'toilet' in Czech. From then on we relied on English rather than our own languages.

It was in Korea that my relationship with Krysia blossomed from friendship tested by time and circumstances into a deep attachment and love. She hailed from Bielsko-Biała in Upper Silesia from a family with strong socialist traditions. Her father, an activist of the Polish Socialist Party (PPS) collaborated with Herman Lieberman, a leader of the Galician PPS, until his involvement in politics was cut short by his rapidly deteriorating health. After his death in 1929, Krysia's maternal grandfather took care of her family. He, too, was a committed member of the PPS. Had he lived beyond 1944 to learn after the end of the war that Krysia had been in the communist anti-Nazi resistance, he would have been greatly disappointed and dismayed. There was no love lost between socialists and communists – they were always political opponents and rivals for the same electorate – and Krysia's grandfather was staunchly anti-communist.

Krysia joined the underground movement towards the end of 1942 through her future fiancé who was a member of the Upper Silesian executive of the communist anti-Nazi resistance movement. He and many others of that underground were arrested by the Gestapo in May 1944. Incarcerated in the notorious Block Eleven (the death block) of the Auschwitz concentration camp, he was executed, allegedly, as stated in the German notification, by a firing squad but, in fact, he was taken to the Birkenau gas chamber and killed there in August of that year. Krysia herself narrowly escaped arrest and certain death for, *inter alia*, her involvement in the production of the movement's under-ground paper and leaflets. However, she was not betrayed under torture either by her fiancé, who owned up to what he had been doing, or by the only other man among those arrested who knew about her.

Soon after the war ended, she learned about all the gruesome details of her fiancé's last weeks from a witness who had come across him in the death block and in whom he had confided in the hope that as a *Häftling* convicted for blackmarketeering he might survive and tell her what had happened. It was a great personal tragedy for Krysia which she found hard to live with, particularly in her native town where there was so much which constantly reminded her of it. The pain was made greater by the fact that she was forced to confront that communist rule was not what she had been led to believe it would be like; the reality proved disillusioning and some of its aspects highly unpalatable.

In an attempt to escape from sad memories and the participation in local party activities that was expected of her, Krysia asked to be sent to the foreign service school run by the Ministry of Foreign Affairs in the capital. On arrival in Warsaw she was told at the party's Central Committee that she was much too young for the very intensive and demanding course, that younger people cracked up under the strain at the preceding course and that they were now accepting only older candidates with complete or incomplete university education. But Krysia would not be deflected. She went to see the wife of Władysław Gomułka, Zofia, who was then in charge of cadres at the Central Committee. Zofia Gomułka, after a long conversation with her, picked up the phone and told those in charge of selection that she had no doubt that Krysia would manage and instructed them to enrol her. Krysia passed all the exams with excellent results, while quite a few people with complete higher education did not, and in the autumn of 1946 was accepted into the foreign service and admitted to the Warsaw Academy of Political Sciences to continue further studies in its Diplomatic and Consular Service Department.

I first met Krysia at the London embassy where she was transferred in 1949 from the embassy in Prague. She was still heartbroken, even though, being an attractive girl who suffered no lack of suitors, she had by that time accepted a marriage proposal. Emotionally, however, she was not yet ready for it, and in the end did not go through with the marriage.

In time I came to know Krysia as a very sensible, reliable, conscientious and broad-minded person, admirably free from any prejudices, including any anti-Jewish sentiments. Like most Poles she came from a Roman Catholic home, but her immediate family were non-observant or, more exactly, agnostic, and so was she. Our views and interests were very similar and often identical, we understood and trusted each other.

Back in Warsaw

Back in Warsaw, my schoolmate, Janek Gelbart, who had survived the war in Romania and was now also in the foreign service, and his girlfriend, Barbara (Basia), knowing of our intentions from our letters from Korea, were delaying their own wedding for us. So it was a double wedding. Guests at the joint wedding reception included the Foreign Minister Skrzeszewski, my wife's sister Irka, my uncle Itzhak and his wife, Franka. (The latter had survived the war by being hidden by a family of Catholic Poles. Itzhak's first, pre-war wife and their child had perished in Auschwitz.)

I resumed work in the British Section at the Foreign Ministry, this time as acting head of the section with my additional duties as interpreter. Krysia was assigned to the International Organizations Department with responsibility for matters dealt with by the UN General Assembly Third Committee (Social, Humanitarian and Cultural).

Soon we were happily awaiting the arrival of our child. We both not only wanted a son but were so sure it would be a boy that we named him Stefan, after the Polish version of my father's name, long before he was born. And a boy, a big and healthy one, it was. Stefan was sheer bliss and the source of unadulterated joy for us. He was a lovely, cheerful baby, had a marvellous appetite and was exceptional in that he never gave us a sleepless night and rarely ever cried. From the first he seemed to take particular pleasure in his daily bath and loved to splash in the water, often drenching us to the skin in the process. He was such an appealing baby that on one occasion when I took him in his pram to the Łazienki Park, a Chinese film crew filmed him for their newsreel from Warsaw. We, his parents, had the tremendous joy of a child, but thanks to his grandma, Krysia's mother Hermina, our professional lives were not at all disrupted. Grandma Hermina, who had become a widow at the age of 29 and, though an attractive woman, had for the sake of her two daughters never remarried, came to stay with us right after Stefan's birth. Until then she had cared for Andrzej, the son of her older daughter Irka, but thought that since Andrzej was four years old by then and Irka, whose husband was a defence lawyer, had no need to work, it was her duty to come and help us. We remember her with gratitude as it was mainly she who gave Stefan all the attention he needed and lovingly cared for him, leaving us free to pursue our professional work. Thus, straight after her three-month maternity leave, Krysia could go to a UNESCO General Conference in Montevideo as a member of the Polish delegation and the following year, in 1955, to the United Nations General Assembly session in New York. And in the same year I left for my next assignment, Cambodia. Unfortunately, I was unable to wait for Krysia's return from New York and Krysia could not join me in Cambodia as my assignment did not provide for it. I was thus separated from Krysia and Stefan for about a year.

The correspondence that Krysia and I exchanged during the period we were separated from Stefan and/or from each other, and letters from Krysia's sister, Irka, with whom he and Grandma Hermina stayed in Bielsko for part of the time I was in Cambodia were a chronicle of how our son was behaving and growing up as a baby and toddler. Though a poor substitute for witnessing our child's progress personally, these letters made our missing him more bearable during the periods when we were away from him. (All these hundreds of letters Krysia has carefully kept, and I have been greatly moved in re-reading most of them after nearly 40 years.)

Cambodia

Following the defeat of the French at Dien Bien Phu in Vietnam in 1954 and the five-power Geneva Conference on Indo-China, three international commissions were set up, one in each of the 'Associated States' of the peninsula – Vietnam, Laos and Cambodia – to supervise the implementation of the ceasefire agreements. They consisted of representatives of three countries: India (again in the chair), Canada and Poland. At the beginning of 1956 I was appointed Poland's representative to the commission in Cambodia, with the rank of minister plenipotentiary. I took over from Mr Wolniak, a future deputy foreign minister.

Having received all the necessary inoculations in Warsaw, I travelled through Paris (to visit Mother), Rome, Beirut, Karachi, Calcutta and Bangkok, stopping in most of these cities for a day or so. Soon after arriving in Phnom Penh I was bed-ridden with a bad stomach pain and fever. Mindful of my past experiences, particularly with the amoebic dysentery I had contracted in Kazakhstan, I feared a serious tropical disease. Fortunately, it was nothing more exotic than gastritis and I was soon on my feet.

Barely did I manage to find my bearings when I was in the middle of gigantic state celebrations. In March 1955 the then 33-year-old King Norodom Sihanouk, who, on the death of his grandfather, King Monivong, in 1941, had been chosen king by the Royal Council, abdicated in favour of his father, Norodom Suramarit, in order to be able to take a direct part in the political life of the country, which he had at first. pretended to shun. However, he effectively continued to rule the kingdom, initially as prime minister and later without that title, as just Prince Sihanouk. The celebrations I witnessed in 1956 marked the coronation of his parents. They were only figureheads though the queen, said to be the dominant and even the domineering one of the two, attempted to exert some influence.

First I had hurriedly to acquire the necessary diplomatic garb for the celebrations. For that purpose I had to go to Saigon, the 'Paris of the East', where a Chinese tailor was recommended to me. Told of the urgency of my order, he took my measurements and asked me to come back a few hours later for a fitting. At the fitting he made the necessary adjustments on a paper coat and told me the tail-coat and trousers, morning-coat and striped trousers and off-white dinner suit would shortly be sent to me to my hotel in Phnom Penh. Unaccustomed to this sort of fitting, I was a bit apprehensive what would come out of it. In the event, what I got was absolutely perfect and people would ask me where I had such an admirable fit made. The remaining accessory, a top hat, and Paris-made at that, I also managed to obtain in Saigon. (All this garb came in handy at my next major foreign assignment.)

The celebrations lasted for a week. The coronation itself was on 5 March 1956. Prince Sihanouk handed the crown to the new king who crowned himself and then crowned his wife. In the evening, the prince – as prime minister – gave a buffet dinner for the diplomatic corps during which he joined the band and played in turn the saxophone, the accordion and sang in Cambodian, French and English. Most of the songs were of his own composition as was Cambodia's national anthem. Sihanouk was also an accomplished painter.

The next day there was a huge, splendidly exotic and colourful royal procession in which elephants played a prominent part. The following day there was a military parade. In the evening we were treated to a Cambodian ballet at the Royal Palace. The gorgeous colours and graceful movement, especially of hands, fingers, legs and feet, held us enthralled. Then, among many other festivities, there was a royal garden party with impressive fireworks and good music. There were also other festivities. Even though the coronation celebrations had ended, the partying did not, and there were cocktail parties, dinners, concerts, film shows and boat trips on the Mekong River, among many other diversions.

Phnom Penh itself struck me as a picturesque combination of the exotic East with modern civilization, but it was also a place of tremendous contrasts: there was great, ostentatious wealth and heart-rending, abject poverty. Next to smart boutiques and jeweller's shops dripping with gold and gems, next to the latest models of American cars, there were beggars, cripples and children sleeping in the street. I had seen something similar in Bangkok and Saigon.

Early on I visited my Polish counterpart in the Vietnam commission in Hanoi, my former boss in London, Ambassador Michałowski. He received me warmly, and offered me some advice on how to be a good boss, as I headed a team for the first time. The advice proved useful, though some of it I thought slightly cynical. Generally, during our occasional meetings, Michałowski was very kind and helpful.

On a later occasion in Hanoi my Polish counterpart in the Laos commission, Janusz Zambrowicz, and I were together officially received by Ho Chi Minh, the president and communist leader of North Vietnam. We talked generalities, as is the case on such occasions, but the president seemed an interesting interlocutor. When the conversation lasted more than half an hour, Zambrowicz and I decided to take our leave so as not to impose on the president's time unduly. We were unaware that we did the wrong thing, that in the case of a head of state it is he (or she) and not the visitor who indicates the end of an official call. Ironically, Zambrowicz later became deputy head of protocol at the Foreign Ministry in Warsaw after having served as ambassador in Moscow and Bucharest. (Incidentally, his boss, head of protocol, Edward Bartol, used to pronounce 'diplomatic corps' embarrassingly like 'corpse'. He was appreciative when privately I drew his attention to this error.)

In Hanoi I also saw officially other North Vietnamese leaders, including Prime Minister and Foreign Minister Pham Van Dong and the Minister of Defence, General Vo Nguyen Giap, the victorious commander at Dien Bien Phu and in other battles. Naturally, they enquired about the work of the commission in Cambodia.

In our spare time my colleagues and I tried, when visiting Vietnam, to see a bit of the country. We visited, among others, a very colourful, richly decorated temple of the Cao Dai sect, one of the more obscure of Vietnam's exotic mix of religions. It has a 'pope' and female cardinals and includes among its saints: Buddah, Confucius, Sun Yat-Sen, Jesus Christ, Victor Hugo, Joan of Arc, Churchill and others. We even attended their service, which I filmed with my newly acquired camera.

In Phnom Penh I stayed in the Hotel 'Royal', the only moderately decent one. It boasted four air-conditioned rooms, the only ones in town. Luckily, I was given one of them. The hotel restaurant was good, that is the meals were tasty, in particular the desserts which were delicious. On the face of it, the standard of hygiene seemed good to me but a little incident proved otherwise. When a waiter whom I asked to exchange my spoon after it had fallen on the floor for a clean one, stuck it in his pocket and went towards the kitchen, I followed him. I did so on an impulse to see what the kitchen looked like rather than to check what he would do with the spoon. As I looked through the door at the forge-like kitchen with fire bellowing everywhere, I saw the waiter taking out the spoon from his pocket and rubbing it with his fingers to clean it. I gave him a piece of my mind when he brought it back to my table.

As for the commission itself, its major tasks under the Geneva Agreement – the supervision of the withdrawal of all French Union and Vietminh forces from Cambodia and overseeing of the political settlement in the country completed with the general elections – had been accomplished before my time there. Yet much remained to be done. My job was a responsible one, though matters were not nearly as controversial as they had been in Korea, if only because, in the case of Cambodia, the commission was not called upon to mediate between communists and anti-communists. Still, at times there were differences within the commission and between the commission and the Cambodian authorities. Differences within the commission followed mainly from the fact that I and the Polish delegation generally reflected the interests of the communist side (that is, principally North Vietnam and China), the Canadians reflected those of the anti-communist side (South Vietnam and the USA), while the Indian chairman attempted a mediating role, sometimes siding with the Polish member and sometimes with the Canadian. Differences between the commission and the Cambodian authorities arose when the latter failed to implement the terms of the agreement.

I had to use my own judgment and initiative. There was nobody I could consult, and Warsaw was far away and relying on me. Assessing that in view of the then political situation it was in Poland's interest, I recommended to my government that it recognize the independence of and establish diplomatic relations with Cambodia, which duly took place just after my return to Warsaw. Poland was thus the first East European country to do so. I was also instrumental in having Sihanouk invited for an official visit to Poland which took place while I was still in Phnom Penh. As Michałowski told me, my political reports, especially in this context, were greatly appreciated.

The commission's chairman, General Das, a former head of army intelligence in India, was a very upright man of rare integrity. A non-smoker and teetotaller, he used to say, 'I don't believe in the small vices'. Occasionally, he would go to Hong Kong without his wife – only he, as commission chairman, could have his family with him. Unlike General Das, my first

Canadian colleague, Arnold Smith (later to become ambassador to Egypt, to the Soviet Union and subsequently, in 1965, the first Secretary-General of the Commonwealth), was somewhat devious. The man who replaced him was much more likeable. (Sadly, soon after his Cambodian stint, he died.)

We, the three-man commission, were dealing mainly with Prince Sihanouk himself. Before going to see him we would thrash out a common position. On an early occasion we differed – General Das and myself holding one view, the Canadian Commissioner another. After a slight concession on the part of General Das and myself, we reached a compromise. Since the Canadian spoke good French he offered to present our compromise position to Sihanouk instead of having it translated by the commission's interpreter, and we agreed to this. General Das was going to the meeting with Sihanouk in his car, the Canadian and myself in a second car. On the way he asked me whether I spoke French, and I answered in the negative which I usually do if I don't know something well enough. When, as agreed, the Canadian was presenting the commission's position to Sihanouk, my poor French was sufficient to understand that what he was putting forward was his original point of view and not the 'compromise' position we had agreed upon. I was flabbergasted and had to do something about it. I whispered what I had heard into the general's ear. He was equally amazed and asked the commission's interpreter who was with us to confirm what I had told him, which he did. The general was furious and from then on, his relations with the Canadian commissioner were rather cool.

I used to see Prince Sihanouk officially also on my own, and socially I saw him more frequently. Most of the time we spoke through my interpreter, but sometimes directly. His English was as poor at the time as my French. But the prince, who was just a few months my junior, wished to practise his understanding of the language as I did that of French, so he would speak in French and I in English and we managed very well without an interpreter.

Sihanouk had an oriental charm, a captivating smile and genteel manner. As a host he was gracious, but as a politician he was often unpredictable, at times impulsive or volatile, not to say erratic. He was known for his frequent swings of mood and petulance. However, to most Cambodians he was the embodiment of the nation and he could not be faulted for his paramount interest in his country and its people.

During the French–Vietminh War he had tried to steer a neutral course. Now Cambodia's relations with France, the former colonial power there, remained good, but with its neighbours – South Vietnam and Thailand – they were rather strained. It was primarily the Americans who vied for influence on the Cambodian establishment not only with the French but also with the Indians, as well as the Japanese, the former occupying power. There were also other forces at play, such as the Taiwan Chinese or the anti-Diem (South Vietnam President) Vietnamese. Unlike his mother, the queen, Sihanouk was rather anti-American. Among other things, he was said to dislike the behaviour of the American Ambassador, Robert McClintock, who was then the doyen of the diplomatic corps. The Americans called Sihanouk, in private, facetiously and somewhat contemptuously, 'Snooky'.

Sihanouk was at the time, apparently, under the political influence of the young Indian chargé d'affaires, Ajai Mitra, a former secretary of the prominent, left-wing Indian politician and Minister of Defence Krishna Menon.

Overall Sihanouk conducted a neutralist policy between the Western powers and the communist bloc, travelling a lot and managing to obtain economic aid from both sides. To some, however, notably the Americans, Cambodia's neutralism was more apparent than actual, because of its inability to prevent the Vietminh from using the country as a troop and supply route to South Vietnam. (Eventually, Sihanouk was overthrown in a coup in 1970. However, in September 1993 he came full circle to the Cambodian throne. *The Times* described him then as 'one of the great political survivors of modern times'. But by 1993 he was hardly ruling over his unfortunate country, whose impoverished population of more than nine million, 90 per cent of which was rural, was further threatened by as many land mines left over from the country's bitter conflicts.)

Socially I became very friendly with Ajai Mitra and his wife. I was surprised to find out that she knew of my Jewish origin from my predecessor, Wolniak – non-disclosure of personal information about your colleagues being an unwritten rule in the foreign service – but even more surprised that she herself was Jewish as I did not know there were any Jews in India. Her's was an interesting story. She had not been aware of being Jewish, she was not even sure she was, but once taunted about it, contrariwise decided to be Jewish.

Ajai was charming and brilliant, and he had a photographic memory. Knowing me he wanted to know my country, so I gave him a book about Poland. He read it in no time and could recite whole pages from memory. Ajai was not a faithful husband; he had a beautiful Filipino girlfriend, a consummate dancer. Occasionally they would take me to the night-club 'Cambodge'. At first Ajai took me there with his wife. Ajai himself did not dance. Sometimes I would dance with his girlfriend, but the really showy dances she did with the Filipino band leader: their cha-cha was superb.

(Later Ajai was a first secretary in the Indian mission to the United Nations in New York. His time in New York partly coincided with my posting in Canada, and my wife and I visited the Mitras there a couple of times. I was very upset when a few years later he was assassinated in Vienna, where he served as a member of the UN Commission on Narcotic Drugs. Reportedly, he had come too close to exposing a drugs ring.)

My colleagues and I made a few interesting trips in Cambodia. On one occasion we went on a fishing boat to a nearby coral island in the Gulf of Siam. We were enchanted with the beauty of the island. It was densely covered with lush tropical vegetation and dotted with gorgeous, colourful flowers. We enjoyed swimming in the sea which was warmer than body temperature, even scorching in shallow places but we had to beware of sharks. The excursion was memorable also for another reason. Not fully aware of the devastating effect the combined exposure to the tropical sun and seawater would have on our skins, we returned to Phnom Penh pretty badly sunburnt.

On a later occasion we went by plane to Kratieh where one of the commission's inspection teams was based. We were a bit apprehensive because the tiny six-seater plane, 'the flea' as we used to call it, was flown by the commission's French pilot who liked to drink even before a flight and was inclined to show off with his aerobatics. This time, however, he spared us, and anyway, he was a very good pilot. On the first day, we drove through the jungle to a rubber plantation and saw how the milky latex was tapped from the trees into cups attached to the trunks and then, in a rubber processing plant, how that milky liquid was transformed into various types of rubber.

The next day we visited a local tribe in the jungle, which was still living in Stone Age conditions. I had never before or since seen such abject misery. At dusk we drove in a larger party accompanied by local hunters into the jungle for night hunting. The area was marked on the map by a special colour denoting that its topography had yet to be explored. It was, apparently, only at night that we could come across some animals. During the daytime we saw only two huge, magnificent birds and one buffalo. At night we saw more animals, that is, their gleaming eyes and it was by the colour of the eyes that these animals could be identified. Greenish eyes, we were told, were those of a panther or deer, red, of a tiger, pinkish, of an Asiatic fox, and so on. We actually saw that night four pairs of eyes. First, from a distance of about 150 metres, we saw what looked like two shining glimmers. When we directed our searchlight at them it blinded the animal which is why it is, apparently, safer to hunt at night but, by the time we came close enough to take a good shot, the animal had disappeared. Of the four animals two were, in all probability, Asiatic foxes and at least one was a panther which we managed to get nearest to, about 10 to 15 metres. One of our party ventured to jump off the vehicle to take a shot at the shining green eyes among the bushes, but the animal managed to escape.

The hunting expedition was an unforgettable experience though a somewhat scary one – we were in the middle of a thick jungle of a radius of at least 100 kilometres. On our way back we saw walls of burning jungle: villagers were burning grass and some trees around their settlement. It was a most magnificent nocturnal sight, which reminded me of the great fireworks in the gardens of Versailles I had seen in 1949.

My most thrilling and, at the same time, frightening experience occurred on another trip to the Gulf of Siam. After having a swim and taking some photographs we went to Mount Bokor on the sea, a distance of some 40 kilometres. The mountain, 1,070 metres above sea level, is covered by thick jungle. The higher up we went, the more beautiful were the views. On reaching the top a breathtaking panorama extended before our eyes: the precipitous rocky mountain-side; the slopes covered with a carpet of luscious green jungle with a greyish patch of an elephant moving among it; the emerald sea reflecting the light of the setting sun; the myriad islets dotting the sea; the fabulous sky at sunset; and the sun itself, a huge ball of fire, slowly sinking into the shimmering sea on the horizon. We were enthralled.

Some tourists on Mount Bokor decided to stay there overnight in a deserted shack so they would be able to admire the sunrise, and also to avoid returning through the jungle in the dark. We set out on our return journey, not expecting anything untoward to happen. After about 40 minutes' drive down the winding jungle road a huge, light grey mass suddenly emerged a few metres in front of us. It was an elephant, perhaps the same one we had spotted from the top of the mountain, moving in the same direction we were. There were four of us plus the Cambodian driver, and we had no firearms, which was probably just as well. We didn't know what to do but told the driver to stop the car. Then realizing the elephant was dangerously close, we asked him to back up. He barely started when he stopped again; it was too dark and we could have tumbled down a precipice or overturned into a ditch. So we just sat there in the car, the tension mounting. The two younger ones among us were laughing nervously; Ewert, who was the oldest, was trying to calm them down. Meanwhile the elephant was plodding on rather briskly, from time to time turning his head as if wondering where this sudden light was coming from. We did not switch off the motor. When he disappeared behind the next bend we waited a while and moved on gingerly. Round the bend we saw the beast again and this went on for a few more bends. Our hearts sank. One of the younger colleagues had stopped laughing, while the other one, apparently terrified, was now laughing hysterically. At long last the elephant moved off the road, but he seemed to be standing in the ditch. We decided to drive past the beast at full speed, though the road was very narrow and bumpy. As we did so we realized that the grey form in the ditch was just a huge tree trunk similar in colour to that of the elephant.

The encounter, though frightening, was an unforgettable experience. Our driver declared categorically that he would never again drive through the jungle at night, while I reproached him for not warning us of such a danger, of which he, as a local, must have been aware. Later we were told that as a rule a lone elephant did not attack unless he was wounded or enraged. We were, however, also told that a single elephant was a rogue elephant removed from the herd and therefore liable to be aggressive. But in any case, had the elephant been moving in the opposite direction, he would have wanted to 'clear' his way and would have pushed the car away even without any aggressive intention.

We made one more trip to the Bokor Mountain. But, as the weather turned foul and it was pouring with rain, we drove down and had a lovely bathe in the cascading mountain river. Then we drove to Kep, also in the Gulf of Siam, and swam in what was, due to the bad weather, a pretty rough sea.

To crown it all, shortly before the end of my stint, I joined my fellow commission members on a visit to the celebrated Angkor Wat. First we flew to Siem Reap where we had one of our meetings and then on to Angkor, the heart of the old Khmer empire. Our French pilot who must have had his usual drink, swooped in our tiny plane over Angkor Wat and circled it. We did not mind too much because we were admiring what we saw. One source decribes Angkor Wat as 'probably the largest religious edifice ever constructed'. It is a twelfth-century Buddhist temple next to Angkor, built originally as a mausoleum for the Khmer King Suryavarman II. From the fifteenth century onwards, when the capital was moved to Phnom Penh, Angkor was like a lost city, apparently kept by monks. It was only when the French colonial regime was established in 1863 that Angkor Wat became a focus of interest, and a programme of research and reconstruction began. When we were there it was still prey to the engulfing vegetation. In some places it was just jungle-covered remnants of temples and ruins of a once-elaborate system of reservoirs and waterways. But we could still admire the magnificent architectural works, remarkable for their striking originality of design and decoration. I can still remember the walls of the galleries decorated with bas-reliefs of extraordinary beauty representing scenes from Indian epic poems and battle scenes.

My assignment was coming to an end and it was time for farewell visits and parties. There were plenty of those, sometimes two or three a day. I was received by Prince Sihanouk who had only just returned from his foreign trip which had included his visit to Poland. I had an interesting and pleasant chat with him. He was very complimentary about my wife whom he had met in Warsaw. At the end of our meeting he presented me with a beautiful farewell gift: a Cambodian silver embossed rose bowl. I was also received in audience by the king.

The diplomatic corps gave me a warm send-off. At the farewell meeting of the commission, the chairman, General Das, addressing me said:

> ...During the course of our association, I have appreciated your sound political judgment, your keen sense of fair play and the realistic manner in which you tried to deal with each case. You have always displayed a liberal attitude towards the views of your colleagues although you might not have been in complete accord with them. You have ably discharged the task of representing your country and have been a helpful colleague. The successful functioning of this commission shows that given good will and honesty of purpose, it is possible for different countries to have better understanding of each other and work fruitfully together in international affairs. I am personally obliged to you for the congenial atmosphere thus created as it helped me a great deal in discharging my task as chairman of this commission with grace and ease... All of us in the Indian delegation and the international secretariat shall feel your absence greatly. You have been a good friend and a cheerful colleague. You have tried to make our tasks lighter by your keen sense of humour and broad-mindedness...

The Canadian commissioner who had only worked with me for about two months said:

> ...I have been impressed by his unfailing sense of cooperation and skill in carrying out his duties, but I think, above all, by his sense of honour and proportion. Of all these qualities I would think surely the most valuable is his ability to see the lighter side of any problem, however difficult...I can truthfully say that my Polish colleague and I have had no differences in the period of our association... Certainly I feel that had there been any differences they would have been dealt with in a pleasant and objective manner; and these differences would have ceased at the conference table and never have been carried into our social activities...

I do not have the text of my own farewell speech, but I remember one story I had in it (about the diplomat's role). It concerned members of four professions arguing as to whose profession was the oldest. First the physician said: surely mine is the oldest, otherwise how could Eve have been created out of Adam's rib? Next the civil engineer argued: yes, but before you had Adam and Eve, you had to create mountains and valleys, lakes and rivers, and who could have done that but an engineer? Then followed the lawyer who said: before you had Adam and Eve, before you had mountains and valleys, lakes and rivers you must have had some order in the universe and who could have done that but a lawyer? And the last, the diplomat, agreed that order had had to come before all those other things, but out of what do you create order? Surely you create it out of chaos, and who could have done that but a diplomat?

The departure itself was very pompous. It was the only time in my career that there was a military guard of honour for my benefit.

On my way back to Poland I stopped over in 12 cities. In Delhi, to which I had been invited, I visited, among other things, the Lok Sabha (parliament) as a 'distinguished visitor', and saw the beautiful sights in the city, but also the squalid life in parts of it. The other cities on my itinerary were Bangkok,

Calcutta, Cairo, where of course I visited the pyramids and rode a camel with some difficulty, Rome, where I tremendously enjoyed seeing the ancient places I had learned about at school and, naturally, Paris, where I was happy to see my mother again.

Note

1   *Polityka* (Warsaw), No. 44, 31 October 1981.

Part Two

5 • Return of Polish Art Treasures: My Most Challenging Assignment

By this time, in late 1956, Poland was in a completely different political climate than when I had left it. Since Stalin's death in 1953 and the mildly liberalizing changes in Moscow which followed it, there had been demands for reforms throughout Eastern Europe. In Poland, in particular, calls for change became increasingly vocal both within the party as well as in the country at large, and particularly among the intellectuals. There were demands for an end to the crude rigidities of Stalinism, for a more flexible economic system, for more consumer goods, for a reduction in the power of the security apparatus and for less subordination to Soviet interests. But it was only in 1956 that those demands greatly intensified, became more widespread and the pace of change itself began to accelerate. In fact, 1956 was a momentous year: the Soviet leader, Nikita Khrushchev's denunciation of Stalin and his crimes; the death in Moscow shortly thereafter of the Polish Stalinist leader, Bolesław Bierut; and the workers' rioting in Poznań for bread and freedom, which was bloodily suppressed with many fatalities.

As a result of Bierut's death, Edward Ochab, who in spite of his Stalinist past was by now committed to moderate reforms, became party leader for a short while and then handed over leadership to Władysław Gomułka, the former leader previously gaoled for not being pro-Soviet enough, and only just politically rehabilitated. In the charged atmosphere only he, a 'national' rather than a Stalinist communist, and a victim himself of Stalin's vengeance, could be expected to gain national acceptance. When in October Khrushchev and some other members of his Politburo arrived in Warsaw to pressure the Polish leadership against any radical changes, Gomułka dared to resist, even under the threat of military intervention, and after some heated and acrimonious exchanges a sort of compromise was worked out including Gomułka's assurances that Poland would not pursue an anti-Soviet policy. Thus what came to be known as the 'Polish October' marked the beginning of a period of relaxation accompanied by a general euphoria. Soviet personnel, including the Defence Minister Marshal Rokossowski, were sent back to Moscow. (Years later Rokossowski was to complain that in Moscow he was regarded as a Pole.[1]) Some liberalizing reforms were also initiated at this time. Most collective farms, the number of which was much smaller than in other communist countries, were dissolved; relations with the Church were improved, and Cardinal Stefan Wyszyński, the Primate of Poland, imprisoned since 1953 was set free; and greater freedom of expression and movement between Poland and the outside world was allowed. Poles cheered Gomułka, they opted for a working realism, accepted the alliance with Moscow, but were determined to work out a better, less brutal, non-Soviet brand of communism. Poland had gained a greater measure of domestic autonomy than any other member of the communist camp, although in world affairs it had no choice but to follow the Soviet line.

I, too, was happy about the turn of events, though I was somewhat sceptical as to whether the aroused public expectations would materialize. (As it turned out, they did not.) In the atmosphere of political thaw, my prospects in the foreign service became brighter. I could reasonably hope to be now considered trustworthy enough not to be sent on a foreign assignment unaccompanied by my family. Krysia, on her part, refused to go for the second year running to the session of the UN General Assembly, making it clear to our superiors that she did not wish to be separated from her family either. Before long I was summoned to see the Deputy Foreign Minister Józef Winiewicz.[2] He commended me for my work in Cambodia and offered a choice of postings: either as minister plenipotentiary in one of the Scandinavian countries, presumably Norway, where Poland had a legation rather than an embassy, or as counsellor and chargé d'affaires in Canada where, for reasons I shall explain, there was only a legation headed by a chargé d'affaires. I preferred Canada, even though it meant accepting a lower rank. It was a much more challenging assignment which, moreover, gave me a chance to get to know America and language-wise presented no problems. I had some doubts, however, whether, given my Jewish origin, I was the right person to be appointed to a country with a sizeable Polish minority, particularly in the context of what the Polish government sought to achieve in Canada. Winiewicz (who, incidentally, was said to have been anti-Semitic before the war) brushed my misgivings aside. He said he would not be guided by such considerations and, anyway, Canadian Poles, unlike their American brethren, were not anti-Semitic. So Canada it was. (As I later learned my appointment, like many others at the time, was made possible by the easing of the rigorous party control over personnel appointments. This allowed Minister Rapacki to assign genuine foreign service staff to postings abroad before his relative freedom in this respect was again severely restricted. Referring to this short-lived period, Winiewicz writes in his memoirs: 'I do not hesitate to say that thanks to that freedom [of making independent appointments] we obtained then one of the best staff at Polish missions abroad.'[3])

The appointment as counsellor and chargé d'affaires was dated 1 November 1956, and my family and I, including my mother-in-law, travelled to Cherbourg and left on the *Queen Mary* on 23 November for New York.

In New York we were welcomed by Ambassador Michałowski, now Polish representative at the United Nations. Evidently we were destined to be 'neighbours' again. We stayed in New York overnight and then travelled by train to Ottawa. There I took over the legation from Edward Kołek, a repatriate from France, and settled in the residence at 323 Stewart Street. Sadly, a few days after our arrival, a telegram brought us the tragic news of the sudden death of Staszek, the husband of my wife's sister Irena. He had died in court of a stroke while defending a client. Their son, Andrzej was barely six years old.

We found Canada's federal capital, Ottawa, which lies on

the Ontario side of the River Ottawa – the other side being the French-speaking province of Quebec – a small rather sleepy city of about 300,000 inhabitants. Ottawa was essentially a civil service community where people lived an unhurried life and practically the whole city was geared in some way to the government and to parliament. The latter's imposing buildings of the House of Commons, the Senate and the Library of Parliament, with their Gothic stone façades and green copper roofs were particularly reminiscent of a mini-Westminster in London. Ottawa with its lovely parks was especially beautiful in the autumn when the maple leaves presented a riot of colours – from pale yellow, through orange to crimson red. A great attraction in the city was the Canadian National Gallery housing not only the largest collection of Canadian art but also an impressive display of American, European, Asian and Inuit painting and sculpture. Especially memorable were the paintings of Canada's Group of Seven, a breakaway from the Royal Canadian Academy, who came to prominence in the 1920s. Most of them were not professionally trained, and their colours and techniques were rather unconventional. It took a long time for the group to be accepted by the establishment.

When I called for the first time at the Department of External Affairs, the then Under-Secretary of State, Jules Léger (brother of Cardinal Emile Léger of Montreal), told me at the beginning of our conversation: 'We have in the department two enormous files, one concerns the Second World War and the other the Polish Art Treasures.' It was the task of retrieving the latter for Poland which made the assignment to Canada so challenging. The Polish government and its five representatives who preceded me in Ottawa had been trying, unsuccessfully, to repatriate these treasures since 1946. The first two representatives, Dr Alfred Fiderkiewicz and Eugeniusz Milnikiel, were fully fledged heads of legation with the rank of minister. Between the two Dr Zygmunt Bielski was briefly chargé d'affaires. The Polish government then, having lost patience with the Canadian government, downgraded the rank of its next representative to that of chargé d'affaires, which was reciprocated by Canada. The first chargé d'affaires was Dr Eugeniusz Markowski, son-in-law of the celebrated writer Jarosław Iwaszkiewicz, who had previously been posted in Rome, and then the aforementioned Edward Kołek.

The odyssey of the Polish art treasures which eventually landed in Canada began in September 1939, shortly after the outbreak of the Second World War. In those anxious days a decision was taken at the Royal Wawel Castle in Cracow – 'the Polish Westminster Abbey', as a Western journalist dubbed it – to spirit away its most precious national relics and art treasures in order to safeguard them against seizure by the invading Germans. Failing any assistance for the evacuation of the treasures from the fast-disintegrating central and local authorities, the custodian and director of the State Collection of Art at the Wawel, Dr Stanisław Świerz-Zaleski, and his assistants had to rely on their own ingenuity and courage and on the help of ordinary people to move them out. They loaded the treasures in the evening on a garbage truck and took them to a coal barge on the River Vistula, which carried them under the cloak of darkness downstream to the city of Sandomierz. From Sandomierz, in order to obviate the risk of German planes spotting the treasures as well as to bypass the main roads which were under constant German bombardment and clogged by fleeing dignitaries and refugees, the treasures were first taken on their way towards the Romanian border by peasants' carts via side roads and finally by military lorries into Romania.

The treasures were under the care of Dr Świerz-Zaleski and architect Józef Polkowski (a draughtsman at the State Collection), who were subsequently named by the Polish government-in-exile as their custodians. In Bucharest it was considered to deposit the treasures for safekeeping with the Vatican. However, the Vatican refused ostensibly on the grounds that they were not Church property but, in fact, to avoid problems with the Germans who would have demanded that they be handed over to them. The German embassy in Bucharest which found out about the treasures was putting pressure on the Romanian government to seize them from the Polish embassy. By then it had been decided to move them to France. A small Romanian ship, the *Ardeal*, carried them to Marseilles from where they were sent for safekeeping to the town of Aubusson in central France, a centre of the tapestry-weaving industry since the Middle Ages. In France other valuable items from the Royal Castle and the National Library in Warsaw and the Catholic Clerical Seminary in Pelplin were added to the collection. When in view of the advancing German troops France, too, became unsafe, the collection was shipped from Bordeaux on the Polish freighter *Chorzów* to Britain. First kept in London it was eventually sent from Greenock in Scotland to Canada on the Polish M/S *Batory*, the flagship of the Polish merchant navy. The ship was also taking British gold to Canadian banks, and was escorted by British boats and planes.

The collection of about 280 items (contained in 24 metal trunks and seven long cylinders) included the celebrated twelfth-century jewel-encrusted coronation sword of Polish kings called *Szczerbiec*, regalia of King Jan Sobieski, maces, sceptres and other royal insignia and robes, royal standards, armour, jewellery, royal saddles and caparisons, and various *objets d'art*. Among the items there was an original Gutenberg Bible, the value of which was estimated at the time by an American expert at half-a-million dollars, and an early sixteenth-century psalter (these were two of the three items in the collection which belonged to the Church), scrolls of ancient Polish chronicles and psalters, the Holy Cross Sermons dating from the thirteenth century, and the oldest extant relic of the old Polish language, the *Chronicle of Wincenty Kadłubek*, covering Polish history up to the year 1206. There was also a precious collection of Chopin's original scores and other manuscripts and, above all, 136 priceless arrases of a larger collection, representing the finest Flemish Renaissance Gobelin art in the world, which were bequeathed by the sixteenth-century King Sigismund Augustus to his sisters with the proviso that on their deaths the wall-hangings became the property of the nation. Some of the tapestries were illustrative of traditions of chivalry or were heraldic in nature, some with the coat of arms of Poland and Lithuania. Many represented biblical themes, the most famous depicted Adam and Eve and the Creation, the Flood and Noah's Ark, the Tower of Babel, and other scriptural topics. Yet another series represented the animal world and mythological beasts. The collection also included a few privately owned items. The overall value of the treasures was at the time conservatively appraised at 60 million dollars.

They are to the Poles as the Crown Jewels are to the British and more. Each item is part of Polish history. And considering the vicissitudes of that history – the wars, defeats, invasions, the partitions, plunder and devastation – it is understandable why the Polish people, whatever their political persuasion, have always been so passionately and deeply attached to their national relics, why they have been so sacredly cared for and why children have been brought up learning about them. The regalia and the tapestries enshrined the memory of a glorious era when Poland had ranked among the most advanced of the civilized states of Christendom and particularly the memory of its golden age under the dynasty of the Jagiellons, when the tapestries had been created, when Poland was one of Europe's proudest empires and Cracow a national capital and cultural centre of great prestige.

Apart from the Wawel art treasures, *Batory* carried an even more precious cargo – hundreds of Jewish children who had been brought to safety from Poland and had been assigned to homes with Jewish families in Canada for the duration of the war.[4]

On the arrival of the treasures in Canada in July 1940 the Canadian government provided a hall for their storage in the Record Storage Building at the Central Experimental Farm in Ottawa. The hall, according to Świerz-Zaleski, 'was an ideal place to store our collection'. And there they lay undisturbed for nearly five years while the Second World War raged elsewhere. However, from the beginning of 1945 the collection was parcelled up and moved out at the behest of Wacław Babiński, the then minister plenipotentiary of the London-based Polish government-in-exile in Ottawa. Most evidently, the purpose was to conceal the treasures in places and in such a manner as would preclude their return as state property to the new post-war communist government in Poland which was soon to be recognized by Canada. The royal *Szczerbiec*, Chopin's manuscripts and a number of other items packed in two trunks were deposited in July 1945 in the Ottawa branch of the Bank of Montreal in the names of Świerz-Zaleski and Polkowski. Previously, in May of that year, 23 trunks and one coffer were moved to the monastery of the Redemptorist Fathers at St Anne de Beaupré near Quebec City. One key to the place where they were stored was held by the Superior General, Father La Plante, and the other by Polkowski. Only persons empowered by Dr Babiński could have access to the treasures deposited there. This was the instruction Father La Plante had received from his superiors in Quebec. In June, eight boxes were taken from the Experimental Farm to the Convent of the Precious Blood of Jesus in Ottawa.

On 6 July 1945 the Canadian government recognized the new Polish government in Warsaw whose first representative, Dr Fiderkiewicz, arrived in Ottawa in May 1946. When he talked to Świerz-Zaleski and Polkowski they declared that they were committed by oath not to divulge the treasures' whereabouts. However, Świerz-Zaleski proved more cooperative a few days later (according to Balawyder 'the next morning'[5]) and handed over a list of arrases and Gobelins brought from Poland, which he had kept hidden away from the others, and a non-negotiable receipt for securities dated 2 March 1945 issued by the Bank of Montreal in Ottawa, on the back of which Świerz-Zaleski wrote: 'I declare that everything in the two trunks is the property of the Polish state and that they contain nothing that is our private property, that is Mr Polkowski's or mine.'

The original custodian, Świerz-Zaleski, though no friend of the new regime in Poland, passionately believed that the treasures belonged to the people in Poland, whatever its government, and was determined, as he later wrote, 'to return to the nation what is national'.

When Świerz-Zaleski went to the monastery to ask for the boxes deposited there he was told they had been moved three days earlier, evidently on Dr Babiński's orders. Father La Plante told Zaleski that, 'any further information he wanted could be obtained from Cardinal Villeneuve'.[6] The Canadian Catholic clergy, however, as Cat-Mackiewicz, Prime Minister of the Polish government-in-exile, later admitted, was 'helping us in hiding the treasures'.

In a statement to the Canadian government Zaleski said:

I declared [to Father La Plante]...the collection belongs to the Polish nation and not to Dr Babiński...When we [he and Polkowski] discussed the matter later with Dr Babiński he told us that I should leave Ottawa altogether and go to New York to look for a position as an art expert there, and to forget all about the Wawel Treasures, while Polkowski should go somewhere to Vancouver, to secure there a position as an architect.[7]

Dr Babiński was so adamant in his opposition to the return of the treasures to the new Polish government that he admitted he preferred the relics to be destroyed rather than to fall into the hands of the communists.[8]

In a reply to Dr Fiderkiewicz's notes, in the first of which the precise location of the the treasures after their removal from their original place of storage had been indicated, the Canadian government declared that by agreeing to store the treasures at the Experimental Farm in 1940 it had not taken any responsibility for them. The Canadian government further stated that until May 1946 it had had no access to the treasures and had not known they had been moved. Now it had issued instructions for new locks to be fitted at the Experimental Farm so that the remainder of the treasures be safeguarded.

That remainder, a tiny part of the treasures, was handed over to Świerz-Zaleski and a representative of the Polish legation at the end of August 1946 for return to Poland. The Canadian government maintained, however, that it had no influence on the decisions of the bank and the monasteries which, according to the legation, were holding the bulk of the treasures. The legation's request to the bank for the release of the two trunks was refused on the ground that it required the consent of both depositaries, that is not only of Świerz-Zaleski but also of Polkowski.

In subsequent notes the Polish legation repeatedly emphasized that under international law the Canadian government was responsible for protecting the rights of other states on its territory and especially their property, particularly as regards national relics. The Polish government argued that the responsibility of the Canadian government had arisen from the mere fact that Canada received the Polish treasures on its territory and agreed to store them in a government building. The exhaustive legal case had been worked out and repeatedly presented to the Canadians and at the United Nations by the head of the Polish Foreign Ministry's Legal Department, Professor Manfred Lachs.[9]

In February 1948 the then Under-Secretary of State for External Affairs, Lester Pearson, informed the Polish legation that the Royal Canadian Mounted Police (RCMP) had traced some of the treasures – that is, those previously held in the Monastery of the Redemptorist Fathers at St Anne de Beaupré. They were at the Hotel Dieu convent in Quebec City. A well-known lawyer, Senator Theriault, representing the legation, went to see the Mother Superior, St Henri, whom he asked to hand over the collection of treasures belonging to the Polish state. He was given a written declaration stating that she had, indeed, received the collection from Dr Babiński whom she had regarded as the representative of the Polish authorities. Following that visit the Mother Superior:

> ...fearing to become involved in court action...contacted the Premier of the Province of Quebec, Maurice Duplessis. With the knowledge and consent of Dr Babiński, Duplessis agreed to take the treasures to the Provincial Museum. This he did on February 25 1948. To provide necessary protection he placed a permanent twenty-four hour guard at the entrance of the room containing these treasures.[10]

On this occasion Duplessis accused the Canadian federal government of '[making] themselves the collaborators of Stalin and his Polish government to the point that they ordered their police to ignore the laws and to violate the cloister...'.[11] In an immediate reply the RCMP Commissioner, S.T. Wood, denied the Duplessis allegations, and the federal External Affairs Minister, Louis St Laurent, rebuked the tactics of the Quebec premier in a sharp statement in the House of Commons. For Duplessis in his staunchly Catholic province holding on to the treasures was not only a manifestation of his fiercely anti-communist stand but also a matter for political use against the federal government.

The Canadian government was of course seeking legal advice. To quote Professor Balawyder:

One legal opinion held that Canada was responsible for the return of the collection on three counts; the immunity from local jurisdiction of the property of a sovereign state, the obligation of one state to respect and protect the property of another state, and the responsibility of a central government in any federal state. Based on these principles the Polish government was under no obligation to use Canadian courts to litigate against those who refused to return the treasures to Poland. Moreover, Canada could not consider herself free from blame nor from responsibility in desisting from pressing Quebec to hand over the treasures since according to international law the government of Quebec and its officials are included in the concept of a federal Canadian state. Despite this advice the Canadian government did not act immediately.[12]

This legal opinion seems valid, though in a letter to Gustave Lanctot, Deputy Minister of Public Works and Archivist, of 1 August 1940 (the time when storage of the treasures was granted in the Public Records Building), the then Consul General of Poland in Canada, Wiktor Podoski, stated:

It is understood that the articles in question will in no way involve the responsibility of the Canadian Government, since they have not been placed in its hands. On the contrary, it is the undersigned who, as the representative of the Polish Government, accepts full responsibility for the space which was placed at its entire disposal for the period during which the articles will be stored.[13]

In his reply Gustave Lanctot said:

I take note of your declaration to the effect that the Polish Government assumes full responsibility for the period during which these articles will be in safekeeping. The Canadian Government agrees to this arrangement and is glad to render that service to the Polish Government...[14]

The Canadian government considered itself a third party to the dispute willing to provide Poland 'any assistance it

needed in locating the national relics and providing the
Canadian courts for prosecuting the culprits' because 'the
treasures in question were removed between 2 March and 27
May 1945 from the storage place at the Ottawa Experimental
Farm, some forty days prior to Canada's official recognition of
the Polish provisional government'.[15]

The treasures were stored in poor conditions, lacking
proper conservation, both in the Quebec Provincial Museum
and in the bank in Ottawa. Polkowski who was, since Świerz-
Zaleski's return to Poland with the first tiny part of the
treasures in 1948, the only curator, regularly reported to his
superiors about their deterioration. This prompted many
organizations and individuals both inside and outside Poland,
including most Polish-Canadian organizations, publicly to
demand their speedy return. However, the head of the Polish
government-in-exile, Premier Antoni Pająk, who visited
Canada in 1957 reiterated his government's position at a press
conference saying that the treasures would 'unconditionally
remain in Canada as long as Poland does not regain complete
independence'.[16]

The Polish government in Warsaw continued to make
strenuous efforts for the return of the treasures not only
through its representatives in Canada, but also internationally
at the United Nations, in UNESCO, through other
organizations and the governments of the big powers, which
had pledged at Potsdam to safeguard Polish national
property. At the same time Warsaw tried quietly to influence
émigré Poles and Polkowski himself to change their minds –
but so far unsuccessfully. It was obvious that the stalemate in
the matter of the treasures had in large measure been the
result of the general political climate between East and West.

The Canadian government, though politically it may have
been sympathetic to the émigré Poles, probably genuinely
wished to remove the internationally embarrassing problem
of the treasures from its agenda. But it was evidently not in
a position to coerce either Mr Duplessis or Mr Polkowski
into releasing the treasures, a fact Warsaw could not
understand.

In July 1956 the Department of External Affairs submitted a
memorandum to the Cabinet which in its preamble contained

a good portion of a Polish note of June 1956 with which the department agreed. According to Balawyder:

> The memorandum stressed that Canada's position of neutrality will be more and more difficult to defend both from the legal and from the moral standpoint. The statutes of limitation of Ontario and Quebec prevented the Polish government from bringing civil proceedings before the Canadian courts. The Canadian recognition of the Polish government in 1945 necessarily included the recognition of the property owned by the previous government. The memorandum reminded the members of the Cabinet that Canada alone, among such nations as the Soviet Union and East Germany who also stored Polish property, continue [sic] to retain Polish collections. It also pointed out that the Polish emigrants outside of Poland and the Catholic Church in various communist dominated countries, including Poland have pressed for the return of the Polish treasures. To avoid further adverse publicity that might result if the topic were introduced to the International Court of Justice, the memorandum suggested that Canada should initiate a procedure to have the two trunks in the Bank of Montreal released... The Cabinet considered these recommendations and accepted them.[17]

When I took charge of the legation in Ottawa in December 1956 the Polish side knew nothing of that change of heart on the part of the Canadian government. (I found out about that memorandum only from Balawyder's book many years later.) For Warsaw the struggle for the treasures was as much on the agenda as before. Thus, from the very start of my assignment in Ottawa efforts to have them returned to Poland were my principal preoccupation. The issue figured in most of my official and unofficial contacts. In fact it was the main focus of my nearly five-year stay in Canada.

In January 1957 I called officially on the Secretary of State for External Affairs, Lester Pearson (Nobel Peace Prize winner later that year), and had a long 'fundamental' talk about the treasures. It was then that, as the Warsaw chronicler of the treasures saga wrote later: '...a friendly attitude of the

[Canadian] government towards the matter of the return of the Wawel treasures was expressed for the first time'.[18] The conversation was amicable and we seemed to have struck up a good rapport. Soon after, Pearson remarked to Ambassador Michałowski at the United Nations in New York: 'At last you have sent somebody we can talk to'.

A month later Pearson talked to Deputy Foreign Affairs Minister Winiewicz at the UN and promised to act towards the return first of the bank deposit. Talks and consultations continued and on 25 April 1957 I received the Secretary of State's written confirmation of the promises made earlier. This was a turning point.

Soon after, however, Pearson's Liberals unexpectedly lost the elections and power which they had held for a continuous 22 years. The Progressive Conservatives took over, led by their recently elected leader John Diefenbaker, a Saskatchewan Baptist who had the reputation of an outstanding criminal lawyer with humanitarian qualities. He had been known to champion the cause of the underdog, defending some of his poorer clients for free. Tall, curly-haired, a non-drinker and non-smoker, Diefenbaker was a very effective speaker with an endless fund of anecdotes, he had charm, a personal magnetism and evangelical fervour. It was largely thanks to him that the Conservatives won the 1957 elections by a small majority and again won the elections in the following year by a landslide. In fact, it was the biggest majority of any prime minister, and he was the thirteenth in Canada's history. By then Pearson had been the Liberals' leader for only about two months and he was at that time no match in an internal political contest for the aggressive and charismatic Conservative leader. Pearson was overwhelmingly elected leader in January 1958 in preference to the more experienced politician Paul Martin, because of his international popularity as a world peace-maker and his Nobel Peace Prize which he had been awarded for the role he played in the 1956 Suez Crisis and in the formation of the United Nations Emergency Force. However, Pearson's knowledge of national problems and domestic politics was said to be limited. Besides, he was not ruthless enough; he did not have the killer instinct a successful political leader requires. He was an accomplished diplomat trained in the art of negotiation and compromise. At the age of 32 he had resigned as history lecturer at the University of Toronto, joined the Department of External Affairs and 20 years later, after various important postings abroad, the then newly elected Liberal leader, Louis St Laurent, persuaded him to leave the civil service and become head of the External Affairs Department. Since then Pearson had been in politics. After his crushing defeat in 1958 he was reported to have said: 'For a time this evening, I wished I were back at the University of Toronto, teaching history.' However, in time Pearson was emerging as a competent leader and a formidable antagonist in the House of Commons. He also impressed people by his honesty and sincerity.

Our efforts *vis-à-vis* the Canadian government had to start anew. Prime Minister John Diefenbaker had the matter of the treasures studied again and agreed to see me himself. He listened attentively to what I had to say, appeared very understanding and promised to resolve the matter, but pleaded for a little more time. My bosses in Warsaw were pleased.

Prime Minister Diefenbaker received me several times over the next couple of years, which for a junior head of mission was no mean achievement, and he seemed to have taken a personal liking to me. When he visited India he spoke very commendably about me to the Polish ambassador there, Juliusz Katz-Suchy who, incidentally, during his many years' service as Poland's representative at the United Nations in New York had also pleaded for the return of the treasures. Warsaw sent me a copy of Katz-Suchy's report on his conversation with Diefenbaker. I wondered whether, in the eyes of my superiors in Warsaw, it was a good thing to be so highly praised by 'the other side'.

I saw, of course, the new Secretary of State for External Affairs, his deputies and other ministers quite frequently both officially and socially. Most of them were trying in various ways to be helpful.

In September 1957 the Polish Foreign Minister Adam Rapacki, who came to New York for the general debate of the UN General Assembly session, talked to his new Canadian counterpart, Sidney Smith, mainly of course about the treasures. As Winiewicz, my immediate superior at the Foreign Ministry, was also there, I was asked to come over to report personally on the progress of my mission. Walking in the lobby of the UN with Winiewicz we came across Diefenbaker, who greeted me warmly. I took the chance to introduce Winiewicz to him, but Diefenbaker just shook his hand, said he was in a hurry, excused himself and left. I was rather amused to read what the above-mentioned Polish chronicler made of that brief encounter: 'On September 23 1957 Deputy Minister Józef Winiewicz conducted a pre-liminary conversation with the new Canadian premier at the UN session in New York.'[19] Winiewicz did have an exhaustive talk about the art treasures with Sidney Smith's successor, Howard Green. In his memoirs[20] he makes much of that talk, overstating its significance.

In the meantime, of course, general political circumstances had changed. The 1956 political thaw in Poland and *détente* in East–West relations had influenced not only the Canadian government but also some hitherto intransigent Polish émigré circles. The latter's political leadership in London had split and while the government-in-exile continued to be adamantly opposed to the return of the treasures some rival bodies began to waver. In these conditions my legation, mainly through the Consul General Edward Więcko, was contacting Polkowski directly. Without his consent the bank would have been unable to release the two trunks deposited there. By then Polkowski, having seen how the treasures were deteriorating, was facing a crisis of conscience. Also the Canadian government had been quietly assured, by Winiewicz and Lachs in their conversation with Howard Green, that when the return of the treasures became possible the actual transfer would be made not to the legation but to a special delegation of art experts from Poland. This approach took into account the sensibilities of the émigré anti-communist Poles who feared that the Warsaw government wished to make political capital out of the return of the treasures.

Yet, despite all these positive developments, the issue remained unresolved. Our efforts continued unabated and that included influencing public opinion. I had extensive contacts with the Canadian press and a number of influential columnists had become sympathetic to the return of the treasures. Similarly, the Consul General in Montreal, Wojciech Kętrzyński, was active in the province of Quebec.

As a result of all the efforts and in particular of unofficial talks with the Department of External Affairs, the management of the Bank of Montreal in Ottawa and Polkowski, the first stage of a resolution of the problem had finally been prepared. It was agreed for the contents of the two trunks in the bank to be inspected jointly by Polkowski and art experts from Poland. The time was thus ripe – December 1958 – to bring over to Canada the delegation of experts. It was headed by Professor Jerzy Szablowski, the director of the State Collection of Art at the Wawel Castle in Cracow from which the bulk of the treasures originated. The other experts were Professor Bohdan Marconi, Chief Conservator of the Centre of Relics in Warsaw; Professor Zbigniew Drzewiecki, president of the Chopin Society in Warsaw (in view of the Chopin manuscripts included in the bank deposit); and Professor Marian Morelowski from Wrocław. Ironically, the latter had been a member of the Polish delegation authorized to take over from Soviet Russia, under the Treaty of Riga of 1921, a collection of arrases which, following the 1795 third partition of Poland, Empress Catherine the Great had ordered to be taken from Warsaw, occupied by the army of General Suvorov. The delegation was joined by the world famous pianist living in the West, Witold Małcużyński, who, at the request of the Chopin Society had even earlier begun talking to Polkowski and some influential émigré Poles both in London and in Canada with a view to reaching some understanding on the return of the treasures. The experts and I spent many evenings at my residence talking, sustained by coffee and cognac to which Małcużyński was particularly partial, until the small hours.

In private consultations with Polkowski it was agreed that if the forthcoming joint inspection were to show that the treasures in the trunks, unopened for more than 13 years, were deteriorating, a report to that effect would be jointly drawn up and Polkowski would agree for the deposit to be taken to Poland. The trunks were opened just before Christmas 1958 in the presence of three bank officials, and Professor Szablowski accompanied by members of the delegation, Polkowski accompanied by his experts (including an American from Chicago) and Witold Małcużyński. Świerz-Zaleski, who had died in Poland in 1951, had transferred his rights as depositary to the head of the Polish legation in Ottawa. These rights were now being exercised by Szablowski.

As Szablowski later told me, the atmosphere during the inspection was solemn and charged with emotion. When the celebrated *Szczerbiec* was being taken out of the trunk all those present instinctively stood up in reverence. In the joint protocol its signatories unanimously concluded that the treasures 'require immediate conservation measures'. Among the signatories, notes Balawyder, 'officials of the Canadian and Polish governments were conspicuous by their absence'.

Thus the way was open for the return of the bank deposit. The technicalities, including the important legal aspects, demanded the legation's full attention. We sought the advice of eminent lawyers, as did the bank. The bank as well as the Canadian government asked for specific guarantees not to hold them responsible for any loss, damage or deterioration suffered by the contents of the two trunks. We had to be extra careful not to create a precedent which would in any way adversely affect future negotiations for the return of the treasures kept by Premier Duplessis in the Quebec Provincial Museum, which might have been depleted by then. These problems caused me a lot of anguish, but I was, of course, in constant touch with Warsaw. In the final stage I had urgently to call Minister Rapacki to obtain approval for the delegation of experts to co-sign the necessary documents with the representatives of the London émigré authorities as there had been no precedent for Poles of the two opposing sides to cooperate in any official way. It was about five in the morning in Warsaw when I called. Woken suddenly in this way, Rapacki, normally an alert and very courteous man, was so confused (which I later found out was usual for him when woken) that he did not know who he was talking to, let alone what it was all about. The only rational thing he managed to say was 'talk to Winiewicz'. Winiewicz from whom after a while I received the go-ahead, refers to this episode in his memoirs. He called Rapacki, who flatly refused to give his consent, and added: 'if you wish, take the decision yourself', which Winiewicz did.[21]

The delegation of experts, including Szablowski, was becoming restless and impatient, for they did not fully appreciate the possible implications of a hasty and imprudent legal guarantee. There was a battle with the bank for words and formulations, but eventually we suggested a compromise formula. The bank accepted it against, as they put it, the advice of their lawyers and probably after some prodding by the Department of External Affairs which outwardly maintained the appearance of non-interference. I signed the document on behalf of the Polish government, which also authorized Professor Szablowski to take charge of the two trunks and give a receipt acknowledging their delivery. On 8 January 1959 I was able to inform Warsaw that Polkowski had formally renounced his rights to the bank deposit.

Technical preparations for the transportation of the treasures and ensuring their security could now go ahead, the security aspect being particularly relevant. We were anxious to bypass the Province of Quebec, through which the train to New York would normally travel, so as not to risk the seizure of the precious cargo by the Duplessis authorities.

At long last, on 18 January 1959, a bitterly cold day with heavy snowfall, the treasures retrieved from the bank and sealed by the Polish legation as diplomatic cargo, set out on their long journey home, accompanied by Szablowski, Marconi, myself and special couriers sent from Warsaw. Loaded in some secrecy on to a lorry they were taken from the bank to the Ottawa railway station to be transported to New York. Security guards from the RCMP provided protection to Fort-Erie on the Canada–US border and from there American rail and ordinary policemen took over, headed by Bolesław Lewandowski, a Polish American who declared himself proud to be participating in this venture. In New York we were greeted, among others, by Jerzy Michałowski, and Romuald Spasowski the Polish ambassador to the UN and to the United States respectively.

In New York the invaluable cargo was loaded aboard the Swedish vessel *Stockholm*. On 21 January we left the US and arrived at Gothenburg ten days later. From there the cargo was taken to Copenhagen, then ferried to Berlin where it was loaded into a sealed train which arrived in Warsaw on 3

February. Thousands of people jammed the Warsaw station to welcome the treasures home. Though the communists were masters at staging and orchestrating mass gatherings, on this occasion it was all genuine and truly spontaneous.

It is hard to describe the jubilation and the celebrations marking the return of the treasures. It was as if the whole nation participated in a big display of joy and patriotism, the more so since Poland was already preparing to begin in 1960 celebrations of its millennium, of which the returned treasures were such an important testimony. There were exhibitions and meetings where warm words of appreciation and special thanks were extended to the members of the delegation of art experts, to Witold Małcużyński and to myself, and there was a festive concert given by Małcużyński playing Chopin at the Wawel Castle in Cracow.

However, the two trunks retrieved from the Bank of Montreal in Ottawa represented in terms of items only about one-third of the treasures originally brought to Canada. The bulk was still held in the Quebec Provincial Museum. So, on my return from Poland I informed the Canadian authorities of the growing impatience of the Polish people with the delay of their return, particularly in view of the forthcoming celebrations of the thousandth anniversary of the Polish state. I also informed the Secretary of State for External Affairs that the Polish government was studying a proposal to have the treasures problem presented for a joint reference to the International Court of Justice at the Hague. This avenue was turned down by the Canadian government which maintained that even if the question was resolved in favour of the release of the treasures, there was no moral means of persuading Quebec to abide by the decisions; force would have to be used.

But the Canadian government was anxious to have the problem solved. So when on 7 September 1959 Premier Duplessis died, a change of heart on the part of Quebec could be expected. The new Quebec premier, Paul Sauvé, an open-minded person, publicly stated that he hoped to have the tapestries returned as soon as he became sufficiently acquainted with the details of the problem. Later at a press conference he admitted that he was being urged by representatives of the Polish government-in-exile and its ministers calling from London not to release the treasures. I saw Premier Sauvé several times, and the Consul General in Montreal, Wojciech Kętrzyński also talked with him. Wojciech and I used to quip that now *la Pologne est Sauvé*. Unfortunately, Sauvé died suddenly on 7 January 1960 at the age of 52.

Sauvé's successor, Antonio Barrette, also promised to 'make sure that this treasure goes back to Poland; it is theirs; they can have it'. Barrette, in turn, was defeated in the June 1960 elections but the new premier, Jean Lesage, was equally ready to seek an immediate solution to the problem.

But it still took time and many strenuous efforts before we obtained a final decision. In the meantime the Canadian Polish Congress had passed a resolution at its board of governors' meeting in November 1959 asking for the immediate return of the collection to Poland. Its president, Dr Brzeziński, a pre-war Polish diplomat and father of Professor Zbigniew Brzeziński who became President Carter's national security adviser, made the request publicly. The impatience was also reflected in the international press. In London *The Times* wrote in its editorial on 21 January 1960:

> ... more important than the artistic absurdity of the present situation or the legal question of ownership is the undoubted feeling of the Polish people over this question. Communist or anti-Communist, Roman Catholic or atheist, they are all passionately attached to their past and its relics. For them, these treasures do not belong to one Government or another, but to the Polish nation. When the rest of these treasures return, as they should, to Poland the Canadians may feel they are rid of an embarrassment; the Poles will have regained part of their history.

The obstacle, of course, was the London Poles. But here, too, things had begun to change, at least in some quarters. While the government-in-exile still continued to be adamantly opposed to the return of the treasures, the rival Council of National Unity headed by General Anders and Count Edward Raczyński and its representative in Canada, Adam Żurowski (who succeeded Dr Babiński on the latter's death in 1957) agreed to the return of the treasures 'in a manner that would not be interpreted as a victory to the Polish communist government'.[22] This change was reinforced by a statement made by the Primate of Poland, Cardinal Wyszyński, at Gniezno on 24 April 1960 that the bishops meeting in a plenary conference had declared themselves in favour of the treasures being returned to the Wawel Castle. This was a change from the position Cardinal Wyszyński held on the matter in 1958, when in a letter to Cardinal Leger, he said that the treasures should be returned to their 'legal owner, the Church'.[23]

According to Balawyder:

> In the fall of 1960 A. Zurowski and J. Polkowski carried out detailed negotiations with Premier Lesage. The Quebec Premier, satisfied with these negotiations, asked the Department of External Affairs to inform the Polish authorities that the Quebec Provincial Museum would be prepared to receive representatives of the Wawel Museum in order to effect the transfer of the treasures stored in the Provincial Museum.[24]

In the meantime, as a result of Polish–Canadian talks the respective legations of the two countries had been raised to embassy level and the Canadian chargé d'affaires in Warsaw, Gordon Southam, had been appointed ambassador. Ambassador Southam called on Minister Rapacki on 29 November 1960 to transmit the happy message that the Canadian authorities had agreed to return to Poland the remaining national treasures held in the Quebec Provincial Museum. Consequently, professors Szablowski and Marconi were sent to Quebec City, where they arrived on 28 December to take them over, while all the necessary preparations were made by diplomatic channels. As Balawyder records:

> The Polish government's representative, M. Sieradski [*sic*], the Chargé d'Affaires at the Polish Embassy in Ottawa, gave a written undertaking that Professor Jerzy Szablowski was fully authorized to give a receipt acknowledging the delivery of the treasures. He further guaranteed that upon the release of the treasures the Polish People's Republic would hold Quebec harmless 'against any claims that may

be made with respect to these objects by any other persons or institutions...on account of any damage or deterioration that may have occurred or taken place to the objects' while held in Quebec. The Polish government requested that the Canadian government 'provide all the facilities and protection of the treasures consistent with the normal diplomatic practice, to insure their safety while on Canadian territory'. Canada agreed to this.[25]

The transfer was effected on 1 January 1961. Similarly to the part deposited in the bank, the 24 trunks containing the tapestries were sealed by representatives of the Polish embassy and travelled as diplomatic cargo. On this occasion, too, the winter was very severe and because of blizzards the departure of the vans was delayed. It took them 26 hours, through the snowstorm, to reach the US border. Up to that point they were escorted by the Royal Canadian Mounted Police and from there by state troopers through Vermont, New Hampshire and Massachusetts.

The Wawel Collection, previously valued at about 60 million dollars, 'was insured by 250 foreign organizations and companies from 28 countries including the Soviet Union, the people's democracies, England and the United States, Switzerland and Egypt, India, Indonesia, Mexico, France, Western Germany, Scandinavian countries'.[26] However Balawyder writes that the collection 'was insured by 28 companies...which included firms from England, France, Sweden, Egypt, Japan, Mexico, the United States, the Soviet Union and other countries from the socialist bloc. No one company was able to adequately ensure the priceless cargo against possible damages or losses the collection could incur on its way across the Atlantic.'[27]

On board the Polish vessel *Krynica* and accompanied by professors Szablowski and Marconi, the treasures were heading home. In Warsaw a special commission was appointed to officially receive the collection.

Thus after nearly 22 years the Polish national relics were coming back from where they had been taken and to where they belonged. It was a triumphal return and very symbolic because of the celebrations of Poland's millennium.

The Canadian government was pleased at the eventual solution of the dilemma of the treasures. The newspapers expressed satisfaction, most of them emphasizing the 'good will' and 'friendly relations' that such a restoration would engender between Canada and Poland. Poland was again jubilant, Poles abroad were relieved and happy. Only the Polish government-in-exile protested. Its foreign minister, A. Zawisza, expressed his regret that Canada agreed to the restoration of the precious relics to 'an alien power occupying Poland which has a long record of infidelity'. He contended that Canada's decision was an act of capitulation of an 'ethical and moral position' and 'a submission to the demands of Communism'.[28]

President Kennedy once said that success has many fathers, failure is an orphan. In the case of the return of the treasures there were many claimants who alleged or on whose behalf it was alleged that their part was decisive in bringing about that result. The claims ranged from the near ridiculous – a Polish-Argentinian activist claimed such a role – through the doubtful, to the exaggerated. Even those who did play a significant part were inclined to magnify it. Deputy Foreign Minister Winiewicz is a case in point.[29]

As for myself, I am fully aware that the recovery of the treasures was the result of a complex combination of circumstances and influences primarily of a political nature – the political thaw in Poland, East–West *détente* and the death of Duplessis. The London émigré Poles and their representatives in Canada played a bigger part, in first withholding and later releasing the treasures, than was generally realized at the time, but also the pressure brought to bear by the Warsaw government and its representatives played a significant part. As one of those representatives I happened to be in the right place at the right time; I did what was expected of me reasonably well and I did not make any errors of judgment or other mistakes which might have jeopardized or delayed the solution of that delicate and complex issue. My contribution was much appreciated by my superiors, which found its expression on my return to Poland in my appointment to departmental deputy director in the Ministry of Foreign Affairs and the fact that an Officer's Cross of the Order of

1. Maternal grandfather, Mayer Berliner.

2. Paternal grandparents, Abram Sieradzki and his wife Bela.

3. The author's mother, Pola Sieradzka, *née* Berliner.

4. The author's father, Szlama Sieradzki.

5. Class at the Jewish secondary school. The author is on the extreme right in the bottom row.

6. Both sides of the author's father's postcard from the Warsaw Ghetto.

OSWIADCZENIE

Ja niżej podpisany Powstaniec Getta Warszawskiego,Komendant
Oddziału Żydowskiej Organizacji Bojowej, stwierdzam niniejszym
że Slama Sieradzki ze Żagurowa był zemną razem w Getcie Warszawskim od początku 1941 roku, i brał udział w powstaniu w Getcie
Warszawskim w roku 1943 w moim oddziale, zginął śmiercią bohaterską
na ul.Nowolipiej dnia 28.maja 1943 roku.
Powyższe dane w razie potrzeby stwiedzić mogę przed Sądem.

/Zylberberg Henryk/
Vel/Malinski Henryk /
Golina n/Wartą rynek 21 pow.Konin
Polska

Prezydium Miejskiej Rady Narodowej w Golinie pow.Konin
stwierdza własnoręczność podpisu Ob. Zylberberg Vel Malinski
Zamieszkały w Golinie ul.Rynek 21.

Z-ca Przewodniczacego
/Kamiński Kazimierz/

7. Certificate recording the author's father's death in the Warsaw Ghetto.

8. The author standing behind the Chinese Prime Minister, Chou En-Lai, waiting to
translate his speech. Also in the picture are, from the left: Bolesław Bierut, First
Secretary of the Central Committee of the Polish United Workers' Party (that is, leader
of the Communist Party and of the country until his death in 1956); Aleksander
Zawadzki, chairman of the Council of State (that is, President of Poland); Konstanty
Rokossowski (in uniform), the then Polish Defence Minister, a Polish-born Soviet
Marshal and one of the top Soviet military commanders in the war with Nazi
Germany, who was sent to Poland to head the Polish military from 1949 until 1956,
when he was asked by the Poles to return to Moscow; and Józef Cyrankiewicz, Polish
Prime Minister.

9. Interpreting for Władysław Gomułka, leader of the Polish Communist Party and the Indonesian Communist Party leader, Aidit. On the far right of the picture is Polish Politburo member, Roman Zambrowski.

10. Interpreting for Polish Prime Minister Cyrankiewicz and Burmese Prime Minister, U Nu. On the left of the picture is the Polish Foreign Minister, Stanisław Skrzeszewski.

11. Interpreting for Bierut, Zawadzki and Pandit Nehru, Prime Minister of India.

12. With Nehru and his daughter Indira Gandhi in the former German extermination camp at Auschwitz (between Nehru and myself is the Polish Deputy Foreign Minister, Marian Naszkowski).

13. Presenting gifts from the Polish government to the King and Queen of Cambodia.

14. Talking to Prince Sihanouk.

15. International Commission in Cambodia (the author is fifth from the right in the first row; next to him are Indian General Das, head of the commission and the departing Canadian Commissioner).

16. With Polish art experts at the Polish head of mission residence in Ottawa. From the left: Professor Bohdan Marconi, Chief Conservator of the Centre of Relics in Warsaw; Polish Consul General in Montreal, Wojciech Kętrzyński; Professor Marian Morelowski; the author; and Professor Jerzy Szablowski, director of the State Collection of Art at the Wawel Castle in Cracow and leader of the experts delegation.

Polonia Restituta was bestowed on me. My involvement in the matter was recorded in the Canadian and Polish press, and in subsequent books and papers on the treasures. The greatest reward, however, was my own satisfaction; the proud feeling that I had participated in a historic process and contributed to what I firmly believed then and believe now was the only right solution, irrespective of the communist regime prevailing in Poland at the time. It was the high point of my career.

Notes

1   Józef Winiewicz, *Co pamiętam z długiej drogi życia* (*What I Remember from [My] Long Life*) (Poznań: Wydawnictwo Poznańskie, 1985), p. 528.

2   Józef Winiewicz, a pre-war conservative journalist who during the Second World War worked for the London-based Polish government-in-exile.

3   Winiewicz, op. cit., p. 548.

4   Aloysius Balawyder, *The Odyssey of the Polish Treasures* (Antigonish, Nova Scotia: St Francis Xavier University Press, 1978), p. 29. This book is an exhaustive account of the subject mainly from the point of view of Ottawa. It contains some inaccuracies.

5   Ibid.

6   Ibid., p. 51.

7   Ibid., p. 42.

8   Jerzy Ros, *Tajemnice arrasowego skarbu* (*The Mysteries of the Arras Treasure*) (Warsaw: Książka i Wiedza, 1963), p. 106. The writer went through all the 'twenty-seven bulky folders' on the matter at the Ministry of Foreign Affairs in Warsaw. From the point of view of the government in Warsaw it was a comprehensive account of the treasures' saga though, of course, it also contained elements of pro-communist propaganda. Since then quite a number of books and papers have been written on the subject. As I have had no access to those folders myself while writing these memoirs I have been unable to go into greater detail about my official activities.

9   Manfred Lachs, a graduate of Cambridge, was later, for many years until his death, judge and, for some time, president of the International Court of Justice at the Hague.

10   Aloysius Balawyder, op. cit., p. 55.

11   Ibid., p. 58.

12   Ibid., p. 61.

13   Ibid., Appendices, p. 91.

14   Ibid., p. 92.

15   Ibid., p. 65.

16   Edward Więcko, 'Sprawa skarbów kultury i sztuki polskiej w Kanadzie' 'The issue of the treasures of Polish culture and art in Canada', Przegląd *Polonijny*, No. 4, 1984, p. 21.

17 Aloysius Balawyder, op cit., pp. 70–1.
18 Jerzy Ros, op. cit., p. 150.
19 Ibid., p. 153.
20 Józef Winiewicz, op. cit., p. 601.
21 Ibid., p. 602.
22 Aloysius Balawyder, op. cit., p. 81.
23 Ibid., p. 80.
24 Ibid., p. 83.
25 Ibid., p. 84.
26 Jerzy Ros, op. cit., p. 180.
27 Aloysius Balawyder, op. cit., p. 85.
28 Ibid., p. 87.
29 Józef Winiewicz, op. cit., pp. 598–603.

6 • My Canadian Experience

Canadian Relations

During my stay in Canada I obviously took an interest in its public life and not just in a political sense worthy of reporting on to my government. I had my special, in some ways, personal interests; I was keen, for instance, to understand Canada's relations with its powerful southern neighbour. Here I want to reflect briefly on that subject. Both countries are huge, stretching from the Atlantic to the Pacific but Canada's population is about one-tenth that of the United States and about 90 per cent of Canadians live (or lived when I was there) within around a 200-mile belt adjoining the United States. This made for a particular closeness and friendliness along the longest land frontier but also for some problems. Most of Canada seemed Americanized; cities differed little from their American counterparts except, of course, Quebec City which has an historic character of its own thanks, *inter alia*, to Château Frontenac and especially the Plains of Abraham. This was the scene of the battle in 1759 between the British forces under General Wolfe and the French under Montcalm, during which both commanders were killed. The British victory there established their supremacy over Canada. (Canada's history was another of my special interests.)

Though Canada had its distinct policies, including foreign policy, political and military interests were very similar and hence cooperation between Ottawa and Washington was very close. Both countries had common goals not only in the wider NATO (North American Treaty Organization) but also in the narrower North American defence: they cooperated in NORAD (North American Air Defence Command), in an inspection system to safeguard against surprise attack across the Arctic, in the uses of atomic energy for mutual defence and in a Joint Defence Committee. They also worked successfully together in the big St Lawrence Seaway project, the greatest of its kind since the building of the Panama Canal. It links the head of the Great Lakes with the Atlantic Ocean enabling large ocean-going vessels to reach the heart of the American continent during the ice-free season. (The Moses-Saunders Dam – a power project closely associated with the Seaway – is one of the largest structures of its kind in the world.)

Needless to say economic relations between the two countries were particularly close, in fact so close that certain aspects were causing resentments and even unrest among Canadians. It was the preponderance of the United States in Canada's external trade, the US disposals programme for its agricultural surplus stocks and the large-scale penetration and control of Canadian industry by US interests that were the cause.

These resentments were most forcefully expressed by Prime Minister Diefenbaker in a speech he made in Hanover, New Hampshire, in September 1957. He said: 'No hereditary animosities or ancestral fears remain to divide us...But we cannot take our relationship for granted...the warm friendship and parallel interests of the two countries enable us to speak to each other with a measure of forthrightness...' And he pointed out that the US took 60 per cent of Canadian exports while it provided 73 per cent of Canada's imports, that the US was buying from Canada largely raw materials or semi- or partially manufactured materials, 'for the US tariff system prohibits any major import of manufactured goods'. He also indicated that Canada's trade with the US was equivalent to 25 per cent of Canada's gross national product, whereas in the US it was only two per cent. Diefenbaker then pointed out the inherent dangers for Canada: 'It makes the Canadian economy too vulnerable to sudden changes in trading policy at Washington. Canadians do not wish to have their economic, any more than their political, affairs determined outside Canada.' Then there was the US surplus disposal legislation which 'made it difficult, if not impossible, for Canada to maintain its fair share of the world's market'. And finally: 'The heavy influx of American investment has resulted in some 60 per cent of our main manufacturing industries and a larger proportion of our mine and oil industries being owned and controlled by US interests.' Of Canadian businesses controlled by non-residents 82 per cent was in US hands. Diefenbaker said: 'Canadians ask that American companies investing in Canada should not regard Canada as an extension of the American market...of American-controlled firms operating in Canada not more than one in four offers stock to Canadians.'

Of course, the Americans had their answers ready. They maintained that in a free trade world the trade imbalance was offset by Canadian export surpluses to other countries and by the flow of investments to Canada, which helped in its economic development. But in Canada there was a sense of disquiet over that situation and over its political implications. This was particularly felt in the French-speaking Province of Quebec. Apart from that, in other parts of the country the ties with Britain and its Commonwealth were still strongly felt, nowhere more than in the westernmost Province of British Columbia where many British pensioners settled to enjoy their last years in its mild climate and among its beautiful scenery.

American influence on Canadian culture was also clearly noticeable, but so was British influence of which it is apposite to mention the impressive Shakespeare Festival Theatre at Stratford, in the Province of Ontario, established in 1953 on the model of the Shakespeare Memorial Theatre at Stratford-upon-Avon in England. My wife and I greatly enjoyed a number of excellent performances at the Canadian Theatre.

Other Preoccupations in Canada

I was, of course, busy with representing my government in other than the case of the art treasures bilateral, mostly routine matters, and in justifying or rationalizing Warsaw's policies, its domestic economic and other reforms as well as its foreign policy with particular emphasis on the danger of 'German revisionism' and the need to uphold Poland's post-war frontiers which were still not fully and universally recognized.

113

Poland's then new initiative, the 'Rapacki Plan' for an atom-free zone in Central Europe was another special topic. One way of presenting those matters, apart from my official encounters, was through contacts with members of the press and letters to newspapers. The latter sometimes produced a lively response. For instance, my letter to the *Gazette* of 14 October 1960 provoked a string of letters, generally critical from Germans (including a former governor of Silesia and

The Gazette

Founded June 2, 1778

MONTREAL, FRIDAY, OCTOBER 14, 1960 ★

Letters From Our Readers

Background To The Polish-German Frontier Question

Sir,—I wish to refer to Mr. Blakely's article from Bonn entitled "The Lost Territories," carried in your distinguished newspaper on Monday, October 10.

In view of the contents of that article, I feel your readers may be interested to know the legal and factual background of this question of the Polish-German frontier.

That frontier was established by the great victorious Powers in the Potsdam Agreement of August 2, 1945, concluded in accordance with international law after Germany had signed the Act of unconditional surrender. The phrase "final delimitation of the Western frontier of Poland should await the peace settlement," quoted by your correspondent from that Agreement, was clearly meant, by any method of interpretation, as a provision only for a formal confirmation of that decision. Obviously it could not have been intended otherwise since, inter alia, the signatories of that Agreement at the same time provided in it for the transfer of the German population from the "former German territories" (this is the phrase used in the Agreement) to Germany proper, and of Poles into those territories, which, by the way, had originally been Polish. The transfer of the German population was thus effected strictly in accordance with the Agreement of the big Powers and, in fact, concerned only part of the Germans living there, since five million of them had left those territories before the end of war operations.

The present Polish-German frontier has been consistently confirmed and guaranteed by the Soviet Union; it has been formally, in an agreement, accepted by the German Democratic Republic; it is formally recognized by many other countries. In fact, all countries recognize Poland within her

present boundaries, although, regrettably, a number of governments have not yet taken the only logical and consistent position in this matter, as did President de Gaulle and Premier Debre of France, who last year clearly stated that France considers all Germany's frontiers, including those with Poland, as final.

Poland's legal and historical rights to those territories have been clearly established. As for Poland's moral rights, she paid for them dearly by the loss of over six million (i.e. 22 per cent) of her population, by the loss of 38 per cent of her national wealth and by the untold sufferings of her entire people at the hands of Nazi Germany.

Those once-Polish territories are now again in every sense an integral part of Poland, inhabited entirely by Poles, about 40 per cent of whom were born there since the war. It must be strongly emphasized that the "fewer than 1,000,000 Germans" reported by your correspondent to be now living there are not Germans: they are Poles, the original inhabitants of those territories who despite the long and arduous attempts at Germanization to which they had been subjected, managed to retain their Polish language and strong Polish patriotism. All these present inhabitants of those territories certainly have the right to what is their homeland.

Despite all these facts and considerations, the German Federal Republic advances territorial claims against Poland and also against other countries, and is the only country in Europe to do so. Mr. Blakely's article provides some evidence of such claims being made.

The contention that these claims are to be realized by peaceful means cannot be taken seriously. For every realistically-minded person knows

that Poland, backed by her allies, would never give up what is irrevocably part of her territory. Consequently, the intensified (as proved by facts) campaign in the German Federal Republic for a change of frontiers, especially seen in conjunction with its ambitious program of militarization as evidenced, inter alia, by the recent memorandum of the, General Staff of the Bundeswehr categorically demanding nuclear weapons for West Germany's armed forces and the further removal of military limitations imposed upon the German Federal Republic by her western allies in 1955, contributes to the aggravation of international tension.

In these matters all Poles, whatever their political views, are of one mind.

As was pointed out by Mr. W. Gomulka, head of the Polish Delegation to the 15th Session of the United Nations General Assembly, there is no problem of frontiers — Poland's frontiers are sufficiently guaranteed. It is solely the problem of peace. That is why Poland considers it necessary to voice her apprehension and warning at the United Nations, in her recent diplomatic notes and representations, and elsewhere, that German irredentism and militarism are a grave peril, not just to Poland, but to peace in Europe and indeed to world peace.

M. SIERADZKI,
Charge d'Affaires a.i.
of Poland.

Ottawa, Oct. 11.

former German ambassador to the Holy See) and generally supportive from Poles, Ukrainians and others, and a number of supportive articles in the Polish-Canadian press.

The question of the final recognition by the Western powers of Poland's western frontiers was over the years one of the major preoccupations of the Polish leadership and of the foreign service. The reasons were well summed up back in 1948 in a note of the British ambassador to the Foreign Secretary:

> In spite of the fact that the Soviet Government have publicly proclaimed their support of Poland's claims to the 'recovered' territories now administered by her, the Poles remain uneasy. They are not and never will be content with only a Soviet guarantee, for they have never forgotten the Molotov-Ribbentrop pact of 1939 and fear that if at any time it should suit Soviet foreign policy a similar pact to the prejudice of Poland might well be made between M. Molotov and the representatives of a puppet German Government of an East-German State, or even with a Communist-controlled unified Germany... They will thus be satisfied with nothing less than a four power pact recognizing and guaranteeing their Western frontiers. They have convinced themselves that a rehabilitated Germany will eventually seek revenge and recovery of lost territories, and the fear they express about Germany is genuine and not to be attributed alone to Soviet propaganda, which would have them believe that the Soviet alone stands between them and Western support of a reconstructed Germany with revisionist demands.[1]

Another way of presenting the Polish position was lecture tours throughout the breadth of Canada, which were organized by the Canadian Institute of International Affairs or the Association of Canadian Clubs. First I made a tour of Canadian Clubs in the province of Ontario. Then my wife and I made an extended trip to the west in March 1960 visiting, among others, Winnipeg, Regina, Saskatoon, Edmonton, Calgary, Vancouver and Victoria. I had speaking engagements in all those cities.

We risked travelling by car though the weather was still

very cold and wintry. Our journey started off inauspiciously. First, after we had been driving for about an hour, my wife realized that she had forgotten her winter coat, so we had to return to fetch it. Next we had to contend with atrocious weather and road conditions. Thirdly we were chased by a driver, who as it turned out, was well-intentioned and wished to warn us that we had been driving on a flat tyre. Changing a wheel in freezing conditions was not something I had bargained for, and with so much unforeseen delay I was afraid I might be late for my first speaking engagement. As we had to go part of the way through the United States, the Canadian cross-country highway not yet being completed, we tried to make up for lost time on the American side, and as a result I was stopped twice by the police. The first time the policeman kindly enquired why I was flying so low and gave us fatherly advice on the dangers of speeding to others as well as to ourselves. I thanked him for the kind way he admonished me and apologized. The other occasion was rather unpleasant. The road through the prairies was completely traffic-free, so I could safely drive faster to catch up on lost time. The policeman who stopped me wanted me to follow him to the station some 25 kilometres back the way we had come, which I refused to do claiming diplomatic immunity. He rightly pointed out that I was not a diplomat accredited in the United States, to which I retorted that I had an American diplomatic visa in my passport. As he persisted I declared that he would have to take me to the station by force. He hesitated and asked me to wait while he went back to his car to get in touch with his superiors. He returned furious and through clenched teeth declared: 'I have been forced to let you go.' I just about got to my first speaking engagement in time.

Driving on the Canadian side through the vast expanse of the empty and monotonous prairies, I was affected by 'highway hypnosis'. Despite my wife's efforts to keep me awake by talking to me or switching on the radio, I had to stop frequently and take a nap to reduce the risk of falling asleep at the wheel. The speaking tour was a great success and provided a unique opportunity for us to see the beauty and expanse of western Canada, its cities, national parks, resorts and the majestic Rocky Mountains.

Later in the year we went on a further speaking tour to the eastern provinces, and on another one to a number of cities in Ontario. Among the letters of appreciation I received was one from the president of the Canadian Institute of International Affairs, John W. Holmes. I knew John very well because he had been for a number of years under-secretary of state at the Department of External Affairs. He was an intelligent and cultured man, courteous and understanding, and it was always a pleasure to talk to him. (I learned many years later he may have been suspected of being too friendly with me. If true, such suspicions would have been a sad reflection of the cold atmosphere in East–West relations.)

I had, of course, the occasional heckler. One such occasion was described in a letter by the chair-person of the Canadian Club in Brantford, Ontario, Helen M. Straith, addressed to National Director, Eric Morse. She wrote:

> ...However, in the question period at the end of the lecture, the questions were – mostly – unrelated to what he had been saying. One man, in very abusive language, harangued the audience for several minutes. This man is a very prominent local person whose brother is Canada's trade commissioner in South Africa. Mr Sieradzki was the unwitting victim of our vaunted 'free speech' at its worst and he stood the test amazingly well. The obvious surprise of it could easily have knocked any man's composure into a cocked hat. Fortunately he and our president kept their heads and the spontaneous and vigorous applause to Mr Sieradzki's reply to the unwarranted attack showed unmistakenly the audience's sense of fair play and willingness to listen to his presentation. My personal suggestion would be to keep him in circulation...Mr Sieradzki's controlled attitude under difficult circumstances would seem to indicate that he is an excellent person to present his country's story.

A letter, dated 10 April 1961, addressed to me by the Ottawa branch of the Canadian Institute of International Affairs said:

> The Executive...has heard from other branches and from

the National Office that you have spoken... in other cities... and have deeply impressed your audiences. We feel that we have too long neglected the opportunity to ask you to speak to our branch and this letter is to invite you to do so in the near future.

As it happened I had to decline the invitation as I was about to leave Canada on the termination of my posting there.

On issues about which I was genuinely concerned, like the art treasures, Poland's western frontiers or the wartime Nazi occupation, I felt I was really convincing to my audiences. Obviously, as communist Poland's representative I had to toe the official line in other matters as well, like relations with the Soviet Union or internal economic, political and cultural developments. I tried to do that by describing the political context of Poland's situation and in a way which would not offend the intelligence of my listeners. The only alternative to somehow following the official line would have been defection and that I decided not to do for reasons which I elaborate on below.

On two occasions I was guest speaker at functions organized by the United Jewish Peoples Order in Toronto. The first, in April 1958, was the opening of an exhibition related to the Warsaw Ghetto uprising and the second in 1960, was the commemoration of the seventeenth anniversary of the uprising. The other main speaker at the second function spoke in Yiddish, and the organization's president, who was sitting next to me whispered into my ear the gist of the address in English. I was sorry for his unnecessary effort as I understood Yiddish, but I did not think it appropriate to reveal my Jewishness – as I was there as Poland's representative and not as a Jew. My address was published by the Canadian Jewish weekly, *Vochenblat*.

There was at least one occasion when I had to act outside my strictly bilateral field. As Poland's delegate to the May 1958 assembly of the International Civil Aviation Organization in Montreal failed to arrive, I had to take his place. I succeeded in reaching a compromise solution to a long-standing dispute concerning Poland's arrears in annual contributions to the organization.

Another unusual function I attended, this time together with my wife, was the presentation of 'the International Lenin Peace Prize' to the Canadian-born American, the Ohio-based industrialist, Cyrus Eaton. The prize was conferred on him 'in recognition of his unremitting efforts to bring about better international understanding'. The ceremony took place on 1 July 1960 in his residence in Pugwash, Cyrus Eaton's place of birth in Nova Scotia. Pugwash gave its name to the Pugwash 'Thinkers' Conferences for which he was responsible. The many conferences of 'international scientists', held from 1954 not only in Pugwash but also in the United States and Europe, brought together 112 authorities from 23 nations of East and West to consider ways and means of diminishing the grave hazards of nuclear, biological and chemical warfare. The Very Revd Clarence M. Nicholson, Principal of Pine Hill Divinity Hall in Halifax, Nova Scotia, presided over the presentation which was made by Professor D.V. Skobeltzyn, director of the Institute of Physics of the Soviet Academy of Sciences. Cyrus Eaton and his wheelchair-bound wife were extremely charming hosts, and my wife and I remember them with affection.[2]

Social Contacts and Occasions

Until the arrival in Ottawa as chargé d'affaires of the first representative of Castro's Cuba – a 29-year-old Jew later replaced by Ambassador Americo Cruz – of the communist-ruled countries only the USSR, Poland, Czechoslovakia and Yugoslavia had diplomatic missions in Canada. Naturally, social contacts between the Polish legation, the Soviet embassy and the Czechoslovak legation were relatively frequent, with the Yugoslavs less close, and with the Cubans very sporadic. We attended parties, film shows and the like at the nearby Soviet embassy, and their staff attended our less frequent ones. The first ambassador when I arrived in Canada was Dmitri Chuvakin, a short, heavy-set, fairly typical Russian who liked to drink and at times tried to ply me with vodka until, on one particular occasion, he realized that I was not a good drinker at all. From then onwards he even discouraged his staff from pressing drinks on me. When he was recalled, the embassy was headed by a fairly primitive but seemingly likeable apparatchik as chargé d'affaires who in turn was replaced by a more sophisticated, swarthy-faced Armenian, Dr Amasasp Aroutunian as the new ambassador.

I never discussed my official business with the Soviet ambassador or any member of his staff. This may seem incredible in the light of the USSR's domination over Poland's affairs, including especially its foreign relations. I was, of course, in no position to know how many of my colleagues in other capitals consulted or reported to their Soviet counterparts and endured their crude political instructions, though I suspected that some or even many did. My colleague at the time in Washington, Ambassador Romuald Spasowski (see below), admits as much in his memoirs, and mentions someone else as well.[3]

There is, to my mind, a plausible explanation why the Soviets did not try their usual tactics on me – I was not trusted. As I have already indicated, I was appointed to this post during the short spell when no strict party and security control obtained in Poland. This in itself would have been reason enough for the Polish security people to distrust me. In addition, as my security record had not been entirely clean since my time in London, they must have regarded me as a potential defector. That suspicion they, no doubt, shared with the Soviets in whose eyes it could have only been compounded and reinforced by the fact that I did not volunteer to report on, consult or discusss my work with them. Possibly, the Igor Gouzenko case in 1945–46 may have been of some relevance as regards their apparent caution.[4] Anyway, the Soviet embassy doubtless had enough information on what I was doing from somebody on my staff who was probably assigned to be in touch with them.

As for the Soviet embassy staff, I remember particularly two of its members – a cultural counsellor and a second secretary – who stood out in their intelligence and knowledge from the rest. (Many years later I learned that they were KGB intelligence officers.)

Frequent partying, cocktails, dinners, lunches, receptions, concerts, exhibitions, state banquets and the like are, of course, an integral part of the life of the diplomatic corps in any capital city. They were particularly frequent, and could drag on for hours, in a small city like Ottawa where there were not too many alternative attractions, such as the theatre. As a well-known Washington hostess aptly observed, there are two kinds of guests – those who leave without saying goodbye and those saying goodbye and seemingly never leaving.

The first social contacts are made on taking up office and it is customary for the new arrival to call on the other heads of mission who later return the call, and similarly, the wives call on each other. That was particularly incumbent on me as a junior head of mission, but rather exceptionally and surprisingly, Michael Comay, the then Israeli ambassador, visited me first. I do not know whether he knew beforehand that I was Jewish, but on this occasion I told him I was and also about my family living in Israel. He intimated that should I ever decide to emigrate to Israel I would be offered a job in the foreign service. (Some 20 years later, when I was already living in Britain, Comay was ambassador in London, and I talked to him again briefly at a Warsaw Ghetto commemorative meeting.)

Comay's successor in Ottawa was Dr Yaakov Herzog, brother of the future president of Israel. I remember him as an observant Jew, so when we entertained him and his wife at our residence we had special food for them. (On his return to Israel Herzog became deputy director-general of the Foreign Ministry. In 1965 he was appointed Britain's Chief Rabbi, but a month before he was due to take up his duties Dr Herzog announced he would be unable to do so because of a 'serious deterioration' in his health. The post went to Rabbi (later Lord) Immanuel Jakobovits. Dr Herzog died in 1972.)

During my time there, Ottawa was visited by an unusual number of VIPs. One of them was Prime Minister Ben Gurion. There was no Israeli ambassador at the time, so in the receiving line greeting the guests at the reception in his honour was the then Israeli chargé d'affaires (in later years consul general in London) and his wife standing next to Ben Gurion. When my wife and I had just shaken hands, I overheard the chargé's wife whispering into Ben Gurion's ear 'Hou Yehoudi' ('He is a Jew'); and the prime minister's rather dismissive remark 'Az mah?' ('So what?').

(That reminds me of a similarly dismissive remark by the then Cracow bishop Karol Wojtyła, since 1978 Pope John Paul II, a distant relative of my wife's (privately she still calls him by the diminutive 'Lolek'), who as a boy and then student occasionally visited with his father her family home. Told with some pride by a common aunt that Minka (my wife's mother) was in Canada with Krysia and her husband who was the head of the Polish legation there, he remarked: 'That does not impress me at all.')

One of the other heads of mission in Ottawa was the kindly Danish ambassador, John Knox. We were to meet again in the late 1960s, when he was ambassador to Poland. (My wife and I are indebted to him for the kindness he showed us at what was a very trying time in our lives, but more on that later.)

Another of my colleagues and neighbour was the Austrian ambassador, Kurt Waldheim, the future Secretary-General of the United Nations and – after his wartime role was revealed – the very controversial President of Austria. (At the time we did not, of course, know of his past. All that we knew was that his wife had been in the *Hitler Jugend* (*Bund der Deutschen Mädchen*), and that he had served in the army, which made me wonder what he may have been doing during the war.) I remember Waldheim as a rather colourless prig, serious-looking not to say morose, with no sense of humour whatsoever; and also that he was disliked by some of his senior embassy staff. Our relations with the Waldheims were similar to those with our other colleagues, though on one or two occasions as neighbours we exchanged some gifts.

Years later, Sir Brian Urquart, a former UN Under-Secretary-General for many years, observed:

Waldheim, emerging as a living lie, has done immense damage not only to his own country but to the United Nations and to those who have devoted, and in some cases sacrificed, their lives for it…We saw him as two people; Waldheim Mark I, a scheming, ambitious duplicitous egomaniac…and Waldheim Mark II the statesman-like leader who kept his head while all about him were losing theirs.[5]

And Sir Robert Rhodes James, principal officer in the executive office of the UN Secretary-General, 1973–76, added:

> Nothing was funny about serving in Waldheim's private office...His qualities and particularly a quite remarkable capacity for hard work, were made unpalatable by his volcanic temper, the absence of anything like a sense of humour, exceptional vanity, and (that least endearing of all deficiencies in a boss) the habit of taking all the credit when things go right and blaming others when they go wrong... It was the revelation that he had consistently lied about his war record that shocked us, rather than the record itself... That such a man should then seek the presidency of his country, and actually be elected, made the situation even more astounding.[6]

The doyen of the diplomatic corps was the French ambassador, Francis Lacoste, whom I remember braving the Canadian cold without coat or hat on his bald head. Inviting the other heads of mission to the customary farewell party at his embassy, prior to my departure from Ottawa, he wrote:

> ...nôtre collègue a été, sans porter le titre d'Ambassadeur, le chef réel de la mission diplomatique polonaise à Ottawa pendant toute la durée de son séjour, et il parait pleinement approprié que nous lui réservions le même traitement qu'au chef titulaire d'une mission diplomatique.

At the party my wife and I were presented with a gift, a silver salver with an engraved presentation centre surrounded by the engraved signatures of all the other heads of mission.

During our stay in Ottawa there were several state occasions. In October 1957 my wife and I met Queen Elizabeth II and Prince Philip at a state reception in Ottawa's Government House, on their official visit to Canada. In August of the following year we met Princess Margaret on her visit to Ottawa. In June 1959 we attended the official opening by the Queen and President Eisenhower of the United States of the St Lawrence Seaway near Montreal.

In 1959 President Eisenhower made a state visit to Canada

accompanied by the powerful Secretary of State John Foster Dulles. At the state reception in his honour I remember heads of mission and top Canadian officials milling round Dulles rather than the President. For, indeed, Eisenhower was known as a not very active president having delegated many of his powers to his 'secretaries' (his ministers), reserving for himself only the most important decisions whereas Dulles completely dominated US foreign policy. A Washington joke had it that Eisenhower had proved the United States did not need a president.

Regretfully, I missed French President Charles de Gaulle's visit to Ottawa as I was accompanying the first part of the art treasures back to Poland at the time. In May 1961 we met President Bourguiba of Tunisia. There were other state visits, but the most memorable one was that by the new President of the United States, John F. Kennedy and his wife in mid-May 1961. First we were invited to be present at their arrival at the RCAF Station Uplands in Ottawa. When the President passed the line of the diplomatic corps, he shook hands and had a brief word with each head of mission. As a chargé I was close to the end of the line. He must have had some soft spot for Poland because he stopped and chatted with me longer than with the others, telling me he had accompanied his father on a visit to Poland before the war; we also exchanged a few words about his sister-in-law being married to Count Radziwiłł. I saw the surprised and somewhat jealous looks of my colleagues, one of whom later asked me whether I knew Kennedy from my student years.

At the state reception in honour of President and Mrs Kennedy people were naturally milling round the couple and Prime Minister Diefenbaker who was introducing them to the honoured guests. My wife and I were keeping ourselves at a distance but all of a sudden I noticed Mr Diefenbaker beckoning in our direction. Wondering if he really meant us, we made our way through the throng. Mr Diefenbaker then introduced us to the President and Mrs Kennedy, and the President told his wife of our brief chat at the airport earlier in the day.

On one occasion when we were waiting at the airport in Ottawa for the arrival of the Australian Prime Minister Robert

Menzies, Prime Minister Diefenbaker chatted with some members of the diplomatic corps and shared with us one of his early experiences as prime minister. He had been visiting Vancouver and was guest of honour at a meeting of a motor manufacturers' association. The president of the association, introducing him, said: 'I have the honour and great pleasure to welcome the Prime Minister of Canada, Mr...er... er...Studebaker.'

Through my frequent contacts with the press my wife and I made a number of journalist friends. I recall particularly our encounters with the Gerald Warings. Gerald, a big, likeable man, worked mostly as a free-lancer. At one time he wrote an Ottawa column called 'Gerald Waring Reporting' for a number of daily papers across the country. For several years he wrote a column about Canada for a number of United States newspapers. He was a top-flight, hard-working newspaperman with initiative and ideas, and became a representative for *Newsweek*, contributed articles to the then *New York Herald Tribune* and also did regular broadcasts for CBC radio and television. He eventually formed with a colleague the Canadian American News Service. We visited each other quite frequently. I remember his pleasant modern country house which he had designed himself at the edge of a wood in Hull, across the river from Ottawa in the Province of Quebec. If he did report on me to the Canadian authorities, which would have been understandable in the circumstance, I did not get that impression.

My wife and I had very few private contacts. However, my cousin from Kalisz, Nathan (Tulek) Berliner, who had survived the war in Germany as a forced labourer, lived with his wife and children in Cleveland, Ohio. They visited us in Ottawa and we revisited them in Cleveland. On a short motoring holiday in the States we met up with my aunt Sara from Israel, and went on a sightseeing tour with her.

I knew that a classmate of mine, Heniek Berlach, lived in Montreal and took the first opportunity that presented itself to see him. He started out as a modest doorstep salesman and by sheer hard work and ingenuity worked himself up into becoming a proprietor of a successful chain of clothing shops. But at that time he and his wife, Lonka, with their three small children, still found it hard to make ends meet. Mindful of the watchful eye of our security people, we dared to visit them in Montreal only on a couple of occasions during our stay in Canada. (Years later, soon after we settled in London in 1969, they visited London and contact with them was re-established. We attended their daughter's wedding in Montreal, spent holidays with them in the Laurentian Highlands where they have a country retreat and in Miami where they have a condominium apartment to which they escape from the severe Canadian winter, and saw each other again in London in 1993. Sadly, this was the last time we saw Heniek alive.)

Such contacts were very risky affairs. To the communist regime and especially to its security services and the party any consorting, on a private basis, with people, including family or old friends, on the 'other' (capitalist) side, was, to say the least, highly suspect. It might indicate a desire to go over to the 'other' side; in other words, you became a potential defector – and hence a potential traitor. Though in the reverse situation of a Western diplomat consorting, on a private basis, with family or old friends in a communist country, let alone having them there, potential security risks would not be overlooked, there is a basic difference. A totalitarian regime owned not only your services and your loyalty but, as virtually the only employer, it owned you, it owned your soul. Yet, whatever the risk, I would not deny myself the pleasure and, indeed, the need, of maintaining at least my family contacts. I never stopped corresponding with my mother in Paris and the security service, of course, knew about it. But I did not maintain any direct contact with my brother and other family in Israel.

We spent our holidays either locally in Canada or toured in the north-eastern states of its southern neighbour. Travel expenses for a holiday in Poland were covered by the Ministry of Foreign Affairs once in two years, so in 1959 we spent our holidays on the Polish seaside where we were joined by my sister-in-law Irena and her son.

For semi-official purposes I used to visit New York at least once a year, usually at the start of the UN General Assembly session, to see my bosses. But I also took full advantage of what New York had to offer: I saw many off-Broadway as well Broadway shows, including *My Fair Lady* with Rex Harrison and the rest of the original cast. A couple of times I also visited Washington and saw my colleague Ambassador Romuald Spasowski. The son of a pre-war, left-wing pedagogue, Spasowski quickly rose in the ranks of the foreign service of communist Poland. At that time – the late 1950s – it was his first stint as ambassador in Washington. (During Reagan's presidency Spasowski was ambassador there for a second time and defected with his family in protest at the introduction of martial law in Poland in December 1981. The Polish authorities deprived him of his citizenship and sentenced him to death for 'treason and espionage' in 1984. In post-communist Poland the Supreme Court acquitted him in 1990 and three years later President Wałęsa restored his citizenship. Spasowski died in 1995.)

We became quite friendly with the Spasowskis, my wife knew them well from the London embassy where he had been counsellor and for a short time she was his secretary. In Washington I used to compare notes with him as regards our respective work as head of mission and we came to the common conclusion as to the difficulties involved in that work. We agreed that the easiest part was to work with the local press, and next came dealing with the Foreign Office of the host country. It was, however, more difficult to deal with our own superiors in Warsaw because they often did not fully appreciate the conditions prevailing in the country in which we were representing them. But by far the hardest part was to work with our own staff, some of whom often were recalcitrant or downright fractious, had their own agenda supported by their security backers or party leaders or were simply personally ambitious and envious. Interestingly in this context, Spasowski relates in his memoirs the 'freest' and 'most relaxed' conversation he had on his second ambassadorship in Washington with his then Soviet counterpart, Anatoli Dobrynin, who admitted that his 'main problem is explaining things in Moscow...They don't understand how incredibly complicated conditions here are.' Both Spasowski and Dobrynin agreed that their respective superiors did not understand how the American administration operated, what it could do and what it couldn't, and that caused 'the greatest difficulties for a post chief in Washington'.[9]

To Defect?

At the very outset of my mission I had been told by 'civilian' and military intelligence chiefs in Warsaw not to interfere in any way with the work of their men on the staff of the legation. When installed in Ottawa, I was told, those 'civilian' men would be identified to me so that I could know, for instance, whose occasional absences I was not to question. (The military attaché's staff needed no identification.) The 'civilian' people were, indeed, identified to me but after a while I realized this had been unnecessary as the men concerned exuded such self-confidence, and, what I called 'mini-power' that they gave themselves away, and I am certain their movements must have been watched and well known to the RCMP.

After some time I ventured, somewhat naïvely, to express to the local intelligence chief the opinion that having around 40 per cent of the legation staff, including the military attaché's office, involved in some kind of intelligence work was hardly conducive to developing good and effective relations with the host country. I understood the need for that work, especially in the circumstances, but I thought the staff proportions wrong. For instance, as far as I could see the military attaché's staff seemed primarily engaged in culling information from newspapers and magazines, military and other, some of which at least could have been done equally effectively back in Warsaw. My remarks to the security chief were not only naïve and pointless but potentially harmful for me for they must have reinforced the security's distrust of me.

It was approximately from that time onwards that I felt, indirectly, the wrath of the security people against me. They were constantly treading on my heels, not necessarily themselves but rather through others so as not to be too obvious. They could not question or interfere with my work where I was the boss and they knew I was well appreciated by my superiors, so they used the party organization at the legation for harassing and plotting against me. There were interminable party meetings, often almost exclusively preoccupied with censuring my conduct. I was variously accused of, for instance, an allegedly wrong attitude to members of staff or of an alleged misuse of the official car. They also conspired against me through the commercial counsellor (Władysław Zawidzki) who was older than I and who had a chip on his shoulder for being, if only nominally, subordinate to me. In fact, he became so obnoxious that I could not stand it any longer and requested Warsaw to recall either him or me. Eventually he was recalled.

As there had been some defections from the Polish foreign service at that time and at least one of the people concerned was Jewish, I got the impression that the security people – in this instance the 'civilian' branch – were anxious to goad me into defecting so as to be able to claim that a Jew could not be relied upon to be a loyal Polish citizen let alone a senior representative. My aforementioned meetings with family and my school mate in Montreal, of which they no doubt knew, must have played into their hands and coloured their reports on me to their Warsaw superiors.

At first the military attaché was Colonel Tadeusz Przybysz who behaved impeccably towards me, and my wife and I became friendly with him and his wife. Things changed somewhat when he was replaced by air force Colonel Mieczysław Roman. He would try to instruct me in the arcana of how to be on my guard against counter-intelligence. I remember during one of our walks (he would not discuss such matters indoors) he told me to avoid or at least be careful about leaving my suits with the dry cleaners. A listening device, he argued, could be sewn into the lapel of my jacket. (Roman later rose high in the air force command.)

His deputy, the assistant military attaché, was the misbehaving Lieutenant Colonel Jerzy Kilanowicz. He was the brother of General Grzegorz Korczyński, Deputy Minister of Public Security, member of the party's Central Committee, a military intelligence chief, and later Deputy Minister of Defence. During the war Korczyński had been one of the commanders of communist, anti-German partisans in the Lublin area. In that capacity, he had ordered the extermination of a detachment of Jewish partisans and their families, whose only survivor was Janek Szelubski. After the war Szelubski joined the foreign service and was for many years deputy head of the Department of Administration in the Ministry of Foreign Affairs in Warsaw. In that capacity he visited our legation in Ottawa while I was heading it, and we became very friendly.

Following the anti-Jewish campaign of the late 1960s (see below) in Poland, Szelubski emigrated to Israel where he was to have written an account of the wartime events. As he knew 'too much' he had to wait much longer than others before he was allowed to leave Poland. Korczyński's deed had been shrouded in secrecy and covered up for many years. It was only in 1992 that the Paris-based monthly *Kultura* got hold of and published a protocol of a November 1954 meeting of top officials of the Ministry of Public Security that revealed some of the truth. At that meeting the minister, General Radkiewicz, answered two questions put to him: one concerned the reasons for Gomułka's arrest in 1950, and the other related to the imprisonment in the same year for a term of 15 years of General Grzegorz Korczyński. In fact, Korczyński was released in 1956, when Gomułka was back in power, declared as having been 'wrongfully imprisoned' and soon again occupied high office. On Gomułka, Radkiewicz said, what had been widely known, that he had been arrested for his 'right-wing and nationalist deviation' which in plain language meant that he was not sufficiently Soviet-inspired like the dominant President Bolesław Bierut and his ilk. It had been assumed that Korczyński, a close collaborator of Gomułka, had been charged with the same 'crime'. But in his reply the minister said:

The case of Grzegorz Korczyński is of an entirely different nature. Korczyński was sentenced...for a crime committed during the occupation when he had been commander of the partisan movement of the People's Army in the Janowskie Woods in the Lublin area. We did not publish a communiqué in the matter nor did we give any information, because the matter is tragic and discreditable. I shall present the case briefly. Behind...Korczyński's detachments there was a supply column which also

provided shelter for more than a hundred Jewish families...
When Nazi troops attacked the Janowskie Woods,
Korczyński concluded that he would be unable to fight his
way through the ring of encircling troops of the occupant if
the supply column with the families was dragging behind.
So he decided to get rid of the superfluous ballast. He
ordered his detachment to retreat and sent the supply
column in the opposite direction, towards the approaching
German troops. When people in the supply column realized
they were heading towards certain death they changed
direction and followed the retreating detachment. Then
Korczyński ordered his men to fire and exterminate
hundreds of defenceless people. No military code provides
for such an alternative...Korczyński's case was brought to
court directly after liberation...by a group of former
partisans whose families had been harmed and those that
were guided by purely humanitarian motives. As long as
Gomułka was [Party] secretary he did not agree to have a
prosecutor's investigation against Korczyński and shielded
him. But later the matter became known and there was no
other way but to bring it before the court.[8]

However, as I said, when Gomułka returned to power,
Korczyński was again at the top of the military establishment
and his brother, Kilanowicz, could have the cosy post of
assistant military attaché in Ottawa.

It was not only the Polish security people who considered
me a potential defector. Apparently, some Canadian authorities and in particular the RCMP thought so too, for they
sought the help of a journalist, Peter Dempson, to persuade
me to remain in Canada. Dempson, whom I had hardly
known before, invited me to a restaurant for lunch under the
pretext of wanting to discuss Polish–Canadian affairs for a
series of articles. As this was not unusual, I agreed. It was
only when he drove me back to the legation in his car and I
was about to get out that he somewhat nervously broached
the subject. He asked me point blank whether it was true that
I wanted to leave the Polish diplomatic service and live in
Canada and if so he could help me. He even stupidly
intimated that I might get a job in the Canadian foreign

service. He showed me my biographical note as evidence that he had his information on good authority. I was thunderstruck and asked him angrily where he got this idea from, why I should want to defect and even if I wanted I would know whom to approach and would not need his help. Naturally, I had no further dealings with him.

Years later Dempson wrote a book, *Assignment Ottawa*, in which he built up this experience with me into an eight-page chapter. First he recounted a chat he had with Revenue Minister George Nowlan who, having spoken 'to someone from External Affairs a few minutes before', 'whispered' in his ear that a 'senior Communist diplomat, serving in Ottawa, planned to defect shortly'. It transpired that diplomat was 'the Polish chargé d'affaires'. If true, Dempson wanted to be the first journalist to write about it. There followed 'clandestine' meetings with officers of the RCMP Security and Intelligence Division who told him that they had been 'onto this for some time' but were 'in no position to make a move unless the diplomat approaches us. Neither is External Affairs.' Consequently, they approved of Dempson's idea of him talking to me and gave him, accordingly, instructions as to how to approach me and also a sheet of paper with my biographical data. He was instructed first to gain my confidence and

> ...when you think you have won him over as a friend, ask him bluntly whether he would like to come over to the West...[But] if Sieradzki runs to External Affairs to complain, or you become involved in a fight of any kind with him that gets into the papers, then you are on your own. We'll disavow any knowledge of the affair...If this works, all we can promise you is the first break on the story, nothing more. No financial reward – nothing...If you encounter some out-of-pocket expenses, such as taking Sieradzki out to lunch, and buying him a few drinks, then we will go good for it.

Dempson agreed. He also received his paper's (the *Telegram*) 'blessing to pursue the matter' and the paper promised it 'would pick up the tab for any expenses' he might incur. That promise regarding Dempson's expenses might explain why in his book he recounted the many meetings he allegedly had with me. In fact, there was only that one lunch. Dempson writes about my nervous and angry reaction and how I stepped quickly out of his car, slammed the door and rushed up the walk towards my office. He also relates how he reported to the RCMP on his meetings with me and particularly on this 'last' one:

> If the RCMP were disappointed, they did not show it. But I was. They thanked me for a job well done... The invitations from the Polish embassy stopped. It was apparent that I was taken off the Poles' list...When I encountered him [Sieradzki] at receptions at other embassies he...brushed right by me. I could tell that he was haunted by fear.[9]

In that he was nearly right; I was greatly perturbed. I was supposed to report an approach of such a nature to my superiors, but their reaction that there was no smoke without fire, that by my behaviour I might have encouraged that approach was more than likely, considering the suspicions fed about me to them by 'my' security staff. My report, which would have been seen by the security superiors in Warsaw, would have played right into their hands, with serious consequences for my future. On the other hand, it might have been worse if I failed to report and they found out about it themselves, which I could not rule out. I was in a quandary.

Quite fortuitously and fortunately, my immediate superior at the Ministry of Foreign Affairs in Warsaw, head of Third Department, Bohdan Lewandowski, was visiting the legation shortly afterwards. Bohdan was a very good friend of mine, I considered him one of the wisest men I had ever known and I trusted him as much as anyone could trust anybody in the circumstances of a communist regime. But, knowing that Bohdan had some highly placed contacts in Warsaw, I was still taking some risk in telling him about my experience and asking his advice as to what I should do about it. He reassured me by suggesting that I leave the whole matter in his hands, which I did. Quite obviously, I owe it to him that I never had to deal with the matter again.[10] However, it is quite probable that that incident made another foreign posting an impossibility for me.

The impression that the idea of defection had never crossed my mind would, however, be wrong. When we had left for Canada, Poland was embarking on a promising liberalizing course. In the intervening years, however, news and private information reaching us and our own observations during a month's holiday in Poland in mid-term of my stint in Canada, indicated a gradual return to some of the old ways of party orthodoxy with its sinister consequences. Why then did I not take the chance of defecting when it was offered to me on a platter? There were a number of reasons. Defection would have been a painful betrayal of the trust placed in me by some personally decent people, like Foreign Minister Rapacki, Bohdan Lewandowski and others. It would have had adverse effects on my wife's family left behind in Poland. It would have been something the anti-Semitic security people wanted and worked towards. I could not give them the satisfaction of proving them right. Moreover, defection would have meant condemning myself and my family to a wretched life of perhaps changed identities, secrecy and fear. (I knew of at least one case of a defector whose life had been cut short.) Besides, I had a very strong intuitive conviction that the time would come when I and my family would be able to leave the regime and the country without harming anybody left behind. (Incidentally, when that time did eventually come, Dempson's book had just been published. Had the security authorities seen what he had written about me it could have seriously complicated my situation.)

In June 1961, having done my share in regaining for Poland its precious art treasures, I completed my mission in Ottawa and left with my family for Warsaw.

Reflections on my Foreign Service Career

By then I had enough experience to look back and reflect on my foreign service career. It had started out as a vague and at the time seemingly unrealizable aspiration combined with my linguistic ambitions. I am not aware of how that aspiration had come to me, except that diplomacy had intrigued me and had an appealing and mysterious aura for me. My interest in foreign affairs, however, had not yet been developed. In time I came to realize that much of what was involved in foreign service work suited my disposition. Of the political complications, contradictions and moral dilemmas I became fully aware only much later.

From a purely professional point of view I greatly appreciated the need and opportunity to learn, to study, to use linguistic and other knowledge, logical thinking and common sense, to exercise precision of words, responsible action, to argue a case convincingly (my alternative ambition had been to be a lawyer). At the same time, the role of a go-between was very much to my liking, I prided myself on trying to understand both sides, on applying moderation when I could and arriving at a compromise. In this context I recall an apt definition of diplomacy as the lubricant that smoothes the crashing of nationalistic gears. As for the language used in public there were some unwritten rules. I was recently reminded of two of them: first, a diplomat must think twice before saying nothing, particularly when being interviewed; and second, when a diplomat says yes he means perhaps, when he says perhaps he means no, and if he says no, he is no diplomat. (Unlike a lady who by saying no means perhaps, by saying perhaps means yes, and if she says yes she is no lady.)

I came to appreciate the variety of postings, the changes of often unexpected circumstances and experiences, the ever new sets of people I had to work with, which was sometimes difficult. Obviously, I enjoyed the opportunities, challenges and relative comfort afforded by those postings, especially after the hardships and privations of the past. On top of that being a diplomat affords a status, not unlike possessing wealth to which I never really aspired nor had the disposition to achieve. Representing a government, meeting a variety of prominent people and taking part in or attending some important occasions, let alone being head of mission, creates a somewhat vain sense of self-importance. However, I never allowed myself to be overwhelmed by it and managed to retain a degree of ironical detachment and humility.

Notes

1 Note of D. St Clair Gainer to Foreign Secretary Ernest Bevin, 7 July 1948, Public Record Office, Ref.: FO 371/71560.
2 'Pugwash' still exists under the name of 'Pugwash Conferences on Science and World Affairs'. Its president, Polish-born British physicist, Professor Joseph Rotblat, and his organization were awarded the Nobel Peace Prize for 1995. The award is presumed to signify condemnation of the French nuclear tests conducted at the time. It is ironic that one of the Nobel awards so often denounced by the former USSR as politically motivated against Moscow has now been granted to an organization which had been consistently supported and sponsored by the Soviet Union precisely for political reasons.
3 Romuald Spasowski, *The Liberation of One* (San Diego, New York, London: Harcourt Brace Jovanovich Publishers, 1986), *passim*.
4 Igor Gouzenko, a cipher clerk at the Soviet embassy in Ottawa, defected in the autumn of 1945. He took away an attaché case full of espionage secrets and turned them over to the Canadian government. It led to the breaking-up of a far-reaching communist spy ring in Canada, the 1946 Royal Commission inquiry into espionage activities, and the imprisonment of ten Canadians, who were secret agents for the USSR.
5 Quoted in *The Times*, 4 January 1995.
6 Ibid.
7 Spasowski, p. 594.
8 'Protokół z Konferencji aktywu MBP' ('Minutes of the conference of senior personnel of the Ministry of Public Security'), *Kultura* (Paris), No. 11/542, November 1992, pp. 25–6.
9 Peter Dempson, *Assignment Ottawa* (Toronto: General Publishing Company, 1968), pp. 210–18.
10 In later years Bohdan Lewandowski became an Under-Secretary-General of the United Nations, among others, under Kurt Waldheim.

Part Three

7 • Back in Poland

On our way back from Canada we stopped in Paris, where my cousin Natek Kempiński, who lived there, helped me buy a Peugeot and learn to drive a non-automatic car again. Thus we drove from Paris to Warsaw, choosing to go through Switzerland, Austria and Czechoslovakia, with my mother accompanying us as far as Vienna. First, we took advantage of travelling by car to visit the French Riviera, where we stayed overnight, and picturesque Monaco. The journey through the Swiss Alps was a memorable experience, and our itinerary led through the Furka Pass. At the beginning of summer the road through the pass which had just been opened, was still wet and partly covered with snow and patches of ice. On the steep and winding way up my wife got pretty scared and urged me to return and take an easier route, while the 'two children' in the car – our son and my mother – wouldn't hear of it; they thoroughly enjoyed the thrill and excitement, thought it was terrific fun and egged me on to continue up the mountain. Not that it mattered one way or the other, as it was impossible to reverse the car. It was rather foolhardy to have taken the route through the Alps as with all our luggage on the roof-rack the car's centre of gravity was misplaced. Luckily we completed the journey without a hitch and having reached the top of the pass were delighted to have done it. There was still enough snow for some skiers to take advantage of the last days of the season. We took a break to enjoy the glorious sun and the magnificent views and obliged our son by engaging in a wild snowball fight.

We parted from my mother in Vienna and, somewhat

apprehensive of what the future had in store for us, proceeded on our way to Warsaw, stopping briefly in Bielsko-Biała to see my wife's sister and her son.

The political climate in Poland had changed by then. The initial liberal impetus of the Gomułka regime had greatly slackened, the period of relaxation was almost over, controls were tightened and disillusionment with Gomułka, the erstwhile hero, had set in. It became obvious that he had no intention of introducing radical democratic change, of extending the scope of political, economic, cultural or religious freedom the majority of the people had expected. Any illusions in this respect were shattered as early as October 1957, when he attacked the liberals and reformists within the party for demanding a second stage of the Polish October, branded them as 'revisionists' who presented a greater danger to Poland than the Stalinists and called for their expulsion from the party.

Thus, even if in comparison with other communist countries the regime in Poland was considered liberal, we found the atmosphere nearly as suffocating as before. The secret police, which had its power curbed during the de-Stalinization process in Poland, regained lost ground and was again ubiquitous. The political straitjacket was still tight, and there was little relief from the monolithic uniformity and the all-pervading indoctrination enforced by the state: the lies concocted from seeds of truth which most people pretended to believe, the obnoxious gibberish and hypocrisy of much of party propaganda (even if some criticism of the evils of capitalist society was warranted) and the occasional mindless chanting at party meetings few dared not to join in. Worse still was the realization that any hopes placed in 'the thaw' had been misplaced and that Poland was doomed to live under a system that was not chosen by but imposed on her by the Yalta Conference, where in the wartime military and political circumstances Churchill and Roosevelt had succumbed to Stalin and Europe was divided into two spheres of influence with Poland coming under that of the Soviet Union.

Everyday life too was as hard for ordinary people as it had been when we left for Canada. Even for us, with comparatively reasonable salaries (my wife resumed her work at the ministry's Department of International Organizations) and some savings from Canada, life was not easy. To make ends meet my wife took on a lot of translating into English and whenever I could spare the time so did I. With the communist state being virtually the only employer, in order to survive the majority of people – as the great Polish writer, Czesław Miłosz, aptly put it – 'temporized and rendered unto an unloved Caesar only so much as was absolutely necessary'.[1] In one way or another most people were working for or with the state. What other choices were there for people convinced as they had by then become that communism was there to stay? But the spirit of the people and their craving for freedom had not been broken, as evidenced by the 1956 riots and subsequent events like the 1968 student demonstrations and in later years the dissent that eventually culminated in the Solidarity movement rightly credited with having greatly contributed to the collapse of communism.

Referring to people's dilemmas in those circumstances a British columnist wrote:

Totalitarian socialism imposes on people a terrifying moral and spiritual pressure. Millions are cowed and crushed by it. Only a tiny handful of very rare individuals are simply compressed by that weight into the very core of their personalities, to become as a result unbelievably strong. It is foolish for any of us, who have not been through such trials, to assume that we would personally be among the latter group, rather than the former. We are subjected to much lesser tests of our ability to know ourselves and to stand out against collective pressures almost every day of our lives. Most of us fail. We take the easy way, of placation and evasion, of joining with the herd rather than following the truth imprinted in our souls.[2]

Following the demise of communism, it became fashionable in Poland

... to demand [of people] that they search their consciences and make confessions... After all those years many of us carry a rucksack full of stones. But many take out stones from their rucksack and, thinking it would ease their conscience, hurl them at others.[3]

My work at the Ministry of Foreign Affairs did not involve me in anything morally reprehensible. In fact, where I could within my narrow field, I tried to make harsh things easier.

In mid-July 1961 I was appointed deputy director of the Third Department in the Ministry of Foreign Affairs, which dealt with relations with the United Kingdom, the United States, Canada and the five Nordic countries. My main responsibilities were the first three. My immediate boss, the director of that department, was Eugeniusz Milnikiel, a former minister to Canada and later ambassador in London. He was a large, coarse man who often used vulgar language, but underneath he was a kindly and basically decent person.

My duties, though for the most part fairly routine, also involved participation in bilateral talks with delegations from countries covered by my department and attendance at other functions connected with such visits. I was also required to attend the presentation to the then Polish President Edward Ochab of letters of credence by newly appointed ambassadors, particularly from countries within my scope, two of which changed ambassadors in my time – the US appointed John Gronouski, whom I had met a year earlier in 1964, when he visited Poland as the US Postmaster General, and Thomas Brimelow, soon to become Sir Thomas, was appointed British ambassador to Poland. (After his return from Poland he became head of the Foreign Office, that is Permanent Under-Secretary of State. Following retirement he was elevated to the House of Lords.) I also attended receptions for foreign VIPs visiting Poland, including, for instance, United Nations Secretary-General U Thant and Yugoslav President Josip Broz Tito. Meeting foreign VIPs at receptions left no abiding memories as these were brief encounters, mostly limited to a handshake and the exchange of a few courtesies.

Official talks were more interesting, and occasionally they involved me in some haggling over the wording of the final communiqué. Apart from bilateral matters, issues which figured prominently in most of them were Polish plans for the limitation of armaments, particularly nuclear armaments in

Central Europe, covering West and East Germany, Poland and Czechoslovakia (variants of the original 1957 Rapacki Plan), and the Polish proposal for the convening of an all-European conference on security and cooperation. In 1975 that proposal materialized in the Helsinki Conference on Security and Cooperation in Europe which marked the beginning of what came to be called the Helsinki Process. The conference (CSCE), renamed in 1994 the Organization on Security and Cooperation in Europe (OSCE), to which virtually all European countries plus the United States and Canada belong, has operated ever since the Helsinki meeting.

The original 1957 Rapacki Plan in particular, but also its later permutations, occupied a special place in Poland's foreign policy and kept its top officials very busy and active for a long time. It was used not only for its intrinsic value and purpose to promote stability and peace in Central Europe and thus between East and West, but also as evidence of Poland's scope of 'independent' initiative in foreign policy since the October 1957 political transformations. It was obvious that all those Polish plans and initiatives were at each step closely discussed and coordinated with the Soviets. At my level I could not claim to have had any inside knowledge of those background 'consultations'. They were conducted by the top people in the Foreign Ministry and the party.

Like others in the foreign service who were kept in the dark on a great many things, as information was dispensed on a 'need to know' basis, I could only peddle the official line, while privately sometimes wondering to what extent those initiatives were in Poland's genuine interest and to what extent they were an implementation by proxy of Soviet interests. However, it seemed that they were genuinely Polish initiatives, and even the British believed so. As documents released by the Public Record Office in London show, the British ambassador, in his annual review for 1964, reported to his government: 'The Soviet Government required considerable persuasion before accepting the Gomułka plan [an adaptation of the first stage of the Rapacki Plan] for a nuclear freeze.'[4] But the West regarded the Polish plan with serious misgivings; they thought it would discriminate against the Federal German Republic, involve a further degree of recognition of East Germany (thus confirming the division of Europe) and it would further affect NATO deployment plans for tactical nuclear weapons to a much greater degree than the Soviets who had ample space for deployment of troops and weapons on the borders of the proposed zone. So while paying some lip service to the plans' official authors – the Poles – the West saw in them a Soviet objective of isolating and neutralizing Germany. Consequently, those plans never went beyond the stage of international discussion, apart from the Helsinki Conference.

In the seven years I held the post of deputy-director of the department, I participated in a number of bilateral talks including in 1964, with a Finnish delegation headed by President Kekkonen, and a Swedish delegation headed by Foreign Minister, Torsten Nilsson. The following year there were talks with a visiting British delegation headed by Foreign Secretary Michael Stewart. In 1966 I participated in talks with a major delegation of US businessmen, financiers, publishers and editors. Also that year I accompanied and took part in talks with the Canadian External Affairs Minister Paul Martin, whom I knew from Canada, during his official visit to Poland.

I was particularly involved in the months'-long preparations for the visit of Michael Stewart, the first visit to Poland by a British Foreign Secretary since 1947 when Ernest Bevin briefly visited Warsaw. I had numerous discussions with the British Number Two, Counsellor R.W. Selby on the programme of the visit and on topics for talks between the ministers. As regards the programme there was one particular problem: the Polish side expected the Foreign Secretary, as any other official visitor, to visit Oświęcim (Auschwitz), the site of the Nazi extermination camp, while the British demurred giving various excuses. As documents released by the Public Record Office show the real reason was that the British did not want to participate in an exercise which they regarded as a blatant exploitation by the Polish authorities of Auschwitz for political, anti-German purposes – which it was. Still Oświęcim figured in the Polish draft programme for some time after the British made their objections. Some of the British suggestions transmitted to higher authorities were simply ignored, which prompted Selby to report to the Foreign Office:

...quite a number of points which we had made orally about the Secretary of State's programme had been either forgotten or ignored. This is not surprising in the case of Mr Milnikiel who speaks bad English and often gets things wrong. It is more surprising in the case of Mr Sieradzki, who is an extremely competent operator. But he has alas gone away on leave. Despite certain misgivings about appearing to dictate to the Poles the details of the programme which we would like them to work out, I thought it best to set down on paper the various suggestions which we had made to them orally... which I handed over to Mr Bartol [Chief of Protocol]...[5]

As for the visit itself, the official political talks between the two delegations were in essence dialogues between the two ministers, Stewart and Rapacki. The main international issues discussed were German reunification, Poland's frontiers, European security and Vietnam. Understandably, there were sharp differences of opinion. Stewart argued for free elections in all of Germany because of the 'justifiable German grievance about the division of their country' and also because he regarded the settlement of problems of European security and of the final delimitation of Poland's frontiers dependent on progress towards German reunification. Rapacki, while not excluding German reunification in future, was decidedly against a Germany reunified on the basis of free elections which would mean the continuation of Federal German policies. He said this would only whip up revanchist feelings and that reunification could only take place through negotiation between the two German states recognized as equal partners. Stewart emphasized, however, that the British government would do nothing to enhance the status of East Germany. On the question of Poland's frontiers, the official British position was that their final delimitation must await a peace treaty with Germany, but the Foreign Secretary repeated in private the British government's confidential, 'unqualified' assurances of 1962 that when it came to the peace conference Poland's western frontiers, would not be a matter of barter for the British government. A public declaration to this effect would not help the situation, things should move forward by degrees and an improvement of

Poland's relations with the Federal German government would help to solve the problem. Rapacki regretted that those assurances could not be made public, if only because such a public declaration would serve to convince not only the West German government but also revanchist elements that claims to a revision of the frontier had no support.

On Vietnam Rapacki argued that the American presence there was illegal and unjustified, and had a disastrous effect on the concept of peaceful co-existence in the world. Stewart blamed North Vietnam for the struggle by Viet Cong against the government in Saigon. The North Vietnamese, he maintained, wanted to win a victory and to get the American troops out. But this, he claimed, was 'unrealistic' and 'to regard such a solution as feasible by military force was a tragic delusion'. (And yet that is what actually happened a decade later.) Both sides hoped the problem could be solved by peaceful means on the basis of the Geneva agreements. In private Rapacki indicated Poland's 'willingness to help resolve the deadlock if opportunity arose'.

Talks on bilateral issues centred on trade and in particular its imbalance – Poland was exporting much more than it imported from Britain, and the Polish side promised to rectify the situation. Also discussed were scientific and technological exchanges, which the Polish side wanted to see increased. Cultural contacts were regarded by both sides as satisfactory. It was agreed to start negotiations on a Consular Convention and a Health Services Agreement.[6]

In February 1967 my wife and I accompanied Foreign Minister Rapacki and his wife on an official return visit to the United Kingdom. It was a strange but pleasant experience to be in London again after so many years. We stayed at the Dorchester Hotel, visited Coventry Cathedral and attended a performance of *Turandot* at the Royal Opera House, Covent Garden in the company of George Thomson, Minister of State for Foreign Affairs (in later years Lord Thomson) and his wife. What struck me on that visit was the occasionally peculiar behaviour of the host, the then Foreign Secretary George Brown, especially when he had a glass or two. He was generally known to be partial to drink and is even remembered by some as 'drunken and tempestuous'.[7]

The talks, almost exclusively between Rapacki and Brown, focussed on the same subjects covered by the previous Rapacki–Stewart talks in Warsaw, and no new conclusions were reached.

(In notes on the officials in Mr Rapacki's party sent to the Foreign Office, the British embassy in Warsaw wrote: 'Sieradzki...speaks fluent English. Is very sure of himself. A tough bargainer. Never departs from the official line, and expounds it willingly and with apparent conviction. Efficient and helpful in day-to-day business. Married to an attractive blonde who also works in the MFA [Ministry of Foreign Affairs] and who has been selected to accompany Mme Rapacki.' One other Polish official was described as a 'hardliner' and another as a 'committed Marxist'.)[8]

Throughout the period I served in the ministry's Third Department I helped in organizing and participated (in Poland) in so-called 'round table' conferences between British and Polish parliamentarians, scholars, journalists and businessmen taking place alternately in Britain and in Poland. They had become a regular, at first annual and later eighteen-monthly, event of lively, unofficial and off-the-record discussion on a variety of topics relating mainly to British–Polish relations. They had been modelled on similar British–German gatherings at Königswinter. For many years the chairman of the British contingent was the MP Bonham-Carter, later elevated to the House of Lords. The list of Polish participants, which we at the Foreign Ministry suggested, had to be approved each time by the Foreign Department of the party's Central Committee. The first conference took place, after considerable delays, in January 1963 at Jabłonna near Warsaw. The British ambassador's assessment of it was, *inter alia*, that

> ...the conference went reasonably well and the experiment is certainly worth repeating...in the Political Committee the Poles wasted a good deal of time in endlessly repeating rather sterile and crude arguments about the wickedness of West Germany and the danger which this particular species of Germans presented. It was only on the last day that the conference was able to get on to more useful themes such as

the Rapacki Plan...informal contacts...proved one of the most useful aspects of the conference...

Although the Poles denied that their delegation had been in any way instructed as to the attitudes they should take up, I am inclined to think that they suffered from over-briefing. From all accounts they showed little inclination to depart from the party line in discussions. I think that we may expect a greater degree of frankness to be shown when the return match is held in England. In the first place, the Poles are likely to be less nervous that government officials might be peeping over their shoulders and, in the second, a degree of confidence has now been established, which should make free speaking easier.[9]

Later Foreign Office documents indicate that the Polish participants did express themselves more freely at the 'return match' in England.

While the British found the repetition by the Poles of arguments regarding West Germany irritating at that first conference, the Poles did not consider voicing their deep concern and arguing their case a waste of time. In this matter no opportunity was ever missed. A Foreign Office confidential briefing of the same year, 1963, shows that the Polish position in this respect was well appreciated:

Poland's main preoccupation in foreign affairs...remains West Germany. Most Poles, regardless of their views about the regime, genuinely fear the growing strength of the Federal Republic and it is widely accepted in Poland that the Soviet alliance is the only guarantee against this threat.[10]

Krysia was occasionally asked to interpret for the wife of Polish President Ochab, and for Mrs Rapacki during courtesy visits by wives of ambassadors newly accredited to Poland by the countries covered by the Third Department and accompanied Mrs Rapacki on the Polish Foreign Minister's return visit to Denmark. She also occasionally accompanied the wives of foreign VIPs on their separate engagements within the programme of the VIPs visit to Poland. In 1964, when Emperor Haile Selassie of Ethiopia made a state visit to

Poland, she was attached to the Emperor's granddaughter, Princess Ruth, for the duration of the visit. On the way to visit Cracow, Haile Selassie invited Krysia to his railway car and engaged her in a pleasant conversation, which made her wonder why his granddaughter seemed so terrified of him. At the end of the visit the Emperor presented her with a gold bangle bearing the imperial emblem.

A number of official photographs, some of which are reproduced in this book, mementos and presents remind us of this phase of our lives. Thus, for instance, the Order of the Lion of Finland and a document accompanying it which stipulates that it should be returned on the death of its holder, remind me of President Kekkonen's visit to Poland on which occasion Polish personalities and foreign service officials involved in the talks were awarded Finnish orders. A key to the city of Los Angeles mounted on wood together with a brass plate bearing a dedication to me brings back memories of the visit to Warsaw of the city's Mayor, Samuel W. Yorty.

Apart from functions connected with official visits, we maintained fairly frequent social contacts with diplomats and their spouses, particularly from the countries covered by my department, attending dinners, film shows and parties given by them. We would also meet some of them who were as keen skaters as we were on the Warsaw ice-rink at times reserved for the diplomatic corps. On one occasion when I returned to the dressing room I discovered that my shoes were missing and instead a similar, somewhat tight-fitting pair was waiting for me. It later transpired that my shoes had mistakenly been taken by the Israeli Ambassador Avigdor Dagan. Among the mementos I particularly cherish is a witty card he sent me together with my shoes which said: 'It's true that from time to time I have to ask your people to put themselves into our shoes, but I never meant it so literally. With apologies and best regards.'

Relations with the US and other Western Powers

Shortly after Gronouski took over as US ambassador to Poland in 1965 I had a chance to meet Averell Harriman, the veteran US diplomat, President Roosevelt's wartime ambassador to Moscow. The war was then raging in Vietnam and he came to Warsaw as President Johnson's special envoy a few days after Christmas to seek Poland's mediation in urging Hanoi to surrender and make peace with the United States. Needless to say, Harriman's efforts were not successful.

A few months later Harvard professor Henry Kissinger, later to become Secretary of State in the Nixon administration, visited Warsaw. I remember chatting with him in the garden of Ambassador Gronouski's residence about the war in Vietnam. I argued that waging that war was not only wrong but against the interests of the United States. It was, I averred, alienating the peoples of the region. Kissinger retorted that when a war was won nobody asked whether it was wrong. He was evidently in no doubt that the war would be won by the United States.

It is ironic that some 20 years after the calamitous end of the Vietnam War Robert McNamara who, as American Defence Secretary from 1961 to 1968, pursued it with such ruthless determination should make the extraordinarily forthright and painful admission in his memoirs that: 'We were wrong, terribly wrong, and we owe it to future generations to explain why.' With the advantage of hindsight McNamara puts forward the reasons and misjudgments which include: viewing the people and leaders of South Vietnam from a Western perspective as thirsting for freedom and democracy; and misjudging 'friend and foe alike' through a profound ignorance of the country and its culture.

Of the countries I had to deal with, Poland's relations with the United States were by far the most significant and most eventful. Following the liberalization in Poland in 1956 Washington became active in an obvious and understandable attempt to help Poland weaken her dependence on the Soviet Union. President Eisenhower offered economic aid to Poland as America had a mission, he said, 'to expand the areas in which free men and free governments can flourish'. At the time the offer was rejected by Warsaw as had been a previous offer of food supplies by the American Red Cross following the disturbances in Poznań. The offers were dismissed by Warsaw as either propaganda exercises or interference in Poland's internal affairs.

However, starting from 1957 agreements were concluded

between Poland and the United States annually. They concerned not only commercial 'lines of credit' through the American Export-Import Bank but, more significantly, the sale to Poland of American 'surplus farm products', payment for which was to be made in Polish currency, the złoty. The złoty balances could be used for a variety of purposes, primarily to cover expenses of the American embassy but also for American projects in Poland. For instance, in 1962 a two million dollar joint medical research programme was agreed, the first such American undertaking with a Soviet-bloc country. This was financed from the 'counterpart funds' created by the Polish payments for US agricultural supplies. Unused złoty balances were to be bought back by Poland in dollars to be paid in annual instalments. But when, in 1959, Gomułka's attacks on US policies intensified again, the sums of economic aid were reduced.

American assistance to Poland also took other forms. For instance, export control regulations were changed to simplify licensing procedures for US exports to Poland. A financial agreement was concluded in 1960 to settle claims of American citizens whose property was nationalized in Poland after the war, and in return the US agreed to release Poland's assets in America. A similar agreement had been concluded with the United Kingdom on compensation for nationalized property as well as on repayment by Poland of some pre-war debts. In fact, they were repaid before the allotted time because of the growth of Polish exports to the UK. Following the restoration of free travel between the United States and Poland, and the growth of trade resulting from the economic aid to Poland, some previously closed consulates were reopened, including those in Chicago and Poznań. The Ford Foundation granted half-a-million dollars to Poland for cultural exchanges with the West, the first direct grant by the Foundation for an 'Iron Curtain' country. When in 1959 Vice-President Nixon visited Poland, huge crowds gave him a tumultuous ovation, though no details of the time of his arrival or the route he would take had been made public beforehand.

A variety of American, as well as other Western, visitors and delegations came to Poland, some of which I mentioned earlier. Eventually, a few American charities resumed their assistance programmes to Poland, among them the Jewish JOINT Distribution Committee.

Despite the fact that the United States provided by far the greatest assistance to Poland after 1957, relations with the Americans were acrimonious and tense. With the British they were much calmer and marked by greater mutual understanding. When, for instance, in 1962, Ambassador Sir George Clutton came to see me, in the absence of my boss Milnikiel, with a complaint about the British consul in Gdynia being under constant surveillance and frequently photographed when going out of doors, he did so unofficially expressing the hope that the matter could be settled satisfactorily, because he believed

> such behaviour was out of tune with the present state of Anglo/Polish relations ... Sieradzki ... said that ... the Ministry of Foreign Affairs knew nothing about the matter, and I am certain he was speaking the truth ... that he would at once investigate the matter and communicate with me further. He continued that the Ministry of Foreign Affairs, as he was sure also the Foreign Office, always deprecated matters of this kind ... [11]

As for the possible reason for the surveillance – a matter which the ambassador did not mention in our conversation – he refers in the above note to a visit to the consul's residence by a seaman, a radio operator at naval headquarters, who

> was proposing to sell intelligence in return for the sum of Zl. 5,000. He was given short shrift ... (probably rightly, for the circumstances of his call were suspicious and he refused to give his name) and sent away. My present guess is that the authorities have caught up with this sailor in some other connexion, and that they are now, like all security services, busy locking the stable doors after the horse has bolted. Forward [the Consul] knows nothing about this ...

The British were of course engaged and closely cooperated with their allies in intelligence gathering. When in 1964 the Polish government, in retaliation against travel restrictions placed on Polish officials in the United States, banned travel by American official personnel in 19 specified areas of Poland,

Ambassador Clutton telegraphed a secret message to London saying:

> The touring programme coordinated between the United States, Canadian, United Kingdom and, to some extent, French service attachés with a view to maintaining maximum intelligence cover of the whole of Poland will clearly have to be adjusted...it is inevitable that we, the Canadians and to some extent the French will in effect have to cover the banned areas for the Americans.[12]

While there was close cooperation with the Americans in that and in other fields, the British whose understanding of the Polish situation and sensitivities was more sophisticated, were not always of one mind with the Americans, and often critical of them. Illustrative in this respect is a report to London by British Counsellor Peter Dalton, on Polish reluctance to the showing in Poland of Colonel Glenn's space flight capsule and on the account of the negotiations as given to him and the French chargé d'affaires by Sherer:

> ...the American Embassy were instructed to ask the Poles whether the latter would like to have for exhibition here, the actual capsule in which Colonel Glenn made his space flight...The Embassy first approached the Polish Ministry of Foreign Trade with the suggestion that the capsule might be shown at the Poznan Fair. The Ministry showed interest and promised an early reply. Nothing happened and after a decent interval...Sherer asked Modrzewski, the Vice-Minister of Foreign Trade, whether he could yet give an answer. Modrzewski...surprised...said he understood that a favourable reply had already been given to the Embassy. He would, however, check this. He subsequently telephoned Sherer to confirm acceptance. An hour later, however, he telephoned again to say that he was sorry to have to go back on his previous statement, but that the matter is in the hands of the Ministry of Foreign Affairs...
>
> Sherer then got in touch with Sieradzki...who said that the matter was being looked into. He subsequently summoned Sherer to say that it did not appear to the Polish

authorities to be appropriate to show the capsule at Poznan and that it would not be of interest to show it in Warsaw, but that it could, if the Americans liked, be shown in the Planetarium at Katowice.

Sherer said that it was no doubt the Polish expectation that this proposal would be declined, or that, if accepted, the capsule could be transported to Katowice and shown in the Planetarium with the minimum of publicity and public interest (he added that the capsule had been offered similarly to the Russians, who had declined, with the intimation that they had plenty of capsules of their own!). Washington, however, had accepted the Polish proposal and had instructed the Embassy to pursue with the M.F.A. the necessary arrangements. The capsule apparently travels in a Globemaster aircraft on a specially constructed trailer with its own tractor. The Globemaster would land in Warsaw and the capsule would make its journey to Katowice by road...Sieradzki's reaction to this information was to say that this raised 'technical questions', which would need further consideration. He promised an early reply, which, however, was never forthcoming and, in the meantime, Washington informed the Embassy that it was now too late to make arrangements for Poland as commitments had been made with other countries.

...Apart from the intrinsic amusement of this story, it, and the context of its telling, are...an illustration of Polish and American attitudes. That of the Poles is pretty well what one might have expected of them, caught between the embarrassment at the American offer (and, no doubt, some interest in the American 'space machine') and the inhibitions placed upon them by their position *vis-à-vis* the Soviet Union, wriggling hard between the two. The American reaction, or, at any rate, that of Sherer, which I think represents the present feeling of the American Embassy, was one of exasperation. He told the story in sorrow, evidently tinged with anger, in the context of 'cultural relations' (our French colleague made the comment that the capsule did not seem to him to be a particularly 'cultural' object), quoting it as an example of what he considered to be the hypocritical attitude displayed by the Poles, who, on the one hand, were urging increased cultural and scientific contacts, but on the other, were unreceptive when the Americans made a practical offer.

... Even allowing for American annoyance at Rapacki's visit to Cuba, which Sherer described as a slap in the face for the United States, I am afraid that his comments on the capsule affair and his criticism of Polish 'hypocrisy' as exemplified therein show a rather poor appreciation of the Polish position.[13]

In a separate handwritten note to the Foreign Office, Dalton said:

It seems to me surprising that the Poles should have proved at all receptive to the idea of displaying the capsule in Poland, and have considered it seriously (even if with no result). The American attitude is not very sensible – obviously, the capsule's main significance is in conferring prestige, rather than cultural advantage.

R. Russell from the Foreign Office adds a comment on the above note saying: 'Amusing. One can just imagine the confusion in the face of the French chargé in referring to the capsule as not being a very "cultural" object. When it comes to space ... the Americans may be as thinned [sic] skinned as the Russians.'

Even more telling is Ambassador Clutton's report to the Foreign Office, dated 6 July 1964[14] on Robert Kennedy, the then American Attorney-General's visit to Poland. The visit was to have been a private one, he was to have been accompanied just by Mrs Kennedy and perhaps one other person. In the event his party consisted of 17 people. And:

... no one seems to have believed other than that Mr Kennedy was visiting Poland as part of the American election campaign. Indeed, Mr Kennedy was indiscreet enough to mention at his first press conference that his brother had owed a lot in his election to the Presidency of the United States to the votes of the five million Poles in the United States.

On the second day of the visit, a Sunday, after mass attended by the Kennedys and their party at the Cathedral of St John in Warsaw:

...jam-packed with Poles...a crowd of probably five thousand had gathered outside the edifice and it was then that Mr Kenendy first adopted a technique of addressing his public hitherto almost unknown in Poland...He mounted the roof of his car and, surrounded by his wife and small children, started addressing the crowd. This performance he repeated wherever he went in Warsaw, Krakow and Czestochowa. How many cars he put out of action is not entirely certain...

A number of interviews with leading personalities were arranged at Mr Kennedy's request...Among others, Mr Kennedy saw [Foreign Minister] M. Rapacki and I have received from Polish sources an account of the interview which was unpleasant in the extreme. Mr Kennedy had various complaints to make, the first of which was that not one word of his press conference on his arrival had been allowed to appear in the Polish press. He also complained that the Polish authorities knew that he had wished to see the youth of the country, but that they had deliberately broken up the schools and sent the children away so that he could not see them. (The Polish school year always ends on the 24 or 25 June [that is, a few days before Kennedy's arrival in Poland].) Rapacki replied with venom that this was perfectly true and that the children had been sent to Siberia.

As a result of this interview M. Rapacki sent [his deputy] M. Winiewicz to represent him at the dinner party given on the same day by the US Ambassador with instructions to be as rude as he could. M. Winiewicz was...M Kennedy arrived one hour late...M. Winiewicz greeted Mr Kennedy by saying, 'Now you must get up on the table and address us. We have been waiting here an hour, while you have doubtless been standing on the car, talking to the people outside. You really must not deprive us of the same honour here.' The dinner party continued with much the same ding-dong stuff...

Mr Kennedy also saw Cardinal Wyszynski...there is no

doubt that by his ostentatious attendance at mass, both in Warsaw and Czestochowa, Mr Kennedy exploited his Faith in a manner uncongenial to many of his co-religionists. By so doing he also gave the regime the opportunity of accusing, quite unjustifiably, the hierarchy of responsibility for the demonstrations.

Some bad mistakes, now freely admitted, were made by both sides, and when it comes to the consideration of whether from the general political point of view the visit did harm or good, it is very difficult to pass any judgement. The answer may well be that it did neither much good nor much harm. On the other hand, the ease with which Mr Kennedy could gather round him spontaneously such large and affectionate crowds must have been a painful reminder to the regime of their own unpopularity and the unbreakable ties between Poland and the West, and particularly the USA. Against this it must be said that Mr Kennedy's performance was neither dignified nor tactful, and it is small wonder that the relations between the US Embassy and the Polish authorities suffer in comparison with those of Her Majesty's Embassy. All in all, it may be that a senior Polish official was correct when he said to the Counsellor that the whole affair only went to prove what he had always felt – that the Americans were still an uncivilised people. Or is it only another proof of the truth of the statement once made to me by a Polish friend that this is not a communist, but a surrealist country?[15]

There was, though, one incident in 1966 which caused some friction between the Polish authorities and the British embassy. It involved the Assistant Air Attaché, Squadron Leader Jones, whom the Polish security service intercepted in the vicinity of a military airport in a closed military area where the attaché's assistant, Mr Toms was seen 'photographing landing aircraft'. Obviously, as was usual in such cases, the version of events I had from the Polish security authorities differed essentially from that of the British embassy with whom I had a couple of less than pleasant conversations on the subject. The letter of the embassy to the Foreign Office quoted below recorded the line I took in the conversation, a line which reflected the position on the matter of the Polish government:

> M. Sieradzki deplored the political 'untimeliness' of this incident, saying that it was the first time British Service Attachés had been found behaving in this way. He was used to such incidents with the Americans, but had been surprised to find our people now acting in the same way – particularly at a time when the Polish Government hoped that Anglo–Polish relations would steadily continue improving, and when a new British Ambassador was just about to take up his duties here.[16]

However, unlike with the Americans, there were no expulsions. Indeed, relations with the Americans were much more tense. While their service attachés were trying to gather as much information as they could, the Polish counter-intelligence services, whose business it was to prevent them doing so, would overreact especially in the mid-1960s, which, I thought, they did deliberately.

They would not only harass the attachés in various ways but occasionally detain them for hours after they had proved their diplomatic immunity, particularly at night. Expulsions became the standard way for United States military attachés. For several years no attaché reached the normal end of his tour. When Air Attaché Colonel George Carey was being expelled for allegedly taking photographs of a jet air base at Bydgoszcz (which he denied, but admitted that he had walked around the base), he spoke of a steady intensification of surveillance on him and said that on that occasion there had been two scuffles between him and plain-clothes policemen. A particularly unpleasant incident occurred in April 1966 involving American Naval Attaché Commander W. Althoff and Assistant Army Attaché Lieutenant Colonel B. Parr and their briefcase which bore the inscription 'Property of the US Navy', during their service trip. Again the Polish security's version of events differed substantially from that of the Americans. According to the Polish authorities the car passengers refused to disclose their identity and it was only at the police station that they did so and were then promptly released. According to the

Americans they were removed from their car by physical force and illegally detained. Their briefcase was illegally removed, it contained various materials, including maps and notes made during their trip, undertaken as part of the normal conduct of their official business. Polish security maintained the briefcase had been found discarded or lost before the incident and was retained as material evidence of espionage activity. It contained, it said, maps, films, plans of production enterprises and military establishments, secret intelligence-type notebooks with information about, *inter alia*, the Polish Navy and WOP (Frontier Guard Forces).

As a result the two service attachés were expelled as was Air Attaché Lieutenant Colonel E. Wooten. In retaliation the United States expelled Polish Air Attaché Colonel Stefan Starzewski, Lieutenant Colonel Wiśniewski and Major Dziedzic. Consequently, there remained only one service attaché in each country.[17]

My official position placed me in the middle of the controversies and complications. I had to transmit findings, charges and counter-charges, complaints and even, more or less veiled, threats, while I myself did not know the true facts. I had to attend a number of meetings either at the 'civilian' Counter-Intelligence Department of the Ministry of Internal Affairs or at its military counterpart to discuss these matters. When at one of those meetings I maintained that it was difficult for me to counter the arguments of the American embassy when I had not been told the real facts of a case, the overall head of the 'civilian' counter-intelligence, Brigadier-General Ryszard Matejewski told me: 'You lie better when you don't know the real facts.' That, of course, shut me up. On another occasion, at a meeting at military counter-intelligence, in which the Foreign Ministry's chief of protocol, Edward Bartol, also participated, when I asked something about an alleged American misbehaviour I was told (if I remember correctly by Matejewski): 'Some people are more interested in defending the Americans than in our own interests.' That was an ominous remark. (Incidentally, years later Matejewski, by then Deputy-Minister of the Interior, was sacked and in February 1972 tried and sentenced to 12 years' imprisonment for 'smuggling and illegal currency deals'.)

I remember having arrived once for a conference at military counter-intelligence, headed then by the not-too-bright Brigadier-General Teodor Kufel,[18] at the same time as the head of the Counter-Intelligence Department of the Interior Ministry, Colonel Michał Krupski. When we both approached the door I stepped aside to let him in first – he was senior and older than I. He returned the courtesy saying: 'As a policeman I like to go behind.'

Another embarrassing matter between the Polish authorities and the Americans was a newly built American embassy which turned out to have been riddled by the Polish security service with bugging devices. Some security people would boast that they knew everything the Americans were saying to each other. The embassy had to bring in their own workmen to rip up the walls and floors and rebuild them. They still used a specially secured top-floor room for sensitive conversations. Officially the Polish authorities denied any knowledge of or responsibility for the installation of the listening devices. The State Department said at the time that more than 130 listening devices had been discovered in United States embassies in communist-ruled countries since 1949. These included, according to the the *New York Times* of 4 November 1964:

> ...a microphone inside a carved replica of the Great Seal of the United States presented to the United States Embassy residence in Moscow by the Soviet Government in 1945. Forty more microphones were discovered inside the walls of the embassy office building in the Soviet capital early this year. The discovery of the microphone inside the Great Seal was made in 1952 but was announced only in 1960.

The paper also reported that:

> [American] officials were inclined to doubt the Polish assertion that the building had been wired without their knowledge. If this were true, the question would then arise whether other intelligence services, such as the Soviet, were operating against United States establishments in a foreign country and, presumably, behind the back of the Polish

security organs...there were similarities between the techniques employed in wiring the embassy in Moscow and that in Warsaw... the nature of the devices found in Warsaw were quite similar to that discovered in Moscow almost six months earlier. In both cases, the listening devices were said to have been installed during the early stages of the construction of the two buildings.

In talking about the cases of the military attachés, as well as other matters with the Americans, almost invariably with the Number Two at the embassy, Counsellor Albert Sherer, rarely with Ambassador Gronouski, I tried to soften, at least in words, the messages and arguments I had to transmit. That is probably why at the end of his stint in Warsaw, Sherer was quoted to me as having said: 'If it were not for Mr Sieradzki as the go-between I would have long ago lost my senses.' He told me once on his return from an extended absence from Warsaw that he had attended a special State Department psychological course for diplomats to prepare them better to endure the exigencies they were exposed to.

It was evidently not enough for the Polish security services at the time to harass and blame the American military attachés. They were out to implicate Ambassador Gronouski himself in the 'campaign of spying'. To that end they concocted a film which included a scene with Ambassador Gronouski saying farewell at the airport to an expelled American military attaché and other shots of the ambassador. The commentary blamed Ambassador Gronouski directly for orchestrating the 'spying campaign'. They could not, however, release the film without obtaining the consent of a number of party and government departments, including the Ministry of Foreign Affairs. For that purpose they convened a high-powered conference of about 25 top people representing not only the 'civilian' and military security services but also, among others, the propaganda and foreign departments of the party's Central Committee. They could have been pretty sure of their support. From the Foreign Ministry, from which they could have expected strong reservations, they should have invited a deputy minister or at least the head of my department, Eugeniusz Milnikiel. However, Milnikiel's state of health was not too good and, since it was I who was dealing at the time with those matters, they invited me, the deputy head of the department. Subsequently, I formed the suspicion that they had invited me in the belief that it would be easier to browbeat me, the Jew insecure in his job, into giving consent to the release of the film on behalf of my ministry. The atmosphere at the conference was, indeed, intimidating for me. All the powerful participants came out clearly in favour of the film. The whole event turned into a strongly anti-American show. When the others had spoken the chairman (I don't now recall whether it was General Matejewski or someone else) turned to me asking for my opinion. I was too overwhelmed and isolated to oppose directly what to me was an idea potentially extremely harmful to Poland's interests. Instead I pretended to agree with some of the arguments put forward by the other speakers, but added that I was not empowered to give consent for the release of the film on behalf of my ministry and that my superiors might have reservations thinking the film could seriously affect our relations with the United States and thereby jeopardize, among other things, the import of badly needed grain and other products on the favourable terms we had arranged. The chairman, visibly displeased with my contribution, said: 'You will then have to use your best arguments to persuade your superiors to give their consent, won't you? We will be in touch with you.' And thus the conference ended with the final decision suspended until I obtained consent from my minister.

Dejected, I returned to my ministry and immediately called on Senior-Deputy Minister Marian Naszkowski. Naszkowski had the reputation of being a 'Moscow's man'. He had come to the ministry in 1952 having served before as Deputy Defence Minister for Political Affairs. He was somewhat pompous and overbearing and his subordinates feared him, but he was known to be at loggerheads with the people now at the head of the security services and especially with General Moczar. Above all Naszkowski being at the Foreign Ministry and working with Minister Rapacki well understood the potential consequences of the game the security services were trying to play. So he approved the stand I had taken, but when I suggested that he himself talk to the security people, he said: 'I won't talk to them but leave the matter with me.' When I was back at my desk, I received a phone call from Michał Krupski, the head of the Interior Ministry's Counter-Intelligence Department whom I mentioned above, asking rather impatiently whether I had obtained the awaited consent. I suggested he talk to Deputy Minister Naszkowski, which he flatly refused to do. As far as I was concerned the matter ended there. Later I found out that Naszkowski had called Artur Starewicz, the secretary of the Central Committee responsible for matters of propaganda and, incidentally, one of the few Jews remaining in the party's wider leadership, who apparently managed to quash the whole idea of the film.

Notes

1   Czesław Miłosz, *The Captive Mind* (London: Penguin Books, 1985), p. 133.
2   Christopher Booker, *Daily Telegraph*, 3 October 1981.
3   Jan Kott, *Polityka* (Warsaw), 6 October 1990.
4   Public Record Office, Ref. FO 371/182656.
5   Confidential note from R.W. Selby to H.F.T. Smith, Northern Department, Foreign Office, Public Record Office, Ref.: FO 371/182670.
6   Foreign Office documents at the Public Record Office, Ref.: FO 371/182671–2 contain an accurate account of the talks. Quotes are taken from those files.
7   Lord Rees-Mogg, *The Times*, 25 May 1995.
8   Confidential Telegram Number 70, 9 February 1967, Public Record Office, Ref.: FCO 28/270.
9   Confidential note from G.L. Clutton to R.H. Mason, Foreign Office, Public Record Office, Ref.: FO 371/171841.
10 Public Record Office, Ref.: FO 371/171843.
11 G.L. Clutton's note to R.H. Mason, Foreign Office, 3 December 1962, Public Record Office, Ref: FO 371/166154.
12 Secret Outward Saving Telegram, 26 March 1964, Public Record Office, Ref.: FO 371/177609.
13 P.G.F. Dalton, British embassy Warsaw, to R.H. Mason, Foreign Office, 13 June 1962, Public Record Office, Ref.: FO 371/166117.
14 G.L. Clutton's note to the Rt. Hon. R.A. Butler, Foreign Office, Public Record Office, Ref.: FO 371/177580.
15 Ibid.
16 Letter from H.W. King to H.F.T. Smith, Northern Department, Foreign Office, 23 August 1966, Public Record Office, Ref.: FO 371/188807.
17 Cf. Public Record Office, Ref.: FO 371/188807.
18 In his book *Poland: Communism, Nationalism, Anti-Semitism* (New York: Karz-Cohl, 1982), Michael Checinski, a former counter-intelligence

officer, refers to him several times: '...Kufel's ignorance matched that of...(he was unable even to write correct Polish), but he made up for it by his impudence and his exceptional gift for intrigue and provocation' (p. 197). '...Kufel acted under the close guidance of Soviet liaison officers...' (p. 199). Kufel was promoted 'despite his lack of elementary education' (p. 200). 'Obeying only Moscow's orders and closely collaborating with Moczar [see below], he could now effectively begin plotting against Spychalski [then Minister of Defence] himself...' (p. 201). In 1967, even before the Six Day War in the Middle East and the official purge of Jews in Poland, Kufel was particularly active in purging Jews from the armed forces. 'At the end of May 1967, General Kufel summoned a special conference of high-ranking army commanders...The main subject on the agenda concerned the need for accelerating the anti-Jewish purge...According to an account given by a high-ranking counter-intelligence officer present at this fateful conference, both Kufel and Urbanowicz [then chief of the Main Political Administration of the Polish Army] pointed out that Israel was going to be annihilated soon, or at least suffer a widespread civilian massacre in the regions to be occupied by the victorious Arab armies. Although the Arab atrocities would be minimized in the Polish mass media, a backlash (characterized as "nationalistic demonstrations" by General Kufel) among officers of Jewish origin was feared. Purging of Jews was seen as necessary to forestall any potential protest to the Six Day War. It also provided a pretext for removing all political unreliables in general' (p. 204). 'Kufel's rise continued even after Gomułka's and Spychalski's downfall. In 1971, Kufel was promoted to Divisional General, the first chief of Polish military intelligence to hold this rank. Only in 1979 was he dismissed by General W. Jaruzelski' (p. 208, note 4).

8 • Anti-Semitism in the Open

It was the June 1967 Six Day War in the Middle East that provided the pretext for bringing the communists' anti-Semitism, flimsily disguised as anti-Zionism, into the open. When back in 1964 Gomułka promoted Mieczysław Moczar, the most vocal advocate of the nationalist trend in the party, to the post of minister of internal affairs, it was a conscious gamble on his part. Moczar and his followers had become useful to Gomułka at a time when he no longer adhered to the 1956 liberalization policy he himself had initiated but gradually betrayed. He may not have counted on Moczar using his newly acquired position and his popular brand of 'nationalist communism', of which anti-Semitism was one of the most crucial planks, if not the most crucial, in a drawn-out, though ultimately unsuccessful, attempt to supplant him in supreme power. One of Moczar's principal tools was to infiltrate his men into sensitive positions in the media and in central and local government departments. He already controlled the security apparatus and the police as minister of internal affairs.

From my vantage point I could see a growing number of posts in the Ministry of Foreign Affairs, including foreign postings, being taken over by people from outside, mostly from the security service, who, we surmised, could only have been Moczar's men. When following the Middle East war Gomułka not only joined in, but led the anti-Zionist, anti-Semitic campaign, accusing 'Zionist circles of Jews who are Polish citizens' of being an Israeli 'fifth column' in Poland, it was thought that he wanted to wrest the anti-Jewish weapon from the arsenal of the Moczarist faction within the party – the Partisans as they were known by then – to use it to his own advantage and that he thereby revealed his own anti-Semitism even though or because, as some wits would put it, his wife was Jewish. That accusation was the pretext for the ousting of Jews from any position of influence and indeed from any job.

In fact, the anti-Jewish policy now so openly pursued had its roots in pre-1956 Stalinist policies and was implemented by various secret and semi-secret measures after 1956. Few people knew, for instance, that the notorious *Protocols of the Elders of Zion* was made available in 1966 to the staff of the Ministry of National Defence. I certainly did not know it. As it turned out a second 'clandestine' edition appeared later at the Ministry of Internal Affairs. Similarly, few people knew at the time that the anti-Zionist campaign unleashed after the June 1967 Middle East war was the result of decisions taken by the communist summit in Moscow on 9 June of that year. However, because of the specific circumstances prevailing in Poland, its communist leadership went further in its anti-Zionist virulence than any other participant of the Moscow summit. The Middle East war provided the opportunity for the full implementation of anti-Jewish decisions taken by the Politburo of the Polish party a few years earlier.

As for the reaction to the war of the general population, some Christian Poles genuinely sympathized with Israel while many rejoiced that – as the saying went – 'our [Polish] Jews beat the hell out of the Soviet-supported and Soviet-armed Arabs'. They did so mostly in private. Polish Jews were particularly on their guard. They were painfully aware that, unlike in democratic societies where many a Jew even in public life could openly profess pro-Zionist or pro-Israel sympathies without being regarded disloyal to the country, or unlike Poles, say, in America who could express affinity with their old country without exposing themselves to accusations of being less patriotic Americans, Jews in Poland could not reveal their pro-Israel sympathies. They could not express such sentiments before without running the risk of being branded disloyal to the country or worse, much less could they do so now when they were already being denounced as traitors, Zionist agents and much else, their reticence notwithstanding.

The official reactions, as reflected in the media and the obligatory, party-orchestrated mass meetings in work places, including of course our ministry, were venomous, vociferous and sickening in their denunciation of 'Israeli imperialism'. It was in this atmosphere of whipped up hatred of Israel and Jews, a hatred seemingly shared by most Poles, that the plans for an all-pervading purge of Jews were being finalized and soon after implemented.

The anti-Zionist campaign was directed not only against Jews. Gomułka was greatly concerned about the criticism on the part of Polish military experts of the poor standard of Soviet strategy and military equipment, as revealed in the Middle East war. First there was a purge of senior officers in the air force and then in other military formations though by then there were very few Jews in senior posts. There was only one Jew among the sacked air force generals, yet the purge was presented later as a measure taken against 'the Zionist conspiracy of Jewish officers' in the Polish forces.

The student demonstrations of March 1968 provided the authorities with another pretext for intensifying the anti-Jewish drive. In a deafening frenzy they were presented in the media and elsewhere as a 'Zionist provocation' designed to spread confusion, weaken the government, bring down the system and even sell Poland out to the West and the Zionists. The officially inspired media and party propaganda spread the idea that the Jews were responsible for all the misfortunes that afflicted Poland. In a public address Gomułka himself spoke of the participation of Jewish youths in the demonstrations and alleged there was a connection between Jews, Zionists, reactionaries and 'revisionists'.

Most people did not see – through the smoke screen – the real aims of the witch-hunt. However, many independently thinking Poles realized that the Moczarite faction had reintroduced and was pursuing anti-Semitism as the most efficient weapon in their efforts to rid themselves of their rivals, not just Jews, not even principally Jews for they were relatively few and not really important, inside the communist establishment and to seize power. Both they and Gomułka, who was the real target of Moczar, also regarded anti-Semitism as a useful safety valve for all the economic and social troubles the communists were unable to prevent or were incapable of dealing with. It was to divert attention from the fundamental problems of the country, shift the blame for all past evils and consequently popular anger on the Jews, thus freeing the Communist Party from responsibility. It was also to 'prove' the national character of the ruling establishment.[1]

I and my circle of friends did not realize at first that the aim as far as the Jews themselves were concerned was not just to remove them from any positions of influence but also to provoke virtually all of them into leaving the country. It is true that in his speech on 19 March 1968 Gomułka offered emigration as a solution, but he divided Jews into three categories and said that those who felt attached to Israel rather than to Poland were free to emigrate. Those of us in government and other 'sensitive' positions, especially, could smell a rat: if we applied to emigrate, and only Israel was allowed as the destination, we thereby condemned ourselves as virtual traitors and confirmed all the anti-Semites' accusations.

At the Ministry of Foreign Affairs there had been a portent of what was to come as far back as the autumn of 1955 when I was in Cambodia. A meeting of 'senior party activists' at the ministry was summoned. My friend Janek Gelbart, to whom I owe the information about it, attended the meeting. The subject was the 'cadres', that is, personnel policy. The speaker, Deputy Minister Naszkowski, surprised and shocked the audience by declaring that the 'cadres should continuously improve by becoming more popular' – that is, they should come from the Polish people. To make it absolutely clear what he had in mind, he added: 'In this connection comrades of Jewish origin must be prepared for the necessity to leave the Ministry.' This was followed by a speech by the deputy head of the Cadres Department of the ministry, Miron, who personally censured several Jewish officials, including Gelbart. He accused him of spreading discontent. Gelbart had previously expressed his dissatisfaction at not being allocated a flat, and said as much at the meeting; he also intimated that

168

he did not understand the new 'cadres' policy. There were two voices of dissent, neither of them Jewish: Bohdan Lewandowski, whom I have already mentioned in these pages, expressed principled opposition to such a discriminatory approach to 'comrades of Jewish origin'; and the other dissenting voice was that of my London embassy colleague, Kazimierz Dorosz. Among those who took the floor there was a contribution from a 'Jewish comrade' who went through the demeaning ritual of self-criticism and supported the removal of those 'Jewish comrades who deserve it'.

The implications of the meeting were disturbing. However, two weeks later another meeting was convened with the same participants at which Foreign Minister Skrzeszewski retracted Naszkowski's declaration and stated that the party could not pursue a policy of discrimination based on nationality and Jewish comrades could safely continue in their work. Apparently, this was the result of the matter having been brought to the attention of Prime Minister Cyrankiewicz[2] by a senior official of the ministry. The entire affair was undoubtedly a reflection of the power struggle that was going on between two wings of the party – the hard-liners, known as the Natolin faction and the moderate reformers, known as the Puławska faction. It was said that Naszkowski had been inspired to make his statement by either Zenon Nowak or Franciszek Mazur, both hard-liners from the Politburo, and that following this experience he declared he would never again allow himself to be used as a tool for such policies. The following year, 1956, ushered in the liberalizing phase of Polish communism and the anti-Jewish policies were suspended.

Now, in 1967–68, the full swing of the anti-Jewish campaign was being introduced in the ministry by a series of party meetings with the participation, *inter alia*, of party Central Committee Propaganda Secretary Stefan Olszowski and one of the deputy ministers of Internal Affairs. These meetings at which Zionism and 'anti-Polish Zionist agents' were vociferously condemned became particularly frantic after the defection of a Jewish foreign service official, Władysław Tykociński.

The witch-hunt proper started soon after the March 1968

student demonstrations with a two-day (or rather two-night) meticulously stage-managed mass party meeting held in a big hall opposite the ministry. It was a nightmare. A suitably selected group of Jewish staff, including myself, became the target of especially vicious attacks. We were individually picked to pieces from the platform and from the floor, accused of pro-Zionist, pro-Israel sympathies, disloyalty to the Polish People's Republic and much else to boot – character assassination being part of the blue-print. Demands were made to expel us from the party and the ministry. We were vilified, denigrated, humiliated and condemned not because we were suspected of being Zionists, though in our hearts many of us had pro-Israel sympathies, but because we were Jews. I spotted a few grim-faced non-Jews obviously distressed and disgusted with the entire spectacle. Minister Rapacki sat with an ashen face on the platform. During an interval he went back to his office and told his secretary 'they are craving for blood'.

Most of those individually pilloried, already traumatized by the drawn-out, unabated anti-Jewish campaign, confused and blinded by mounting fear of what fate was being prepared for them, felt they had somehow to defend themselves. A wartime, battle-hardened partisan broke down when he took the floor.

Among the charges levelled against me much ado was made of the fact that my step-father, Zineman (who had died two years earlier), had been a well-known Zionist – the transparent implication being that with such family connections I could only be a Zionist and traitor. My wife, sitting next to me, tried to dissuade me from taking the floor but, fearing possible consequences, I decided I had to rebut some of the accusations that had been made against me. I promised her that I would not give them the satisfaction of breaking down in the process. We did not yet realize that any attempt to refute the charges was an utterly futile exercise, that our fate had been sealed beforehand and this was just a charade to create a semblance of legitimacy for further measures against us. When at a similar meeting at the Institute of Nuclear Research a 'defendant' who was 'accused' of having a brother in Israel declared that he was an only child, the meeting's chairman, nonplussed, retorted: 'Never mind, we shall find something else.'

This ordeal was followed a few days later by an individual grilling at the ministry's party executive committee. At my grilling the arch-anti-Semite Kazimierz Sidor, a close collaborator of Mieczysław Moczar and former ambassador to Egypt, referring to my keeping in touch with my mother in Paris, affected appreciation of the fact that one had only one mother but why two motherlands (Poland and Israel)?

My wife was anxiously waiting for me outside the ministry. When I finally emerged after about two hours of interrogation, totally drained and alarmed by the thinly veiled accusations of pro-Americanism in my work and remembering all the fake trials of the past, I told her I did not expect to be alive by the twenty-fifth anniversary of my father's death in the Warsaw Ghetto, which was a month away. It was only much later, with hindsight, that we could see that our fears had not been justified but at the time, with the authorities' intentions unbeknown to us, we expected the worst. Subsequently I was told I would not be expelled from the party but administered the next severest punishment – 'serious admonition'.

It was obvious that the meeting and the subsequent grilling were just a prelude to dismissals from work. To spare myself that humiliation I tendered my resignation to Deputy Minister Wolniak (my erstwhile predecessor in Cambodia and successor in Canada) who was in charge of the dismissals campaign in the ministry. He was so pleased that I was quitting myself that he offered me six months' severance pay instead of the usual three. Thus my 23 years in the Polish foreign service came to an end.

My wife, utterly disgusted by what had happened and outraged at hints that she should divorce me so that she could continue with her career, resigned at the same time. She was not allowed to leave straight away – presumably because that would have looked like a protest – and had to continue to work for a further five months. This was a harrowing time for her. Ostracism on the part of those who showed their true colours during the whole sordid campaign, or the easily recognizable few who debased themselves for the sake of a promised reward – a posting or a trip abroad – did not bother her, but she could not stomach having to deal with people whom she held in total contempt and the feigned politeness towards her of the ringleaders. Luckily in her own room which she shared with Danusia Cosma (whose father was Romanian), a colleague and friend working in the UNESCO section, she could breathe freely. Danusia, a deeply devout Catholic who never joined the party, was unreservedly opposed to the anti-Jewish drive and later, fully aware that she was risking losing her job, made a point of coming to the railway station to bid farewell to her former Jewish colleagues driven out of the country, including even those with whom she was only remotely acquainted. Not surprisingly, such defiance did not go unnoticed and she was sacked.[3]

Before the dismissals were under way a list of Jewish staff to be dismissed was presented to Foreign Minister Rapacki for him to sign. He not only indignantly refused to do so but entered his own name on top of the list. He was so disgusted with the whole campaign that he soon resigned. He had, of course, opposed it in the party's Politburo along with Edward Ochab, the then President of Poland, who subsequently also resigned. (Incidentally, Rapacki was also against the armed intervention in Czechoslovakia.[4]) Similarly, a few other members of the Central Committee protested against the anti-Jewish campaign, but these were cries in the wilderness, and it proceeded relentlessly towards its goal of making the administration *judenrein*.

Senior-Deputy Minister of Foreign Affairs Naszkowski, a staunch adversary of Moczar, was the target of fierce attacks at the above-mentioned mass party meeting for allegedly employing the 'Zionists', even though he was on official business abroad at the time. We had considered Naszkowski an abrasive character but he turned out to be more decent than the affable Winiewicz. It was Winiewicz who in the circumstances was appointed acting foreign minister. It is symptomatic that in describing that meeting in his memoirs Winiewicz does not say a word about its anti-Zionist or anti-Jewish nature. He only speaks in general terms of 'mutual accusations', of the ministry's personnel policy being attacked and about 'totally justified censure' being mixed with 'slander'.[5]

Practically all my former non-Jewish colleagues and 'friends' did not know me any more, most of them probably because they feared they would harm their careers if they were seen talking to or even greeting me. But I remember meeting Minister Rapacki in the street who doffed his hat to me before I had a chance to do so first.

Our prospects were bleak and we were particularly concerned about the future of our son. While determined to leave Poland, we thought it wiser, however, not to apply for emigration straight away lest it be taken and used in the smear propaganda as proof of Zionist and pro-Western inclinations and intended treason by Jews who had been working in such a sensitive field as foreign affairs and had been privy to some 'state secrets'. Believing that at least 12 months would have to elapse from the end of my association with foreign affairs for the authorities to grant us permission to leave the country, I decided to stick it out until then, while preparing ourselves for the plunge.

Getting another job was not easy. For one thing, as everything was either directly or indirectly controlled by the state or the party, not many employers dared to employ Jews in the prevailing atmosphere. For another, the authorities had stipulated that Jews should not be offered more than a meagre 3,000 złotys per month (my salary had been twice as much). My wife and I were fortunate in that there was always great demand for translators into English. To lessen the risk to themselves, those who gave us translation work would for the most part commission it in my wife's name. But there were three people courageous enough to commission me directly. One was Bohdan Lewandowski's wife who worked in a publishing house. She was of Ukrainian-American origin. She later divorced Bohdan when he was Under-Secretary-General at the United Nations and stayed in the United States. The second was Mirka Dorosz, whom we knew, as well as her future husband Kazimierz (already mentioned above), from our embassy days in London. She now worked at the Polish Press Agency. Ironically, I also received commissions from the Foreign Department of the party's Central Committee. This apparent paradox was due to the fact that a Canadian-Jewish communist was then still in charge of its English-language

publications. I delivered the translated material to his flat
rather than to his office. Thanks to these translations my wife
and I were earning more than twice our combined previous
salaries at the ministry, but others were not so lucky.

Meanwhile all sorts of rumours were flying around.
According to one, camps were being prepared in the region of
Bieszczady for Jews who were not in regular employment.
(We realized only later that this was part of a security-inspired
'whispering propaganda' designed to scare and provoke the
Jews into leaving the country.[6]) To be on the safe side, I began
looking urgently for some work that would provide me with
proof of regular employment. I found a cooperative of foreign
language teachers in Warsaw which, on my passing the
necessary tests, employed and provided me with the
necessary document. After an official inspection of my class
by a Warsaw University lecturer who highly praised my
teaching methods and results in his report, the cooperative
wished to employ me for more than the initial few hours a
week but I declined. While preparing ourselves for leaving
Poland and being in no doubt that we would be skinned in the
process, I needed all the time for the better-paid translation
work to save up enough cash to defray the costs.

In the meantime Krysia left the ministry. Her familiarity
with United Nations' affairs and good command of English
stood her in good stead in obtaining a relatively well-paid job
at a United Nations Development Fund office in Warsaw
which ran a potassium salt exploration project in Poland.

The Exodus

When Jews, first those who had worked in non-sensitive
posts, began to apply for emigration and were in most cases
granted permission to leave within a month, I decided it was
time to join them. It took several weeks of incredible hassle to
procure all the documents, certificates and attestations which
had to accompany the applications before I was finally ready,
in early spring 1969 – almost exactly a year since I had left the
ministry – to submit our application, and I was the first among
our circle of close friends to do so. The documents required
were further proof that the anti-Jewish drive had been

thoroughly premeditated and thought out in great detail up to and including the exodus of the Jews. One requirement was particularly indicative of the authorities' cynicism. We were all forced to apply to the Council of State for permission to renounce our Polish citizenship, which was promptly given. This meant, among other things, that the applicants, the majority of whom were middle-aged or old people, lost their entitlement to old-age or retirement pensions to which they had contributed throughout their working lives.

Having crossed the Rubicon we now braced ourselves for the waiting period, for living in a state of suspense and uncertainty as to what the decision in our case would be. Our anxiety grew after two, then three, months of waiting only to become even greater when towards the end of the fourth month (July) my wife and mother-in-law received their exit permits, but I did not. By sheer malice rather than any administrative oversight, as the entire operation was very efficiently run by the Internal Affairs Ministry, mine arrived some ten days later.

Yet, it could have been worse and in comparison with some other applicants we considered ourselves very lucky. For instance Jan Szelubski, whom I have already mentioned above, was kept waiting for almost a year, while Bronek Rabczyński for several years. Szelubski simply 'knew too much'. I spoke to him shortly after we received our permission to leave and he was shattered; he doubted whether he would ever be allowed to go. Even more hopeless seemed the case of Bronek Rabczyński. He had once worked in the Foreign Ministry and also in Prime Minister Cyrankiewicz's office. But his latest post had been as head of a Ministry of Health department dealing with charities. He was accused, among other things, of allowing the American Jewish Joint Distribution Committee to bring goods for distribution in Poland without payment of import duties. The charge was nonsensical – I remember a file in my office containing explicit instructions signed by Prime Minister Cyrankiewicz exempting the Joint from paying any duties on its charity supplies.[7] I shuddered to think that if such preposterous charges could be levelled against Rabczyński on what would have been a technicality, how much more vulnerable to trumped up charges was I whose department

175

had political supervision not only over American charities in Poland but over relations with the United States in general. It was some relief to learn from Rabczyński what an official at the party's Central Committee had told him: 'If the international situation were different you would have been brought to trial and convicted.' In other words, in view of the then prevailing atmosphere in East–West relations, the Polish communist leadership could not afford to stage fake political trials.

Happy though we were to have received our exit permits we still lived in a state of tension and under immense psychological pressure. Having our permits was no guarantee that we would actually leave the country, and anything could still happen. We were on the point of becoming stateless persons, as we had already applied for permission to renounce our Polish citizenship, a condition we had to meet in order to be granted travel documents. We had to be cautious and tread carefully so as not to jeopardize our chances.

For these reasons we, regrettably, had to decline a private invitation from the British ambassador with whom I had had official dealings, which he extended to us through my wife's British boss at her UN office, presumably in order to see how he could help us. We feared how such a private contact with a Western ambassador might be interpreted and used against us by the security authorities.

The ambassador enquired, through the same channel, whether he could help us in arranging our entry to Canada, assuming that having spent five years in that country on my last foreign assignment, we would probably wish to settle there. Our preference for Britain evoked some surprise as economic conditions and hence prospects were then much better in Canada than in Britain. Anyway, the ambassador promised to help. We preferred Britain for a number of reasons: I had my university degree from London, which I hoped would make it easier for me to find a proper job, London as a big metropolis seemed to offer more possibilities of finding suitable employment (I had the BBC, among others, in mind). We knew Britain and the British, and felt we had much in common with them and Britain was still Europe which would make it easier for us to visit my close family and for Krysia's sister and her son in Poland to visit us, should it one day become possible for them to do so. That is why and how we eventually managed to land in London.

Why not Israel? I thought it the only natural destination for me. But since my wife is not Jewish and fearing what might happen to Stefan, our only child who was 15 years old by then, in the precarious Israeli circumstances, we decided against it.

Ostensibly, however, we were going to Israel, as this was the only country for the emigration to which Jews were granted exit permits. We picked up our British visas only after we had left Poland. Visas for Israel were obtainable from the Dutch embassy, as Poland had severed relations with Israel following the Six Day War. I had some difficulty persuading staff at the Dutch embassy that I was Jewish as my surname, my first name and my appearance provided no indication to that effect. Eventually, when I produced my birth certificate with my original first name and that of my father, I was believed.

We decided to give to Krysia's sister some of our furniture and sell the rest as well as anything else that could be replaced, but to do our utmost not to leave behind things which were of great sentimental value to us. We suspected that getting the authorities' clearance for some of them would, in the best case, involve much additional aggravation, but more likely than not we would not get it. That was particularly true of our 28 rolls of half-hour 8mm films. Sending them by post to my cousin Natek in Paris seemed the best, indeed the only, solution. Only two post offices in Warsaw would accept such parcels. In order to avoid suspicion I mailed, within the space of several weeks, one film roll at a time, making sure not to deal with the same clerk too often and alternating between the two post offices. Occasionally I had to take out the roll and show a bit of the film against the light to the clerk to convince him that it was a harmless family film. Extra caution was necessary to avoid the entire exercise getting me into trouble. One film, for instance, included shots of some Polish navy vessels, which I had taken on a return trip to Poland by boat. Filming those, let alone sending such a film to a Western country, was a grave offence. The caution paid off and, all our films were safely dispatched.

177

Clearance for some of the gifts connected with our foreign service years was also problematic, for instance, the Cambodian silver bowl I had received from Prince Sihanouk and the silver salver given to me by my colleagues, heads of mission, as a farewell gift on my leaving Canada. We plucked up enough courage to take them to the Danish ambassador in Warsaw, John Knox, my erstwhile colleague in Ottawa, and ask him whether he would do us the favour of transmitting them to Paris where they would be collected by my mother. My wife hid the salver under her jacket and carried the bowl in a shopping bag. We approached the Danish embassy with some trepidation, particularly as it happened to be situated opposite the Interior Ministry and its notorious prison on Rakowiecka Street. The ambassador not only remembered and recognized us straight away but when told of our predicament had tears in his eyes. It did not need any pleading on our part for him to accede to our request. He took the two silver items and walked across the room to put them in his safe. The safe was opposite the window through which we could see the Interior Ministry building. My wife and I exchanged somewhat panicky glances and positioned ourselves between the ambassador in front of his safe and the windows. In due course my mother received a letter from the Danish embassy in Paris that she could pick up our two items.

Later we received from John Knox a letter which deeply moved us. In it he said:

> ... you and your wife have been in our minds. Often I have been wondering how you are faring and in what way you two have been mastering your hard and implacable fate. I would like to think that this Memorial Plate will be a sign to both of you that everything is turning for the better.
>
> ... There must be nearly 1800 of your compatriots up in Denmark and I know that their presence carries with it much hardship for these people, but we are doing our best to have them integrate in the Danish society and I am sure we can absorb most of them.

My wife left her few items of jewellery with her British boss, which, after we had settled in London, she gratefully received back from Scotland.

We were allowed to take with us our hard currency savings, deposited with the Polish National Bank, to the amount of 622 US dollars. This was all the money we had to start our new life with.

Most of our belongings were to be sent by rail to Vienna. Packing them into crates at the station was a long drawn-out process with innumerable complications and much aggravation. The packers had to be handsomely tipped not to delay it too much. They and their supervisors as well as the customs officers were all controlled by the security service, and every item was carefully checked as to whether it was 'exportable'. We knew that our two or three paintings had to have stamps of a state art authority so that they could be taken out of the country and we had obtained these in advance. But when it came to packing our china tea set we were told almost at the last minute that it too needed such stamps. I had to take the set and rush in my car at break-neck speed, as the crates were about to be closed, to the Art Conservator's office to get the necessary authorization. To my dismay the queue was inordinately long and I did not have time to wait. So I knocked on the door of my erstwhile acquaintance, Chief Conservator Professor Marconi, one of the experts to take over the Polish national art treasures in Canada. He did help, though somewhat reluctantly.

Earlier I had difficulty in having two other items approved. One was a 16mm film I had received as a gift from Canadian External Affairs Minister Paul Martin during his visit to Poland. Evidently his advisers had told him I was a film buff but were unaware that I was making only 8mm films and consequently had only an 8mm projector, so the 16mm film, an uninteresting documentary on Polish-Canadian émigrés anyway, was useless to me. But as a matter of principle I did not want to leave it behind. The second item was much more important, it was our 8mm projector. When I argued with the customs officer about it he, being in a somewhat accommodating mood, explained why he could not approve its 'export' by showing me his extremely bulky official list of items allowed for export, which had been compiled, if I remember correctly, back in 1952. 'Look', he said, 'this list does not include an 8mm projector, so for me, officially, there is no such thing as an 8mm projector. Consequently, I cannot allow the export of something that does not exist.' I was silenced by his 'logic' and decided to go to the main customs office to plead there about the two items. I saw a senior official who was not prepared to change the ruling of the station customs officer. In the course of the argument I asked whether I should go to the Canadian embassy and tell them that the Polish authorities would not allow me to take with me a gift from their External Affairs Minister. He paused for a minute and then asked me to wait while, evidently, he went to consult someone. When he returned he was more accommodating and arranged for both items to be cleared.

In this as in some other instances at the station itself I was in a combative mood and ready to fight my corner. I felt we were out of danger and our departure was more or less assured. But my wife still cautioned me against being too optimistic. Indeed, one more aggravation was still in store for us. A couple of days after our crates were, to our great relief, finally closed and nailed up and we were about to start packing our suitcases, we learned that the crates had been opened during the night for one of the spot double-checks that were occasionally carried out on instruction from above. We were furious: this was sheer spite as everything had already been thoroughly checked. When we opened the crates in London we saw that they had obviously been badly repacked, many fragile objects were broken and, most painfully, my wife's university degree certificate was missing. It had either been officially confiscated, as happened in many instances, or simply stolen, as such documents were sought after and sold for good money to forgers.

At long last we were ready to leave in our Fiat 1500. (This, bought in Poland in 1966, is now insured as a vintage car and still serves us well.) We bade farewell to Irka's son Andrzej, who was in a Warsaw boarding school at the time, and a few friends and were on our way. Our last stop in Poland was in Bielsko-Biała to pick up my mother-in-law, who was waiting there for us and my wife's sister who accompanied us to the Polish–Czech border which we crossed at Cieszyn. We had feared some last-minute stringent checks – body searches were not uncommon – but were let through with little fuss and even some politeness. Our parting with my sister-in-law was very emotional. Not knowing whether she would ever see her elder daughter and her beloved grandson Andrzej again was particularly hard on my mother-in-law. She had no other regrets about leaving People's Poland which had in 1945 deprived her of her widow's pension because her husband, the father of her two daughters, had been a Piłsudski legionary. She had been granted the pension before the war because his death in 1929 was the result of tuberculosis he had contracted in the trenches shortly before his long internment by the Austrians for refusal, along with most other legionaries, to take an oath of allegiance to the Central Powers, and because he was a legionary who distinguished himself in battle and held military decorations for valour. My mother-in-law never forgave the communists for not honouring Poland's debt to widows of Piłsudski's legionaries who valiantly fought and sacrificed their lives for Poland's independence.

We passed quickly through Czechoslovakia, as the situation there was still tense a year after the Soviet-led invasion, and crossed the Czechoslovak–Austrian border on the easily memorized and memorable date of 6.9.69. It was only then that, with the 'Iron Curtain' behind us, we felt safe and relatively happy, despite the uncertain future that lay ahead of us.

(When many years later a newly established democratic Poland officially deplored the 1968–69 purges and virtual expulsions, and apparently wanted to mollify Western and Jewish critics, it allowed the Jewish expellees to apply for their pensions. In reply to my enquiry as to the conditions for a successful application, I was informed by the central Office of Social Security in Warsaw that one of the first conditions was to prove that I had worked in Poland for at least 25 years. Considering that I, and others like me, started working there in mid-1945 (just when the new Poland was being established) and finished when I was dismissed and virtually expelled in 1968–69, I could only claim to have worked there for a total of 24 years, which disqualified me from the start. Moreover, even were I granted rights to a pension I would not have been able to receive it unless I was registered as a resident in Poland. In the circumstances I consider the apparent 'gesture' of the Polish authorities to be illusory and hollow.)

Notes

1 For a detailed account of the anti-Semitic campaign, see Josef Banas, *The Scapegoats: The Exodus of the Remnants of Polish Jewry* (London: Weidenfeld and Nicolson, 1979).

2 Cyrankiewicz, a pre-war socialist, spent two years as an inmate in Auschwitz where he was said to have been active in the underground organization. He was a slick orator, intelligent and a cynic. In the party he had the reputation of being a liberal, though during the strikes in Poznań he showed himself to be a merciless brute. He was known in Warsaw as an avid womanizer and had a weakness for ingenious Western gadgets. He was not anti-Semitic.

3 Michael Checinski quotes Władysław Bieńkowski, an erstwhile close friend of Gomułka, a non-Jewish Marxist, 'who lived through this gloomy period but has had the courage to come out openly to denounce the perpetrators... The anti-Semitic campaign intimidated, pushed out, and forcibly silenced all those who had retained their capacity for thinking, for common human decency, and for patriotic concern over their country's fate. Corrupt elements had surfaced...who were ready to march in any direction.' Op. cit., p. 224, note 18.

4 Rapacki's political profile is aptly drawn by M.K. Dziewanowski, professor of history at Boston University, in his *Poland in the 20th Century* (New York: Columbia University Press, 1977), pp. 193–4: 'Adam Rapacki, a former socialist, the only post-war Polish minister of foreign affairs...was a colorful as well as courageous and independently minded personality. Rapacki was a member of an old Polish family with a long liberal intellectual tradition and with social-democratic ties...Being a realist, Rapacki viewed Poland's international position as it was, not as it might be. He believed, therefore, that all moves in the field of foreign relations should take as their point of departure the rigid international structure of the postwar world and the existing balance of forces. Instead of unrealistic efforts to achieve impossible dreams, the government should use all avenues to raise the living standard, national culture, and political education of the Polish people...In a world divided between two superpowers, neutralism was an impossibility. The first purpose of Polish foreign policy, according to Rapacki, should be to contribute as much as possible to the relaxation of tension between the two camps, encouraging small steps to bring about international *détente*. In a relaxed world there would be a greater role for the smaller states that must exist and cultivate their own way of life in the shadow of the

superpowers. Rapacki's ideas provided the philosophical background of the plan to create a nuclear-free zone in Central Europe.'

5 Winiewicz, op. cit., p. 576.

6 Michael Checinski (op. cit., p. 221) writes on this issue that: '...according to confidential information received by the author from absolutely reliable sources, preparations were already being made for large scale anti-Jewish measures. They were patterned partly after the plans submitted in 1953 at the time of the Kremlin doctors' plot, but in certain respects went even further: all "Zionists" were to be assembled in forced-labor camps and employed in hard labor. Jews were to be expelled from all major cities, or at least from certain districts, denied private phones, and their letters officially restricted and censored. The *de facto* and *de jure* status of Jews in People's Poland would then closely resemble the situation in Nazi-ruled Europe on the eve of the "final solution". It was only due to circumstances beyond their control that the survivors of the Holocaust were spared this final outrage.'

7 Michael Checinski writes in this connection the following: 'Prime Minister Cyrankiewicz, in fact, personally requested the AJDC to resume its activities in Poland. In 1957, the AJDC Vice-Chairman Jordan was invited to visit Poland and was welcomed by the prime minister, who requested increased financial aid to Polish Jewry...' (p. 128). 'The AJDC alone provided some $700–800,000 annually, thus contributing considerably to ameliorating Poland's shortage of foreign currency' (p. 134, note 16).

The author also writes that 'Józef Kutin, deputy minister of foreign trade...an old Communist, veteran of the Spanish civil war and of the French resistance movement...was...charged with waiving import duties on goods sent by the AJDC for Jewish workers' cooperatives affiliated with the Cultural and Social Association of Jews in Poland' (pp. 220–1).

9 • Building a New Life in Britain

We stopped at the nearest road-side café to shake off our emotions and the tension of crossing two borders on that day, and to savour the first moments of freedom unspoiled by the uphill struggle of building a new existence that awaited us. The past – with all its tribulations and upheavals, with all our illusions and disappointments, mistakes and regrets – was momentarily forgotten and all our thoughts concentrated on the future. The odds were against us – we had no financial resources, no relatives or close friends in Britain and most importantly no concrete profession by which we could make a living. Yet we were not despondent and hoped that we would somehow make it. The fact that we were granted the rare privilege of settling in Britain seemed a good omen.

In Vienna we were 'processed' by Jewish organizations. I remember my pained explanations to Israeli representatives as to why we decided against settling in Israel. The American Hebrew Immigrant Aid Society (HIAS) which was helping those who wished to make their home elsewhere advised us to apply to the Jewish Refugee Committee on arrival in London.

We left our crates which had by then arrived in Vienna in storage for future transportation to wherever we would eventually settle, and set out on our journey to London stopping over for a week in Paris to see my mother and cousin Natek and his family. They were relieved and happy to see us safe and sound. I felt a special affection for Natek; he was a man after my own heart, had a great sense of humour and was well liked by all who knew him. Our common wartime experiences in Lvov had brought us particularly close together, and throughout the 30 or so years my mother lived in Paris he was of tremendous help to her. In later years we visited each other and spent several holidays together with his loving wife Genia. It was a real pleasure to spend time in their company. (Natek died in 1988 aged 74 of heart failure and Genia a year later of breast cancer. My wife and I still sorely miss them.)

We arrived in London in the late afternoon and went straight to the Jewish Refugee Committee, as advised by HIAS, to seek their assistance. We spoke to the committee's secretary, Mrs Epstein, an elderly Austrian-Jewish lady, who seemed to be in charge. She was warm-hearted and understanding. My East European pre-war Jewish background had not prepared me for the widespread phenomenon of mixed marriages in the West, so I was trying to explain to her why ours was and she reassured me that that was of no consequence. She was also an efficient organizer: it took her just a few phone calls to find temporary accommodation for us at the house of a Hungarian-Jewish couple in Stoke Newington, north London, and she also arranged a small loan for us to tide us over the worst period. In the next couple of days she found a job for Krysia at the Institute of Jewish Affairs, a research body of the World Jewish Congress, where Krysia began working a week after our arrival in London and has continued to work ever since. Mrs Epstein's assistance was invaluable and we remember her with gratitude. Within a few days we enrolled Stefan in the local comprehensive school which provided him with the compulsory school uniform free of charge. Admittedly, life was not easy in our temporary cramped and damp lodgings, with no facilities for any cooking, but it was all we could afford to pay for at the time, and it was a beginning.

I was not nearly as lucky as Krysia in finding employment. Mrs Epstein introduced me to a number of influential people, while her boss, Mr Oscar Joseph, tried to be helpful and thought that with my background I should be able to get a proper job. I met a number of times with Mr Abraham Marks, who was the secretary of the Board of Deputies of British Jews at the time. He took me to see Cyril Stein, a very influential businessman, and invited me and my wife to a party to meet some other influential people in the Jewish community. One of them was the head of the Legal Department of the American-Jewish organization *B'nai B'rith*, who was visiting London, with whom I had a long conversation. He seemed impressed with me and thought I was a suitable candidate for the post of European representative of his organization (presumably vacant then) and promised to make arrangements for me to obtain it – however nothing came of it. I also had a long talk with a representative of the well-known international conglomerate, the Anglo-American Corporation, based in South Africa. He thought I could be employed in its team of international analysts, but when, as promised, he got in touch with me again, the reply was disappointing. I was considered well qualified for the job, but unfortunately too old. The corporation was granting large pensions and at my age – 49 – I was too close to retirement age. I also sought a job with the *Jewish Chronicle* and saw its then chairman, David Kessler, and the paper's editor, William Frankel; however, although they were very understanding, they had no vacancy for me.

After three months of fruitless job-hunting I was so disheartened that I even contemplated reverting to my wartime forced occupation of docker or some similar manual job. In fact, I was ready to accept any job – but even that eluded me. At one point, it occurred to me that an acquaintance of mine living in London could perhaps lend me a helping hand. He was the elder brother of the pharmacy assistant who had saved my life in wartime Djambul by supplying me with the only effective remedy for my amoebic dysentery. I knew that he had a prosperous business and was very well-off. When I called him up he asked disbelievingly: 'Mietek from Djambul?' Reassured that it was really I, and told of my predicament, he regretted he had nothing for me. The only vacancy in his business was for a messenger boy of sorts with a wage of about £15 a week. Despite my assurances that I would not mind taking the job in the least, he said he could not employ me in such a lowly position. And that was the end of it.

It all looked pretty hopeless, and by then we were in great financial straits. Krysia's salary did not go nearly far enough to meet our basic needs, modest though they were. My brother, who had at that time worked as an Israeli expert for an International Labour Organization (ILO) project in Venezuela, sent us a few hundred dollars, though we had not asked him for any assistance, but we could not accept his offer of providing us with a couple of hundred dollars a month for as long as I was unemployed. He had his own family of four to provide for and we knew he had to save as much as he could to be able to buy a decent flat on his return to Israel.

After his arrival in Tel Aviv in 1948, my brother started out by joining the army. He took part in some difficult fighting missions during the War of Independence and in the 1956 Sinai Campaign. During his military career he was first a physical training officer in the air force in Haifa, was a top cadet in the first course of the air force officers' school, but having been rejected due to his inadequate sense of smell for the pilots' school he became an instructor in the air force officers' school and later commanding officer of an air force training base.

When he left the army my brother studied political science and international relations at the Hebrew University of Jerusalem. In 1957 he was chosen to represent the ruling Mapai Party as a special emissary in London where he worked mainly with Jewish students for three years. He was then offered and accepted the post of head of Mapai's Human Resources Department, a very central political and professional position which allowed him to participate in major decisions in the party. However, he was not cut out for a political career; as Moshe Sharett, whom he consulted, put it, in this 'manipulative and power-stricken environment' a person of integrity would not be able to reach the peaks of his ability without paying a very high price. He resigned and became a member of the executive board of the Israel Productivity Institute responsible for technical assistance to developing countries. In this capacity he travelled extensively, directing various programmes, and he was so successful that he was invited by the ILO to represent it in Venezuela where he spent three years as an adviser to the government and a further year as a private consultant. Although offered further highly remunerative assignments in Venezuela, he felt homesick and returned to Israel in early 1970 via London where we saw each other. We had last met in Paris in 1966 after the death of Jakub Zineman.

I had to persevere in my quest for a job and continue applying for any vacancy I got wind of, where there was any chance that I could be accepted. When, in mid-January 1970, I was offered the job of a clerk in the Overseas Branch of the National Westminster Bank, Head Office, it was a breakthrough. With my confidence restored I believed that from then on things could only improve. Naturally, I could hardly derive much satisfaction from addressing envelopes, shuffling papers, cheques or even, on rare occasions, acting as English–German interpreter for the management, but a bird in the hand was worth two in the bush.

Although I did not abandon my search for a more fulfilling job, I began reading some books on banking, just in case I was destined to spend the rest of my working life there. I did it half-heartedly, however, as a career in banking never appealed to me and I felt I was too old to start afresh now. In addition, I was put off by the social segregation within my particular institution – the separate restaurant and other quarters for the management, a canteen for lesser mortals. Thus while trying to familiarize myself with banking, I never stopped pursuing my real interests and remained, as before, an avid reader of publications on current affairs, closely following developments on the world scene, while at the same time continuing my quest for a job where my experience in this field would be of use.

With this objective in mind, I got in touch with a number of professors and institutions. My contacts with Professor Alec Nove from the University of Glasgow, Professor Finer from the University of Manchester, the Royal Institute of International Affairs, *The Economist* and other institutions brought no positive results. On the other hand, Professor Leonard Shapiro, the eminent authority on Russia at the London School of Economics, where I had attended lectures in the late 1940s, tried to help me in getting a foothold there. He arranged interviews as a result of which I was offered, as a start, participation in a seminar on East–West relations in Europe and a commission to write a book based on my past experiences. For reasons which my interviewers, well-versed in communist affairs fully appreciated, I hesitated to commit myself to doing it at that time, but the offer was there in case I changed my mind.

Also, Professor Richard Hiscocks, an old acquaintance of mine from Canada, who now lectured at the University of Sussex in south-east England, helped in arranging for me, again as a start, a series of lectures on Eastern Europe and participation in seminars at his university. As this offer coincided with my awaiting the outcome of my application for a job with the BBC's External Services, I accepted it gratefully but provisionally.

With the BBC

My first attempt to obtain employment at the BBC's Polish Section, the best option from the point of view of my qualifications and preference, failed. Though a vacancy in the section invariably attracted scores and sometimes hundreds of applicants, I had reason to believe that other considerations rather than an abundance of suitable candidates accounted for my not being shortlisted and even being told that there was no vacancy at all. Soon afterwards, however, I was accepted, after an exhaustive examination, by the BBC's Monitoring Service based at Caversham near Reading. I began work in the Polish-language team in September 1970 and was before long included in the Russian-language team as well.

As the work involved day and night shifts I travelled from London once a week spending working shift nights in Caversham. Later on we managed to arrange a mortgage and bought a house there, and then it was Krysia who commuted to work in London. Stefan was enrolled in the grammar school in nearby Henley – the transport to and from school being provided by a special school bus service.

Listening in to Polish and Russian broadcasts and selecting items meriting translation into English was an interesting and demanding job. On one occasion I was complimented on quickly identifying and supplying a text which permitted the service to produce a significant news item about 20 seconds ahead of any other news agency. That kind of 'feat' is important in the news business.

189

My overall boss, the head of the Monitoring Service, was generally referred to as HMS, which was also used in all communications. As this happens to be the acronym of 'Her Majesty's Ship', someone once wrote beneath his communication pinned on a notice board, 'and God bless all who sail in her'.

Well before my contract with the Monitoring Service was up I asked HMS to enquire unofficially at the BBC's Polish Section in London, where there was a vacancy, whether I now had any chance of being accepted. The reply was 'none whatsoever'. I applied anyway and when my application went further than before I was admitted for an examination (much less stringent than that of the Monitoring Service) and accepted, beating the other candidates for the vacancy at the interview. Thus by September 1972 I was with the Polish Section in Bush House where I had wished to be in the first place. I was looking forward to being able to take part in an activity of a political nature which I knew would permit me to interpret events in an unbiased and objective way. Incidentally, Poland's security people evidently could not stomach my having made good and presumably in order to blacken my name spread the rumour – clearly meant to reach my BBC colleagues and superiors – that I had been adviser on Far Eastern affairs to Poland's Stalinist leader, Bierut. I learned about this rumour from a BBC colleague on her return from a visit to Poland.

At first I was involved only in preparing and broadcasting texts (in Polish). For broadcasting I adopted the name Marek Styczyński. I found the work less demanding and at the same time more creative and much more gratifying than monitoring. Preparation consisted of translating into Polish and editing centrally distributed material in English. In time I started writing my own texts: talks and features mainly on British and Polish topics. Increasingly, I was asked to translate my own texts on the then frequent major Polish developments into English for use by other language services and the World Service. I also covered some events, such as annual conferences of British political parties. I took part in discussions on the air on Polish, British and international topics and also chaired such discussions, often having linkups with other cities and countries, with the participation of Polish-speaking experts, including professors, political commentators and politicians.

After a few years I was on a six-month attachment with the Central Talks unit of External Services, providing talks in English for translation to all the language services – about 40 in all. I wrote talks on a variety of international topics, mainly on East–West relations, the United Nations, the Soviet Union and Poland. I relished the opportunity of expressing my real views, of being free to be myself, although some degree of conformity had to be observed. I could easily identify with the BBC's principles of objectivity, impartiality, balance, accuracy and reliability – qualities for which the BBC External Services received the Athinai Prize in 1984.

There were the odd occasions when my private views on major events differed from those generally prevailing. General Jaruzelski's imposition of martial law in Poland in December 1981 was widely condemned as a brutal move against the Solidarity opposition and the Polish people in general, and as an act tantamount to doing the Soviets' dirty work for them. I believed that Jaruzelski, irrespective of what his political past had been, and apart from wanting to preserve his power, acted, at least to some extent, out of patriotic motives in the sense that he wanted to avert a much greater catastrophe for his country – that is, a Soviet invasion – though the methods employed were harsh and even brutal. In other words, I believed then that he chose what he would later call 'the lesser evil', and, when on the tenth anniversary of martial law he told an interviewer that, 'it was necessary to pass through what has sometimes been called purgatory, that is martial law, in order to avoid ending up in hell', I did not doubt his sincerity.

There was little doubt in my mind at the time that the petrified Brezhnev leadership, fearing that Poland's successful separation would have an infectious effect and threaten the disintegration of the Soviet bloc – as it eventually did – would have used every means to retain control over Warsaw. Thus Soviet military intervention with consequences much more disastrous than those in Hungary in 1956 or Czechoslovakia in 1968 seemed to me imminent. My views were in a way vindicated ten years later by public opinion surveys which showed that more than 50 per cent of Poles agreed that 'Jaruzelski was right to impose martial law because it saved Poland from Soviet military intervention'. It seems that this opinion was also shared by at least one former leading Solidarity stalwart and martial law internee, Adam Michnik, who argued in his editorial in the newspaper *Gazeta Wyborcza* that, 'the entry of the Red Army would have been a hundred times worse for Poland than martial law, and could have caused tens of thousands of deaths'. What is more, the Primate of Poland, Cardinal Glemp, was at the time among those many people who foresaw no end to communist power and were convinced that martial law was the lesser of two evils, the only way that Poland could avoid a Soviet armed intervention. However, obviously, Polish opinion at all levels remains divided on the issue.

I had my own views, shared by other people, on Wałęsa becoming president of Poland. Nobody could doubt his immense contribution to the victory over communism and the introduction of democracy in Poland. He had been a courageous and very effective revolutionary, he had an unmistakable political instinct and was even capable of the occasional flashes of genius. But he was not suitable for the role of state president, and once he took office this became particularly obvious. While in many respects ignorant, he became obsessed with his own wisdom and importance, and sometimes acted in a way that made him the object of ridicule and discredited the office of president and his country abroad. He was unpredictable, secretive, given to sudden stunts, he tried to divide and rule, and he surrounded himself with yes-men and shady advisers. He has become, as a close observer of the Polish scene and author of his biography put it, 'the master of chaos, interpreting democracy as a process of continual confrontation'[1] and, as a leading article in *The Times* remarked:

Mr Walesa, who so eloquently symbolised resistance to the abuse of power during the 1980s, increasingly appears to put his own pursuit of continued power ahead of the health of Polish democracy.[2]

No wonder that in 1994 (and subsequently) Wałęsa, the Nobel Peace Prize laureate, was lagging far behind others in public popularity surveys, even behind General Jaruzelski, the man responsible for martial law. Before the 1995 presidential election Wałęsa recovered from rock-bottom, single-figure popularity ratings chiefly because many Poles were determined to block his main rival the former communist, Aleksander Kwaśniewski. And yet Wałęsa eventually lost the presidency because many Poles voted for Aleksander Kwaśniewski out of Wałęsa-fatigue.

I did not agree with the criticism of Gorbachev. For what he did and accomplished, he was censured and debunked in his own country and admired in the West but criticized for not going far or fast enough. Just suppose another septuagenarian had followed Chernenko, or the tough hardliner Grigori Romanov, the Leningrad party boss, had become Soviet leader instead of Gorbachev; the 'evil empire' could have existed for quite some time yet. After all 'permanence of existence' was the general premise of Western Sovietology.

For a product of Soviet upbringing, Soviet education and Soviet power Gorbachev appeared to me a man of exceptional intelligence, drive and above all courage. He realized the system did not work and had to be dismantled, but he had to act with caution and cunning for, apart from anything else, he was faced with powerful and evil vested interests – hence the relatively gradual progress, his pragmatism and the compromises he made. As a result he was the Bolshevik reformer who destroyed the hated system. To my mind, Gorbachev's achievements were properly defined by Andrei Sinyavsky, the exiled Russian writer, who wrote:

What did Gorbachev do? 1: He withdrew the troops from Afghanistan. 2: He gave us freedom of speech. 3: He allowed eastern Europe to regain independence. 4: He freed Andrei Sakharov and other political prisoners. 5: He put an end to the cold war.[3]

And I fully subscribed to the view that:

But for his unravelling of communism, the Soviet Union

would still be standing today...He can be argued to have done more to change the map of Europe by peaceful means than any other statesman since Metternich.[4]

However, as is made clear in his 'Memoirs', Gorbachev modestly regards himself more as an instrument of inevitable historic forces than as an initiator of change.

On my return in 1980 to the Polish Section from the six-month Central Talks attachment there was an opening for the post of the section's deputy head, then officially designated as Senior Programme Assistant. I applied for and was appointed to the post which I held until my formal retirement in 1984.

As deputy head I shared an office with my immediate superior, Krzysztof Pszenicki, the first section head of the younger generation, a veteran of the 1968 student protests in Warsaw. His predecessor, Jan Krok-Paszkowski, the son of a pre-war Polish general, a fair-minded boss, had been moved upstairs and became deputy head and then head of a service in External BBC. Very bright, remarkably articulate, eloquent and ambitious, Krzysztof too was eventually promoted to the post of deputy head of service and a few years later promoted again.

I drew great satisfaction from knowing that my work was appreciated. This found expression not only in words and bonuses and in that in 1981 I was retained for another three years beyond the BBC retirement age of 60, but also in the official thanks I received on retirement from the Managing Director:

On the occasion of your retirement, I should like to send you my good wishes for the future and my thanks for your work over the past fourteen years.

You joined the Corporation as a Monitor at Caversham Park in September 1970 and rapidly made your mark as an able and conscientious member of staff. However your transfer, two years later, to the Polish Section at Bush House, offered broader scope for your varied talents, backed by a profound knowledge of international affairs, much of which had been gained at high level and in person during your previous long and distinguished career as a diplomat.

You swiftly adapted yourself to what must at first have seemed a very strange profession in an equally strange environment. Soon you were noted for a fluent and distinctive radio style, elegant translations and for the forceful but moderately expressed arguments which characterise your original writing on political subjects. As a broadcaster, you were especially effective in presenting the British political and social scene to listeners in Poland, notably during the 1979 British General Election.

In 1980 as a man of 'exceptional competence and dedication', you were appointed, without competition, Senior Programme Assistant of the Polish Section and, in further recognition of your merit, offered three years of extensions beyond the Corporation's normal retirement age.

Perhaps the greatest test and demonstration of your sustained high calibre performance in conditions of great professional and emotional stress came as events in Poland erupted and remained a world news story. Throughout this long period – the emergence of Solidarity, its suppression and the imposition of martial law – your sensitivity to events in Poland and your clear understanding of the BBC's role at all times were of great value to your PO [Programme Organizer, i.e. head of section] and to your Head of Service.

Your career with the BBC has, by force of circumstances, been comparatively short but you have won the respect and affection of your colleagues to a greater degree than perhaps you yourself realise.

Thank you very much for all you have done to sustain the high reputation of the BBC and the Polish Section. Please accept my warm wishes for a happy and active retirement.

Though formally retired, I continued to work in the section, full-time, for another eight years, first on a renewable contract and later without it. For the last four or five years I acted as a kind of 'quality controller' and adviser to the management of the Polish Section, although these functions were not officially provided for. On a number of occasions higher management sought my opinion on Polish affairs.

After the fall of communism in Poland and particularly on the setting up of the British Know-How Fund many Polish institutions sent their workers and managers to Britain to acquire new skills and/or familiarize themselves with British practices and expertise. Among them were employees and executives of Polish Radio. The head of Polish Radio, who attended a couple of the *post mortems*, the daily programme evaluation sessions I conducted, asked my boss to 'lend' me for several months to Warsaw to run a course in radio journalism. I was flattered but not interested. One of my primary motives for ruling out going back to Poland in that or any other capacity was not to be again in a position where my Jewishness would be thrown back at me.

Again I shared an office with the head of the section. By that time it was Eugeniusz Smolar, also a veteran of the 1968 student protests in Warsaw. I thought he was clever, extremely well-versed in Polish affairs and very enterprising; in short, a great asset to the section and to the BBC in general. Personally, I was particularly impressed by some admirable qualities of his character, which are rarely found in a boss. It was not unusual that, being some 20 years my junior, he often sought and accepted my advice. What was exceptional was that he would not present my ideas or suggestions as his own but would give credit where it was due. Moreover, on the rare occasions when I felt my private criticism was called for, his reaction would not be one of piqued *amour propre* but of appreciation. It was truly gratifying to work with someone endowed not only with a sharp mind but wisdom as well.

Although when I first joined the Polish Section I sensed a certain hostility towards me on the part of some of its staff, in time I got on very well with practically all its members. Among them were some amiable, intelligent and gifted men and women, including the very knowledgeable Krzysztof Dorosz, son of my former foreign service colleague, a man more in the mould of a philosophical thinker than a political animal. I also got on very well, from the very start, with my superiors outside the section.

When aged over 70 I finally retired for good, I was asked by the section head to write and broadcast a weekly political commentary. On reflection, I decided it was time to call it a day and declined, although I was grateful for the offer.

I am proud to have been associated with the BBC's External Services, later renamed World Service, in general and its Polish Section in particular. In my view the World

Service has reflected some of the best values of British society and projected them to the world at large. Its impact is difficult to gauge but I believe its role is important and its work impressive. For instance, Oxford Professor of Modern History Norman Stone, writing about the BBC External Sevices said:

> Their post-war role has been a brilliant one in a very British way – the practical, the humane, the unflappable, and the good humoured have gone together with that peculiar chemistry that gives the British such a good name in this battered century... They represent the best that this country does.

Dame Peggy Fenner, describing herself in the House of Commons as a devotee of the World Service, commended it even as 'a fine example to the BBC Home Service'.

The BBC World Service's international popularity is unrivalled. It has an audience of over 130 million, and more people listen to it than to its five closest competitors combined. What must in large part explain its enormous audience and unique reputation, concludes an observer, are features which chiefly distinguish the BBC from its main competitors in the field of external broadcasting:

> ...its political independence and impartiality. Although financed by... the Foreign and Commonwealth Office... the External Services are totally free of any editorial interference by the Government... No other major external broadcasting organisation enjoys such freedom... The first language service was in Arabic because it was being used by the Italians at the beginning of their Abyssinia campaign. Its opening news bulletin on January 3, 1938 carried an item about the execution in Palestine of an Arab by the British authorities for possessing a rifle, exactly the kind of information that would not have been broadcast on a government-run service.[5]

One of the greatest compliments paid to the BBC World Service was that by Mikhail Gorbachev, who called it his lifeline to the outside world during the 1991 coup. And as people working in overseas countries have attested over the years, 'for millions of people who are oppressed, persecuted, displaced, who live under tyranny or in war zones, it [the BBC World Service] is a lifeline to the outside world. Often it is the only way they can find out what is happening in their own countries, let alone elsewhere.'[6]

My own attachment to the service began in the early 1950s following my return from London to Warsaw. I regularly listened to its English broadcasts as much for the language as for the comprehensive and reliable contents. Early one morning in 1953 after Stalin's death I heard in the BBC's news bulletin that the Soviet police chief, Lavrentii Beria, had been shot dead in the Kremlin. On arrival at the office I shared this almost unbelievable news with my colleagues. When I asked Janek Gelbart: 'Do you know what has happened in Moscow?', he, in an allusion to the recent 'doctors' plot' affair, half-jokingly replied: 'The Jews have assassinated Stalin.' It was not long before I was summoned to the head of the Department of Cadres (personnel) and asked to explain myself. As a member of the British Section at the Foreign Ministry my listening to British radio (as opposed to the American Radio Free Europe)[7] was excusable but the piece of news I had brought sounded so preposterous as to be incredible. I repeated that that was what I had heard on the BBC. I myself did not doubt the accuracy of the news item but I nevertheless spent some anxious hours before the news was confirmed from Moscow.

The BBC's Polish Section has its own impressive record. It started out in 1939, and its wartime broadcasts carried to the Poles under Nazi occupation not only true and reliable information, thereby keeping up their spirits and courage, but also coded military messages for the Polish underground. Throughout the period of the communist regime in Poland the BBC's measured and detached broadcasts were a source of reliable, comprehensive and hence invaluable information which strengthened people's defences against the official media propaganda. It was so important that in time more and more people of the political establishment either listened to it directly or read it in special bulletins in closely restricted circulation. But officially it was taboo, though not as much disapproved of as the American Radio Free Europe.

After I joined the section in 1972 some people in Poland were already daring to lend their voices to its broadcasts. At first they were just voices of dissidents but in time also official representatives considered the BBC acceptable enough to be interviewed by it. I myself interviewed, among others, the sharp-tongued Polish government spokesman Jerzy Urban.

The section played a particularly significant part in times of dramatic events or crises in Poland, and there were many of those, the most historic being the birth of Solidarity, martial law introduced by General Jaruzelski in December 1981 and the collapse of the first communist regime there eight years later. The section not only provided Poles – incidentally not only in Poland – with objective and accurate information but also made its expertise available to others. The head of section and I were frequently consulted by different World Service units and also by domestic BBC radio and television. I was interviewed on numerous occasions for World Service English transmissions, for BBC domestic radio and several times appeared on television. I gave interviews to BBC regional stations, to Canadian and even Australian radio, wrote talks in English for distribution to other language services, and broadcast commentaries or interviews in the BBC Russian Service. I was consulted by leader writers of some quality British papers including *The Times* and the *Independent*. It was gratifying to see the following day that much of what I had said was included in the leading article. Some of my Polish Section talks were reprinted in the London *Polish Weekly*, and I also wrote a few analytical briefs on Poland for *Oxford Analytica*.

Work in the section had its lighter moments too. Mistranslations, faulty audio-transcription, slips of the tongue during broadcasting or anecdotes and jokes used in talks were the source of much merriment. The latter two were a bit of a problem when those present in the studio during broadcasting who had not heard them before could barely manage to keep their spontaneous laughter inaudible. With laughter being contagious and the sight of people struggling to contain it being rather funny, it was a strain on the broadcaster to keep a straight face. I experienced it on several occasions. When I was reading in front of the microphone my talk on 'Wit in Parliament', my colleagues present in the studio could barely contain their audible laughter at the exquisite story about an irate Lady Astor telling Winston Churchill in the House of Commons: 'If I were your wife, I'd put poison in your coffee', and his riposte: 'If I were your husband I'd drink it.'[8] There were similar reactions when I spiced my continuity with jokes or anecdotes. For instance, in introducing an item on hospital treatment I told the joke about a schoolboy who when asked in class why a surgeon wears a mask during an operation replied: 'So that he is not recognized when the operation is not successful.'

Sometimes people had great difficulty in pronouncing a word or phrase. It happened rarely in the case of professional broadcasters who, when it did occur during a live transmission, could wriggle out of it by either amusingly apologizing or quickly using a substitute word. It was more frequent though in the case of outside contributors with little broadcasting experience. Thankfully they were usually pre-recorded, but some of their seemingly unending repeats provoked fits of laughter, especially when the tape was replayed in the culprit's absence.

In the rush of broadcasting work and with occasional insufficient knowledge, some mistakes, including those in translation, are inevitable. One of our tasks in management was to reduce the number of such errors, howlers in particular, to a minimum. I frequently checked translations, and found some of the mistakes hilarious; like when, for instance, 'a man crossed the Atlantic single-handedly' was translated as 'a one-armed man...', or 'the West Bank' of the Jordan was translated as 'the western bank'.

Mistakes also occurred in the transcription in London by typists frequently unfamiliar with distant locations of dispatches filed by the BBC's foreign correspondents. Thus a dispatch from Bonn referring to the German–Polish border 'along the Oder and Neisse rivers' was transcribed as 'along the older and nicer rivers'. We had also to watch out for simple typing errors which turned 'least effective' into 'least defective', 'discuss' into 'disgust', 'the Koran' into 'the Korean', 'kosher' into 'kosha', and the like.

In the 1970s, while with the BBC, and especially during my visits to Israel in 1974, I renewed my friendship with Victor Grajewski, by then head of the East European Broadcast Department in Israeli radio, *Kol Israel*. Victor was contributing occasional, especially Christmas, programmes from Jerusalem for the BBC Polish Section. He also visited the BBC a couple of times on official business.

I knew Victor from wartime Djambul. Later, in the early 1950s, we used to meet in Warsaw where he worked as a journalist for the Polish Press Agency, PAP. In 1957 he emigrated to Israel where he rejoined his parents who had moved there eight years earlier.

In March 1994 it was revealed that Victor had been responsible for what has been described as 'the leak of the century'. In 1956 he secured the text of Nikita Khrushchev's secret speech denouncing Stalin, delivered at the 20th Congress of the Communist Party of the USSR. Divorced from his first wife, Victor had a girlfriend working in the party's Central Committee in Warsaw whom he persuaded to 'loan' him for a few hours the 58-page Russian text made available to the Polish leader by Moscow. Victor gave the text to the Israelis who apparently photographed it and then he returned the document to his girlfriend. Although, according to press reports, Western intelligence services were offering up to a million dollars for a copy of the speech, Victor never received any payment or even thanks until the whole matter was publicly revealed in 1994. The then Israeli Prime Minister, Ben Gurion, decided, for political reasons, to hand over the document to the American CIA, who leaked it to the media. It was broadcast in full over Radio Free Europe and Radio Liberty which, as one observer remarked, '...had a devastating effect and may well have marked the beginning of the break-up of the Soviet Union and its East European satellites'. Press reports point out that the procurement of the text was for a long time considered an American accomplishment. It was only later in the 1980s that it began to emerge that this was Israel's success, but Victor's crucial role in it was only revealed and acknowledged in 1994, especially in a 60-minute Israeli television documentary, broadcast in June of that year.

I should add here, however, that there have been other claimants to the leak. The then (1956) First Secretary of the Warsaw Party Committee, Stefan Staszewski, has been quoted as saying that he ordered many additional copies of Khrushchev's secret speech to be printed and handed copies of it

> ...personally to Philip Ben, correspondent of *Le Monde*, to Gruson of *Herald Tribune* and to Flora Lewis of *The New York Times* – three friendly foreign journalists, who telexed it straight away to the West. In this way I broke all principles of party discipline...Khrushchev attempted to deny, saying the document was falsified...but that was of no use, Khrushchev's report had become an open secret.[9]

However, Sydney Gruson questioned about it by Dan Raviv and Yossi Melman, the two authors of a fundamental book on Israeli intelligence, did not confirm having received the text of Khrushchev's speech from Staszewski. The two authors could not question Philip Ben who had died in the meantime but they suggest that it was he who had provided the text to the Israeli intelligence.

Anyway, the two claims of Grajewski and Staszewski do not rule each other out and apparently Victor's copy was the first to reach the West.

Notes

1 Roger Boyes, *The Times*, 6 February 1995.
2 *The Times*, 7 February 1995.
3 *Guardian*, 19 October 1993.
4 *The Times*, 8 December 1993.
5 Ian Bradley, *The Times*, 3 February 1982.
6 From a letter in *The Times*, 5 July 1996.
7 It is interesting to read in a Foreign Office document (E. Youde to Sir G. Harrison, 29 July 1964, Public Record Office, Ref.: FO 371/177612) what the British thought of R.F.E.: 'We have now been asked for advice on whether Sir Winston Churchill should accept an invitation from Radio Free Europe to send a short message to commemorate the [Warsaw] Uprising [of 1944]. There can clearly be no objection in principle; but I think we should enter a warning that Radio Free Europe programmes often go further in aggravating the Polish regime than we or the BBC

think wise. I am also doubtful whether Radio Free Europe is an appropriate channel for a message from someone of the stature of Sir Winston.'

8 Quoted from Adam Sykes and Ian Sproat (comp.), *The Wit of Westminster* (Frewin, 1967), p. 52.
9 Teresa Torańska, *Oni* (*They*) (London: *Aneks*, 1985), p. 145.

10 • *Reflections on Polish Anti-Semitism*

Past experiences have made me particularly sensitive to anti-Semitism in general and to Polish anti-Jewish prejudices in particular, though I have tried to be objective about it.

While I was at the BBC, Polish–Jewish relations cropped up from time to time in our current affairs output. One such issue was the protracted conflict between the Polish Catholic hierarchy and world Jewry over the Carmelite convent on the site of the former Auschwitz concentration camp. This conflict, and in particular the protest staged at the site of the convent by the maverick New York Rabbi Weiss, prompted Primate of Poland Cardinal Józef Glemp to deliver a homily at Częstochowa on 26 August 1989, which contained anti-Jewish utterances. He said, *inter alia*: 'Esteemed Jews ... Your power is the mass media, at your disposal in many countries. Do not use it to spread anti-Polonism ... If there is no anti-Polonism, there will be no anti-Semitism here.' Moreover, he stated that: '... as a result of wartime events ... there has remained a resentment [with the Poles] towards the Germans and the Jews.'[1]

The question may be asked: What had the Jews done to hurt the Poles during the war as the Germans had? Earlier, in February 1987, Cardinal Glemp seemed even to deny the Holocaust. Answering a question in public in Brussels he said: 'The statement that during the Second World War six million Polish citizens perished does not preclude that there were Jews among them; if you can define the number of people of Jewish origin among those Polish citizens, this can be taken into account.'[2] Those were the views not of a parish priest but of the spiritual leader of the Polish nation.

On the other hand, I was dismayed by Israeli Prime Minister Yitzhak Shamir's sweeping accusation that 'Poles suck anti-Semitism with their mothers' milk'. While I fully understand the bitterness that prompted him to make this statement – his father and sister had been murdered by Polish 'friends' to whom they had turned for shelter from the Nazis – it was utterly wrong for the leader of the Jewish state to express such views in public, quite apart from the injustice of such an accusation against the Poles *en masse*. Did Yitzhak Shamir include in his statement the 'two thousand Poles', out of a total of 'some 8,000 persons'[3] granted the title of 'Righteous among the Nations of the World' by the Jerusalem *Yad Vashem* Holocaust memorial centre, who 'had risked their lives to save Jews during World War Two'? My aunt Franka was hidden and saved by a 'righteous' Polish family. Some of those Poles and their families not only risked but lost their lives together with the Jews whom they had sheltered. Even some known anti-Semites helped Jews during the war. Jews often reproach the Poles for not having done enough to save their Jewish compatriots, oblivious of the fact that Poland was the only occupied country where sheltering Jews was punishable by death. This begs the question so rightly put by the German Jewess, Else Rosenfeld in a postscript to her book: 'At any time in human history there has only been a minority of true heroes and their actions known to very few people; we should all ask ourselves to what extent we would have been able and willing to act heroically.'[4]

Some historians believe that in the Middle Ages and during the Renaissance when Jews were being persecuted in other countries, Poland probably saved Jewry from extinction. That is why such a large proportion of the world's Jewry lived in Polish territories – though even then there were some anti-Jewish disorders. But later when new ideas of religious tolerance were spreading in Western Europe, the situation of Jews in Poland was deteriorating. 'Why', asks one historian, 'did the French and Polish revolutions of 1789 and 1791 respectively, differ in their responses to the rights and status of Jews?'[5] To which a reviewer of his book, replies:

...In 1789 there were, at most, 50,000 Jews in France, but more than a million in Poland. Jews in Poland were more numerous than the nobility or the non-Jewish commercial class. To grant full legal equality to Jews on the French pattern would have been a revolutionary step far too disruptive of the balance of Poland's public life.[6]

By the nineteenth century about 70–75 per cent of the world's Jews lived in Poland. From the last decades of that century up to 1940, the Jews of Warsaw never constituted less than a third of the city's total population. At one point in 1917, nearly 50 per cent of its inhabitants were Jewish, and Christian Poles began to fear for the 'Polish' character of the capital. The situation was similar in some other Polish cities and towns. There were the inevitable commercial rivalries, economic, social and other differences. All these, in addition to the general decline of the country and the increasing role of the Catholic Church, contributed to the growth of anti-Semitism which in the inter-war period, and particularly in the late 1930s, became widespread and at times vicious partly as a result of modern nationalism. Its prime exponent was the National-Democratic Party (*Endecja*) founded and led by Roman Dmowski. He and his party advocated an alliance with Russia and preached hatred towards Germans and Jews. (No wonder there was such a close ideological affinity between the Gomułka regime and the pre-war *Endecja*, despite the fact that the latter was a right-wing party. Some say Gomułka realized Dmowski's dream of a nationally homogeneous population, free from Jews.)

The ensuing discrimination and persecution alienated many Jews from Poland and undermined the allegiance to the country of some of them to the extent that they at first welcomed the invading Soviets in 1939 and helped them organize Soviet rule in Poland's eastern territories. This fact, grossly exaggerated in popular perception and ascribed to all Jews, further intensified anti-Jewish feelings in the country. This is testified by a report, dated 30 September 1941, by the leader of the Polish underground, General Grot-Rowecki, to the Polish government-in-exile in London:

Please accept as a real fact that the overwhelming majority of the country is disposed in an anti-Semitic way. Even the Socialists are no exception. Differences relate only to tactics of dealing [with the Jews]. Practically no-one suggests following German methods. These methods evoke spontaneous sympathy [with the Jews] which has, however, diminished after the merging of the two [German and Soviet] occupations and after the general public learnt about the conduct of Jews in the east.[7]

There were some Poles who approved of the Germans doing the dirty work for them; there were the *szmalcowniki*, that is those who betrayed Jews to the Nazis, robbed and even killed them; there were those who showed 'spontaneous sympathy'; and the relatively few very brave 'righteous' ones who risked their lives to rescue Jews. However, the overwhelming reaction to the Holocaust was indifference, silence and an attempt to forget. It is hard to tell how many shared the views of the eminent Polish writer, Jerzy Andrzejewski: 'To all honest Poles the fate of perishing Jews must have been particularly painful, because there were people...dying, whom our nation had no right to look straight in the eyes and with a completely clear conscience...'[8]

Referring to Polish attitudes to the Jews immediately after the war – a period in which hundreds of Jews who survived the Holocaust in hiding, in the forests or had been rescued in time from concentration camps, Jews who could hardly be identified with the hated communist authorities, were murdered in pogroms in Kielce and elsewhere – the same author writes: 'Polish anti-Semitism did not burn itself out in the fires and smouldering ruins of the ghettoes. The death of several million Jews did not prove a horror sufficient enough for its impact to eradicate Polish mental and emotional habits.'[9]

One explanation, though by no means a justification, offered by a Polish-Jewish writer is that, unlike other German-occupied countries, Poland did not experience the moral shock of the Holocaust because of the six million Polish citizens who had perished at the hands of the Germans some three million had been ethnic Poles. That is why most Poles – so the argument goes – have not been sensitive to the fact that in the case of the Polish Jews almost all of them had been exterminated.

It should, however, be borne in mind that it was the Polish underground which set up a special organization, *Żegota*, the only one in any of the German-occupied countries, for the specific purpose of rendering assistance to the persecuted Jews. And what is more significant, that underground kept the Polish government-in-exile in London informed of the extermination of the Jews, which was naturally transmitted to the Western allies. Moreover, an underground emissary, Jan Karski (after the war he became a US citizen and a professor at Georgetown University in Washington),[10] who had twice been smuggled into the Warsaw Ghetto and also bribed his way into the Bełżec extermination camp disguised as a Latvian guard in order to see everything with his own eyes, was sent to England and America. He briefed their leaders, including Foreign Secretary Anthony Eden and US President Franklin Delano Roosevelt, on the fate of the Jews in Poland and conveyed to them the urgent pleas of the Jewish underground leaders. But the politicians were not interested and all his efforts produced no practical results. No action was taken, not even the bombardment and destruction of rail lines leading to extermination camps, while factories in the proximity of the death camp were bombed:

> ...the I.G. Farbenindustrie, situated next to Auschwitz concentration camp, was destroyed by Allied bombers in August 1944. The purpose of the bombing was to destroy a German armaments factory. This was successfully achieved. Given that the Allies were fully aware of what was going on within Auschwitz at the time, why did they not divert some of these bombs to destroy the gas chambers, crematoria and railway lines leading to them, despite appeals from Jewish organisations in the free world to do so? I am not suggesting that the 1.6 million deaths at Auschwitz would have been averted, but this action would have certainly slowed down the killing process.[11]

In utter despair at the futility of all the combined efforts and in protest against the indifference of the Allies, the Jewish member of the Polish National Council in London, Szmul Zygelbojm, committed suicide.

It is often argued that the main reason for the upsurge of anti-Semitism in post-war Poland was the participation of many Jews in the Soviet-imposed Polish regime. From its very inception Polish Jews played a significant role in the communist movement. Trying to escape from their closed community and the external enmity towards it, they discarded their Jewishness and embraced the communist ideology in the misguided belief that communism would deliver on its promise of universal brotherhood and other utopian ideas.

In the immediate post-war conditions, Polish Jews, grateful to the Soviet Union for saving their lives from the Nazi Holocaust, socially isolated, culturally uprooted and sensing the enmity of their environment, became suitable and ready material for active participation in the new regime. Apart from the old communists who occupied leading positions in the party apparatus, in the security services, in the media and a few in the foreign service, other Jews were also picked for office because of their perceived loyalty, not because of their national origin.

In my own ministry the total number of Jews throughout the period from 1945 to 1968 when it became virtually *judenrein* amounted, by the reliable reckoning of my friends who also worked there, to between 134 and 140 out of a total staff of between about 800 and over 1,000.[12] They included in the initial post-war period two consecutive Jewish deputy ministers, Józef Olszewski and then the hard-line Stefan Wierbłowski. (There were none at that level later.) There were 12 Jews who were ambassadors and 13 who were other heads of mission such as chargés d'affaires. There were thirteen departmental directors and 12 deputy directors, though they were frequently the same people who held the senior posts abroad (like, for instance, myself). Over the years the rotation of personnel was considerable; generally speaking, the overall number of staff increased while the number of Jews, and hence even more their proportion, considerably decreased.

Some emigrated to Israel, especially in 1956–57, up to ten defected. (Incidentally, as I later found out, defections of non-Jews were, as a rule, hushed up while those of Jews were broadcast.) By the mid-1960s there were about 30 Jewish staff left in the ministry and only a handful in foreign postings. A document of the Ministry of Internal Affairs of October 1969 on emigration to Israel, which was made public in 1992 and 1993, gives a breakdown of people who had applied for emigration in the period from 1 January 1968 to 31 August 1969 and of people who had been refused permission to leave in the period from January 1968 to October 1969.[13] The list of people from the Ministry of Foreign Affairs – all of them summarily dismissed in the 1968 purge – contains 28 names, including one of ambassadorial rank, five departmental directors or deputy directors (including myself) and five heads of section.

As a matter of fact, Jews had been over-represented but not inordinately so and one could hardly use in this instance the joke once applied to the Soviet Foreign Ministry that the difference between it and Palestine was that there were no Arabs in the ministry. Most Jews were of course in later years removed from the Soviet foreign service. So, when on his official visit to the United States Khrushchev showed his 'democratic credentials' by telling his hosts how many Jews there were in his foreign service and then asked about the respective number in the State Department, he was told: 'We do not count them'.

But in Poland, even five years after the collapse of communism, they apparently still counted how many Jews there were in their Foreign Ministry. A parliamentary sub-committee for the assessment of personnel in that ministry, which consisted mainly of left-wingers, criticized the ministry's staff, *inter alia*, for their aristocratic, 'Solidarity' and Jewish origin. The sub-committee's report was adopted by the lower chamber (*Sejm*) as an official document.

(In this context it is worth pointing out that at the time of writing, 1994, the United Kingdom has a Defence Secretary, Malcolm Rifkind,[14] and a Home Secretary, Michael Howard, who are Jewish. The predominantly Catholic country of Peru has a prime minister, Efrain Goldenberg, who is Jewish and a Japanese, Alberto Fujimori, for president into the bargain. The allegedly anti-Semitic Ukrainians have an acting prime minister, Yukhim Zvyagilsky, who is Jewish. According to the *Jewish Chronicle* of 26 August 1994: '...the only nationalist Russian state outside the Russian Federation, the Dnestr Republic, was created and is ruled by a Jewish colonel called Mikhail Bergman.' Even in an Arab country, Morocco, there is a tourism minister, Serge Berdugo, who is also president of the Moroccan Jewish community; King Hassan's economic adviser, André Azoulay, is also Jewish. And these countries are not falling apart because of it.)

However, the principal object of the wrath prevalent in Poland was the security service, held responsible for the regime's atrocities and in popular perception virtually identified with the Jews. On the issue of the number of Jews in that service the historian Krystyna Kersten, quoting from a November 1945 communist leadership document, writes the following:

> Out of a total of 25,600...there were 438 Jews, that is about 1.7 per cent. Out of 500 leading posts 67 were held by Jews, over 13 per cent. One can say that...the Jews were over-represented; it is, however, necessary to part with the myth that the UB [*Urząd Bezpieczeństwa* – Security Office] *are* the Jews.[15]

Certainly some of them did take part in atrocities against political opponents of the communist regime, including many wartime anti-German underground fighters. Among their victims were also communists, including Jewish communists.[16] But they were not acting alone. Moreover, as Lieutenant Colonel Winiawski stated at the 1954 security personnel meeting referred to above: 'Everybody knows...that the real managers of the policies of repression and operational intelligence are the Soviet advisers, for without their approval no superior will sanction any case.'[17] Years later the former intelligence officer Winiawski would elaborate:

> There existed a general belief, promoted by the media, by all kinds of party propaganda...and special disinformation cells that the Jews and the UB were responsible for all the

misfortunes that had befallen Poland. This was convenient not only for the former Politburo and central state authorities, but for various circles of party intellectuals, writers, journalists, literary critics, historians, etc. The policy of repression was managed within the 'bloc' by a KGB command centre in Moscow, leaving the particular countries a certain freedom of manoeuvre, depending on local conditions and situation. The Politburo, the government and the *Sejm* endowed these instructions with a theoretical and legal force – ordering the UB to implement decisions. The UB did not act on its own it was totally subordinate to the highest party authorities.[18]

This may look like an attempt to whitewash the security services but there are other sources which confirm the gist of what Winiawski has written. For instance, the already quoted former military counter-intelligence officer wrote:

The fact of the matter is that neither the military nor the civilian security service ever acted on its own but always obeyed orders and directives received from Moscow and usually took good care to have all their actions countersigned by Bierut, Berman, or Mazur.[19]

However, this does not exonerate the security people from responsibility for what they were doing.

Moreover, the man responsible for the security services in the Polish Politburo in the Stalinist period was Jakub Berman, a Jew. A former high-ranking communist functionary, Andrzej Werblan, has given a revealing account of the Politburo four-day discussion in 1956, after the atrocities of the security services had come to light, on whether to accept Berman's resignation. His resignation was finally accepted, by one member reluctantly and another being, initially, against it. These two argued that there was 'collective responsibility' of the entire Politburo for what had happened. Some Politburo members, including Marshal Rokossowski, maintained that Berman alone – or 'at most' together with Bierut, the Stalinist leader of Poland who had just died, and Minc, another Jew who also resigned in 1956, the so-called 'big three' – was responsible for what the security service had done. One of them, Aleksander Zawadzki (who later became president of Poland), while admitting that when thinking of Berman's case he asked himself 'whether it is hatred or anti-Semitism that puts the words into my mouth', accused Berman of staffing top posts with 'Jewish comrades'. 'Is a Jew really more trustworthy than a Pole? Why do we speak of Polish nationalism and not of Jewish nationalism which is more dangerous?', he asked.

The majority of members, while not denying Berman's responsibility for 'certain decisions', were against burdening him with exclusive responsibility. They pointed out that

> Poland's limited sovereignty and the great influence the USSR, Stalin and Beria had on the operations of the security service, took into account the part played by Soviet advisers in the MBP [Ministry of Public Security] and in military information [counter-intelligence].

Edward Ochab, the then party leader and future state president, said:

> ...I know there was much good in his [Berman's] work, he restrained many adventurist tendencies, he often cautioned not to be influenced by investigation protocols...We all know that in relation to Jakub [Berman] there was a course to destroy him...However, his responsibility for security matters is greater than that of other members of the Politburo.

Replying to arguments put forward by Rokossowski, who had tried to shift the blame from the Soviet Union and his own Polish military intelligence, Ochab 'reminded the Marshal of his own responsibility [for that intelligence] where 19 innocent people had been shot'. Prime Minister Cyrankiewicz said:

> Berman himself was one of the candidates for liquidation... Poland was in danger of an anti-Semitic trial like that of Slánský's. As for the security personnel, many of them had

been 'planted' by the NKVD...The period we have gone through was too complex for us to blame one man for it.[20]

According to a former *Informacja* officer, the military counter-intelligence, the *Informacja* 'responsible for...the murder of dozens of innocent Polish officers', unlike the civilian intelligence, 'acted independently of the Politburo' and hence of Berman, and 'was staffed virtually exclusively by Soviet officers'.[21] According to the same source:

Contrary to popular belief, there was only a token number of native Polish and Jewish officers in the *Informacja*: from 1949 to 1954 (at the time of the most intensive terror), out of almost 120 senior posts in the entire *Informacja* network there were at most 15 to 20 Poles, among them 5 to 7 were Jews. The only exception was the Fourth (Investigation) Department...a virtual 'state within a state'...The absolute ruler of the Investigation Department was Colonel Anatoly Skulbaszewski, who, together with Voznesensky, played a major role in the reign of terror in Poland.[22]

And further, the same author writes:

To my own surprise, I discovered what a small share the Jews had had in the entire network of the *Informacja* apparatus, and particularly in the investigation department. There had been only four men of Jewish origin among the several score of investigation officers...and of those four only one was in a senior position.[23]

Elsewhere the author wrote: 'On the other hand, the number of officers of Jewish origin who fell victim to this arm [the investigation department] exceeded 40 per cent of the total number of victims.'[24]

There can be no doubt that whatever the degree of shared responsibility, Berman and the other Jews in the security services were responsible for what they had been doing as communists, as human beings, but not as Jews. Some security officials were then dismissed and imprisoned, but, significantly:

...nobody was put on public trial (even Różański [a Jew], who was sentenced to five years imprisonment for using sadistic methods to extract evidence from political prisoners, had been tried *in camera*). The reason was that no such trial could have sustained the spurious claim that the only people to blame for all those crimes were a handful of Jewish officials in the Ministry of Public Security. The role played by both the party leadership in Poland and by their Soviet supervisors could not have been passed over in silence, and the official version of the past 'errors and distortions' of the security apparatus would have been that much less credible.[25]

The 'authorized version' approved by the Ninth Plenary Session of the Central Committee in May 1957 assigning responsibility for the misdeeds of the security service mentioned only Jewish officials 'with the single exception of the former minister of public security, Radkiewicz, whose role could not conceivably have been overlooked (and who had a Jewish wife anyway)'. There was no mention of either non-Jewish Polish leaders, 'whose responsibility was at least equal to Berman's', or of the powerful Soviet KGB officials in Poland or, finally, of any of the non-Jewish security officials. 'The Jews alone were to blame.'[26]

Anyway, whatever their responsibility was, Jews should not be blamed collectively. Nobody has blamed the Polish people for the fact that Feliks Dzierżyński, a Pole, founded the Cheka, later renamed NKVD and subsequently KGB. Nobody has blamed the Georgian people for the atrocities and crimes of Stalinism though both Stalin and his NKVD chief for 15 years, Lavrentii Beria, were Georgians.

In Poland, however, to quote the historian Krystyna Kersten again:

In wide circles of society there was a deep-rooted belief in an osmosis between the Jews and the authorities. In this view not only Minc and Berman but also Bierut and Radkiewicz [Minister of Public Security] were Jews. Already then it was not so much that the Jew was the enemy as the enemy was the Jew, that is how it was encoded in the collective consciousness, thereby generating that paradoxical anti-Semitism without Jews, that so astounds foreigners...Jews were [seen] everywhere...and were a danger to Polishness. This view was shaped spontaneously, it grew on...phobias, prejudices...it was enhanced by Poland's situation...by helplessness...Not being able to attack the real perpetrators of the Polish defeat they turned on a vicarious enemy – the Jews. They were ideally suited for this role...They were weak, defenceless and at the same time could be identified with the forces which were the real source of the frustration, and on which a frontal attack would be dangerous...The myth of the omnipresence of Jews in the apparatus of power...emanated from the collective psyche and...mental habits...which led to a deformed perception of reality...There was no need for Jews to appear in the authorities for the wave of anti-Jewish sentiments to swell alarmingly.[27]

As the regime stabilized and under the impact of Soviet anti-Jewish policies Jews were replaced by nationally 'pure' Poles, just as ideologically the regime became more nationalistic. And yet in some other communist countries of Eastern Europe where the part played by Jews was even greater than in Poland there were no officially organized anti-Semitic campaigns. In Hungary the top Stalinist leaders Mátyás Rákosi and later Ernö Gerö and the chief of police Peter were Jews. Out of 25 members of the party's Central Committee in 1945, nine were Jews.[28] In Poland the ruling Politburo of over a dozen men included three Jews. Romania even preserved its relations with Israel after 1967 when all the other satellites followed Moscow's line. Why then was Poland different? Arguably because the nationalist past was superimposed on the communist present. The already quoted Michael Checinski ascribes it to 'a coincidence of factors peculiar to the political situation in the country', including 'steady and growing pressure from various Soviet sources to introduce anti-Jewish restrictions into Poland's public life'.[29]

Following the 1968 events to which I referred earlier, most of the remaining Jews left Poland. That produced a lull of sorts in Polish–Jewish relations, apart from the occasional angry rebuttals of Western denunciations of the anti-Jewish campaign. Still, in its drive against political influence from the West and particularly in an attempt to discredit in the eyes of the Poles the tremendously popular Radio Free Europe broadcasts in Poland, the communist propaganda made use of the Jews so recently squeezed out of the country, blaming them for 'the anti-Polish campaign waged by anti-Communist and Zionist centres'. In a note written on the subject in 1971, I described it as a 'kind of external anti-Semitism for internal purposes'.[30]

However, in a 1972 note on current developments in Poland,[31] I pointed out that the Sixth Congress of the Polish party held in December 1971 proceeded, unlike the previous one in 1968, without the words 'Jews' and 'Zionists' even being mentioned:

> Even as regards Israel, all Gierek [the then leader] said was: 'Poland supports the nations of the Arab countries in their aim to restore peace in the Middle East on the basis of the UN Security Council resolution of November, 1967.'... to continue to exploit the antisemitic scapegoat in whatever form or guise would have been futile and risky in addition to being externally compromising... [But] why was there no reference at all to that embarrassing past [the anti-Jewish and anti-Zionist campaign]?... That such a reference was called for was recognized by Edward Ochab, Poland's former President, the man who for the first time in the history of communism, voluntarily handed over Party leadership to another man (Gomułka in 1956), [and who was] one of the rare species of honest and believing Communists in power. In a letter to his Party branch in Warsaw (naturally unpublished in Poland, but printed in the Polish émigré Paris monthly *Kultura*)... he condemns Gomułka's autocratic... and despotic system... based, like Stalin's on a deformed security service... dissemination of legends and myths... and nationalistic tales... resorting to the poisoned weapon of antisemitism (e.g., the case of the Zionist doctors' 'plot', the Zionist 'centre' of Slánský, or the threat to socialism in Poland from the 'Zionist fifth column').
>
> Ochab then calls for 'remedial measures...' [suggesting,

inter alia, that]...a proposal should be made to the Sixth Congress to include in the central Party authorities all Communists groundlessly removed from these authorities during the Fifth Congress under the pressure of the autocratic regime of that time. All former members... should be fully made use of in all spheres of Party and trade union activity, in local authorities, and various social commissions, editorial offices and publishing houses.

Ochab also calls for the 'removal from the Party apparatus and government bodies of incorrigible bureaucrats, careerists... antisemites, nationalists, people of no principles or moral scruples... of those... who... distinguished themselves by a particular... zeal in the struggle against the 'Jewish-Communist conspiracy' (of course under the cover of the struggle with Zionism)...'

In Gierek's political calculations there was no need for reference to the past. The mass of the workers may not stand for further antisemitic nonsense as an explanation of their plight, but they are simply not interested in any form of condemnation of antisemitism as such. Indeed, the majority are not against Poland having rid herself of the Jews... any such, even indirect, condemnation would have amounted to an admission that antisemitism... was employed in a Communist state, that all the Western, Jewish 'anti-Polish' propaganda was at least partly justified. Moreover, it would have been fiercely fought by the Party apparatus and would have certainly been nipped in the bud by Moscow. Not that Gierek is likely to have contemplated it, but even if he had, it would not have been feasible.

And thus from the Polish leadership's point of view it is advisable to act as if there had been no anti-Jewish campaign, as if there had been no Jewish problem... However, unofficial information which has trickled through from Poland in recent months indicates that with the entrenched antisemitic cadres, with the anti-Jewish poison injected in the recent past and... with the example from the USSR, antisemitism in Poland is alive, though it is obviously less intense and demonstrative than of late... Jewish emigration has in a way cleared the air inside Poland... Below the leadership level, however, anti-Jewish sentiments are being kept alive and fostered. And this undercurrent tolerated by the leadership is likely to prevail in the foreseeable future. Anti-Israeli policy will obviously continue to conform to Moscow's current needs.[32]

When on a state visit to France in October 1972, Gierek was asked in a press interview about the 'Jewish question in Poland', he replied that 'there never was any racial discrimination in Poland...We have no problems of this kind.' Regarding the 1967–68 campaign, he said:

Decisions taken by our government in the wake of the Israeli aggression against Arab countries were criticized by many people of Jewish origin. This attitude was not approved by the population...One can therefore say that in 1967–68 we had to face differences of opinion concerning the Israeli aggression...these animosities have since calmed down. Some of those who were politically active in the most aggressive manner have left Poland of their own free will...Today we see nothing that could cause problems. The issue you have raised does not, therefore, exist any more.[33]

In fact, anti-Semitic propaganda never ceased to appear in the mass media, in trashy novels, thrillers or non-fiction reports.

After the imposition of martial law in December 1981 the communist authorities made some friendly, cosmetic gestures towards Jewry with a view to breaking out of their international isolation, obtaining credits and better media coverage. Nonetheless, they used anti-Semitism as a weapon against the opposition in order to discredit it by pointing to its allegedly Jewish connections and alleged services to world Jewry, to German revanchism and American imperialism.

Even within the democratic Solidarity movement there was an anti-Semitic wing revealed by the embarrassing outburst of one of its leaders, Marian Jurczyk. In 1981 he alleged that most people in top posts were Jews and that they betrayed Poland. In post-communist Poland, his splinter faction – Solidarity-80 – has not renounced its anti-Semitic stance, though it has been less pronounced, while within the mainstream Solidarity anti-Jewish tendencies increased.

But there has also been, since the late 1970s, a positive revival of interest in the Polish-Jewish past, largely as a result of the desire to come to terms with chauvinism and anti-Semitism. This preoccupation, strong among a section of the Polish intelligentsia, was best articulated by the literary critic Jan Błoński in a widely discussed article in 1987:

> We did take the Jews into our home, but we made them live in the cellar. When they wanted to come into the drawing-room our response was: Yes, but only after you cease to be Jews, when you become 'civilized'...There were those among the Jews who were ready to adhere to this advice. No sooner did they do this than we, in turn, began talking of an invasion of Jews, of the danger of their infiltration of Polish society. Then we started to put down conditions...that we shall accept as Poles only those Jews willing to cooperate in attempts to stem Jewish influence in our society...Eventually, when we lost our home, and when in its premises the invaders set to murdering Jews, did we show solidarity towards them? How many of us decided it was none of our business? There were also those (and I leave out of account common criminals) who were secretly pleased that Hitler had solved for us 'the Jewish problem'. We would not even welcome and honour the survivors, even if they were embittered, disorientated and perhaps somewhat tiresome. I repeat: instead of haggling and justifying ourselves, we should just consider our own faults and weaknesses. This is the moral revolution that is imperative when considering the Polish-Jewish past. It is only this that can gradually cleanse our desecrated soil.[34]

After the demise of the communist regime, freedom of expression also meant freedom to voice openly old prejudices and hatreds, and to use them politically in the new democratic conditions. There were some anti-Jewish incidents and vicious anti-Jewish propaganda.

The Auschwitz convent controversy provoked another

upsurge of anti-Semitism, which intensified after Cardinal Glemp's sermon, referred to above.

Anti-Semitic propaganda was used by extreme nationalistic parties in political warfare to discredit liberal opponents, and anti-Jewish innuendo was employed by some of the mainstream parties – the Centre Alliance or the Christian-National Union. Anti-Semitic publications, such as *The Protocols of the Elders of Zion*, were openly sold on bookstands and in bookshops, including in such prestigious places as a Warsaw church.

Even the non-anti-Semitic Lech Wałęsa was not averse to using indirect anti-Semitic stereotypes instrumentally in his presidential campaign of 1991, though he later repudiated his behaviour (and, probably with a view to the forthcoming 1995 presidential election, was slow and half-hearted in denouncing the outrageously anti-Jewish sermon and statements of his confessor, Father Jankowski. But, as it turned out, the 1995 election campaign was reportedly almost free of anti-Semitic rhetoric). However, the first free parliamentary election of 1991 and that of 1993, in which all extreme nationalistic parties were routed, showed that militant anti-Semitism had no future in Poland.

It has been pointed out that what has been manifesting itself in post-communist Poland is not mass anti-Semitism but mass tolerance of anti-Semitism. For many Poles anti-Jewish stereotypes are presumably not central considerations, but they are tolerated, in one's own thinking as well as in that of others. Yet after one of its polls on the attitude towards Jews in 1991 the respected Centre of Public Opinion Research, CBOS, commented:

> In a country almost devoid of Jews, where no lobby or Jewish organisation with the smallest political ambitions exists, large numbers of people feel they are being ruled by the Jews. This is evidence of strongly rooted negative stereotypes, which even the most obvious facts are unable to change.

There have been some other developments which give grounds for cautious optimism and not least a change in the attitude of the Catholic Church, largely under the influence of Pope John II, of which the pastoral letter of the Polish bishops, issued on the twentieth-fifth anniversary of the Papal *Nostra Aetate* declaration and read in all of Poland's churches in January 1991, was the most significant manifestation. The letter had been drafted during the Conference of the Episcopate held in October 1990 but, significantly, its reading in churches was delayed until after the presidential elections, presumably because the Church, which supported Wałęsa's candidature, did not wish to assist the candidature of Mazowiecki, a devout Catholic, against whom anti-Semitic innuendoes were directed.

The pastoral letter was generally hailed as the first unequivocal condemnation by the hierarchy of anti-Semitism, although it may take a long time for that change of attitude to percolate throughout the clergy and the people.

It may be apposite here to quote from the letter:

> ... With the Jewish nation we Poles are linked with special ties and, since as early as the first centuries of our history, Poland has become another homeland for many Jews. The majority of Jews living all over the world at present derive from the territories of the former and present Republic of Poland. Unfortunately, it is exactly this land that became the grave of several millions of Jews in our century, not by our will and not at our hand ... Many Poles saved Jewish lives during the last war. Hundreds, if not thousands paid with their own lives and the lives of their families for that assistance ... there were also people who remained indifferent to that inconceivable tragedy. We particularly suffer because of those Catholics who were in any way instrumental in causing the death of Jews. They will for ever remain a pang of conscience for us ... If there was only one Christian who could have helped a Jew in danger but did not give him a helping hand or had a share in his death, we must ask our Jewish sisters and brothers for forgiveness.
>
> We are aware that many of our compatriots still nurse in their memory harm and injustice inflicted by the post-war Communist rule, in which people of Jewish origin participated as well. But we must admit that the source of

inspiration for their actions hardly lay in their Jewish origin, or religion, or Communist ideology from which Jews suffered much injustice too.

We also express our sincere regret at all cases of anti-Semitism that have taken place on Polish soil. We are doing this deeply convinced that all signs of anti-Semitism are contrary to the spirit of the Gospel and, as John Paul II has recently underlined, 'will remain totally contrary to the Christian vision of human dignity'.

While expressing our regret at all injustice and harm inflicted on Jews, we must mention that we feel it unjust and deeply unfair that many use the notion of the so-called Polish anti-Semitism as a particularly dangerous form of anti-Semitism in general, or that sometimes concentration camps are attributed to Poles in Poland occupied by Germans instead of to their actual originators... also Poles as a nation became one of the first victims of the same criminal, racist ideology of Nazism...

... The crucial way to overcome the still-existing difficulties is... dialogue which will lead to the elimination of distrust, prejudice and stereotypes, which will allow us to get to know and understand each other better on the basis of respect for separate religious traditions and open up the road to cooperation in many fields.[35]

A Polish-Jewish writer living in Israel, Natan Gross, wrote in 1993:

In the Poland in which a part of the Jewish community sees only (a growing new wave of) anti-Semitism, there is spreading (a continuous uninterrupted wave of) the cult of memory of the people that over centuries lived on Polish lands, maintained its national culture, but also became an inseparable part of Polish culture. This cult manifests itself, *inter alia*, in a very abundant historical literature, memoirs, in an extensive polemical journalism, in works of fiction and poetry. He who does not see that (and some other activity as well) – simply does not want to see.[36]

Opinion polls conducted in Poland since the overthrow of

communist rule confirm that while anti-Semitism remains a fairly widespread phenomenon, opposition to it is equally widespread. This prompted a remark by a Jewish journalist that Poland is in the forefront of both anti-Semitism and the struggle against it.[37] There is little doubt that the enlightened, liberal-minded elements in Polish society face an uphill struggle.

At the end of 1996 an editorial in the Polish-Jewish biweekly *Dos Jidisze Wort* said:

...Extreme nationalism combined with an outright zoological anti-semitism ceases to be the domain of the political fringe, it enters the mainstream of Polish politics.

There have appeared large, politically significant parties, which have become havens for notorious anti-semites, there exists a sizeable number of large-circulation, national papers, which see it as being in their interest to curry favour with their readers through anti-semitic propaganda, there are publications specialising in publishing books which brand the Jews with infamy for all the world's sins.

In Poland where after the Holocaust a small remnant of Jews remained this violent and primitive eruption of brutal anti-semitism seems to be gigantically stupid. Who needs it and why?...The tiny Jewish community presents neither a political nor an economic force.

...Nothing, however, happens without a reason. Under the anti-semitic call the parties' electorate is rallied, a battle-front is set up against political opponents, who are being discredited by reminding or imputing to them their alleged Jewish origin. An atmosphere of Jewish threat is being created.

...Let us hope that in the next elections these balloons will burst like a soap-bubble. Not for the sake of the Jews. For the sake of Poland. For it is primarily Poland that they harm.[38]

It should, however, be pointed out that Polish anti-Semitism was never mediaeval, there were no mass expulsions, there was no Inquisition, there were no Nazi 'solutions'. It has been a product of historical, political, economic, demographic and religious circumstances. There has been nothing inherently Polish about it and Poles should not be found collectively guilty of it.

When reflecting on the olden times when Polish kings not only allowed Jews to settle in their lands but also gave them rights, admittedly not for altruistic reasons (they needed them), when Poland was generally tolerant of Jews, when later many Jews were able to prosper and Jewish culture flourished, when they were contributing to the well-being and cultural life of the host country, I recall what a rabbi wrote about the Ancient Egyptians. Despite their inhumanity to Jews, he said:

> ... the Torah enjoins the Hebrews not to forget the debt of gratitude they owe the Egyptians for the pre-slavery years, when they had extended a hand of friendship and hospitality to a landless people: 'Thou shalt not abhor the Egyptians, for thou wast a stranger in their land'. (Deuteronomy 23:8)[39]

Notes

1 Quotations translated by the author from the original text of the sermon. Cf. BBC, *Summary of World Broadcasts*, EE/0548, 30 August 1989.

2 Quoted by Konstanty Gebert in an article 'Trochę mniej w domu' ('Somewhat less at home') in *Polityka*, 9 September 1989.

3 Figures quoted by *Yad Vashem* director, Yitzhak Arad, at a press conference in Warsaw in June 1990. These figures have since grown. According to later information there are about 4,500 Righteous Poles, nearly 50 per cent of the total.

4 Else Rosenfeld, *Verfemt und verfolgt* (1945), republished as *Ich stand nicht allein: Leben einer Jüdin in Deutschland 1933–1944* (Germany, 1988).

5 Professor Hillel Levine in his *Economic Origins of Anti-Semitism: Poland and its Jews in the Early Modern Period* (New York: Yale University Press, 1993).

6 Zeev Ben-Shlomo, *Jewish Chronicle*, 23 April 1993.

7 Krystyna Kersten, *Narodziny systemu władzy 1943–1948* (*The Birth of the System of Power 1943–1948*) (Paris: Libella, 1986), p. 172.

8 Jerzy Andrzejewski, 'Zagadnienia polskiego antysemityzmu' ('Questions of Polish anti-Semitism'), *Martwa fala* (Warsaw: Wiedza, 1947).

9 Jerzy Andrzejewski, op. cit.

10 Karski received the *Yad Vashem* award of 'Righteous among the Nations'

and on 12 May 1994 was made an honorary citizen of the State of Israel.

11 Quoted from a letter by Brett Radley in *The Times* of 10 February 1995.

12 In 1994 the total staff amounted to some 3,250, including over 1,000 in the ministry itself and the rest in foreign postings, *Polityka* (Warsaw), 16 April 1994.

13 Jerzy Poksiński, 'Pomarcowa emigracja' ('Post-March emigration'), *Literatura*, No. 5, 1992 and 'Banicja marcowa' ('The March banishment'), *Literatura*, Nos. 6, 10, 11, 12, 1992 and No. 1, 1993.

14 In July 1995 Malcolm Rifkind became Foreign Secretary, the second Jew to hold the post. The first was the Marquess of Reading, Rufus Daniel Isaacs, in Ramsay Macdonald's national government of 1931.

15 Krystyna Kersten, 'Władza–komunizm–Żydzi' ('Power–Communism–Jews'), *Polityka*, No. 27, 6 July 1991.

16 Michael Checinski, pp. 71–2 and 84–5, notes 23, 24, 25.

17 'Protokół z konferencji aktywu MBP' ('Minutes of the conference of senior personnel of the Ministry of Public Security'), *Kultura* (Paris), No. 11/542, November 1992, p. 9.

18 'Głos uczestnika konferencji aktywu MBP' ('Voice of a participant in the conference of senior personnel of the Ministry of Public Security'), *Kultura* (Paris), No. 5/548, May 1993, p. 33.

19 Michael Checinski, p. 96.

20 All preceding quotations relating to the 1956 Politburo discussion are taken from Andrzej Werblan, 'Po śmierci Bieruta' ('After Bierut's death'), *Polityka*, 15 June 1991.

21 Michael Checinski, pp. 57–8.

22 Ibid., p. 53.

23 Ibid., p. 101.

24 Michael Checinski, 'An Intended Polish Explanation, December 1956', *Soviet Jewish Affairs* (London), No. 3, May 1972, p. 84.

25 Michael Checinski, *Poland: Communism, Nationalism, Anti-Semitism*, p. 99.

26 Ibid., pp. 100–1.

27 Krystyna Kersten, 'Władza – kommunizm – Żydzi'.

28 According to Checinski, *Poland: Communism, Nationalism, Anti-Semitism*, '...the Hungarians refused to exploit the Middle East war and anti-Zionism as a pretext for Jew-baiting in their internal and personnel policies – even though in both these countries [referring also to Romania] there was a much larger Jewish minority and incomparably more Jews in leading party and state posts than in Poland' (p. 210).

29 Checinski, pp. 209–10.

30 'A Footnote on Poland 1971', *Soviet Jewish Affairs* (London), No. 1, June 1971, p. 43.

31 'Current Developments in Poland', *Soviet Jewish Affairs* (London), No. 3, May 1972, pp. 76–80. (The note was reprinted in part in the *Jerusalem Post*, 4 October 1972.)

32 Ibid.

33 *Le Monde*, 3 October 1972.

34 Jan Błoński, 'Biedni Polacy patrzą na ghetto' ('The poor Poles look at

the Ghetto'), *Tygodnik Powszechny*, No. 2 (1959), 11 January 1987. Quote taken from Antony Polonsky's article, 'Loving and hating the dead', *Financial Times*, 2 May 1991.

35 Quoted from translation of the Letter supplied by the Press Office of the Polish embassy in London.

36 Natan Gross, *Poeci i Szoa. Obraz zagłady Żydów w poezji polskiej* (*Poets and Shoah. The Picture of the Extermination of Jews in Polish Poetry*) (Sosnowiec: Offmax, 1993), p. 45.

37 Charles Hoffman, 'Polish anti-Semitism', *Jerusalem Report*, No. 7, March 1991.

38 *Dos Jidisze Wort* (Warsaw), No. 22 (126), 1 November 1996.

39 Rabbi Dr Jeffrey Cohen, *Jewish Chronicle*, 28 January 1994.

11 • *Personal Reflections*

I am by nature a moderate, suspicious of any ideological dogmas. I have known some dogmatic communists in Poland who, having emigrated to the West, have become equally dogmatic anti-communists. I am in favour of all the fundamental freedoms of a modern democracy, but am sceptical, not to say cynical, about politics and politicians. Since leaving Poland I have not wanted to join any political organization; I even avoided becoming a member of the National Union of Journalists. But then exuberant ambition, the pursuit of power and hypocrisy are by no means restricted to politicians. The greed of some money-makers, of 'the charlatans of the stock exchange' or, as former Prime Minister Edward Heath put it 'the unpleasant and unacceptable face of capitalism', I find even more reprehensible. But, at least in a democracy they can be publicly exposed. And, anyway, isn't it all part of human nature? Are we not just high-grade animals – high-grade in intelligence if not in morals?

The religious can blame God for the injustices and horrors of life. Leo Rosten tells the story about a legendary Jew who put God on trial:

He appointed nine friends as judges, himself being the tenth...and summoned the Almighty to the witness stand...For six days and nights this remarkable jury tried the Lord: they presented charges, defenses, prayed, fasted, consulted Torah and Talmud. Finally, in solemn consensus, they issued their vedict: God was guilty!...He had Himself created the spirit of Evil, which He let loose among innocent and temptable people.[1]

I believe in the need for more tolerance all round, though tolerance may not be enough. I have read a very critical description of tolerance by a black academic who sees it as 'a spiritually defunct state' and he quotes Rabbi Boteach from Oxford who said that

> ... tolerance is really a repugnant state of mind. Rather than find any redeeming virtue or positive element in another person, we tolerate or bear him. We stomach, or suffer his right to be different. There is something immoral about this.[2]

I have experienced that kind of tolerance myself. And yet in the real world we live in, more of even that sort of tolerance would be very beneficial.

I fully subscribe to the view so aptly expressed by Arthur Koestler that

> The continuous disasters in man's history are mainly due to his excessive capacity and urge to become identified with a tribe, nation, church or cause and to espouse its credo uncritically and enthusiastically, even if its tenets are contrary to reason, devoid of self-interest and detrimental to the claims of self-preservation.[3]

Alas, man seems never to have derived any lessons from history. As Chesterton put it, opening his first novel *The Napoleon of Notting Hill*: 'The human race, to which so many of my readers belong, has been playing at children's games from the beginning, and will probably do it till the end, which is a nuisance for the few people who grow up.'

However, group identification like modern nationalism is but a form of collective selfishness. And just as genuine communists and other utopians have dismally failed to change human nature, they and others are hardly likely to do away with group identification. It can only be curbed to the extent of being tolerant and understanding of other groups' identification. So the operative words in Koestler's quote are 'excessive' and 'uncritically'.

In this context, I consider Zionism and its outcome Israel to be a manifestation of not just group identification, a form of nationalism and a means for normalization – Theodor Herzl dreamed in his '*Altneuland*' of a Jewish state with everything from Jewish policemen to Jewish thieves – but, in the light of the Jews' history, it is also the surest – perhaps the only – way of their self-preservation. For as the veteran Israeli politician Dr Yosef Burg said: 'There are two important things to remember about the Holocaust: that it happened and that it was possible, which means it could happen again.'[4] And assimilation is no solution, as the fate of German Jews clearly demonstrated: nobody was more deeply assimilated than the German-Jews. But my sympathies are with the Zionism of Abba Eban and Shimon Peres rather than that of Yitzhak Shamir or Ariel Sharon.

When my wife and I visited Israel for the first time in 1974 my brother took us round the country. The visit was a deeply emotional experience for me: both on account of meeting, after so many years, those few of my family (and school friends) who had escaped the Holocaust and of setting foot for the first time on the soil of the Jewish state.

I was totally loyal to my native country, Poland, whatever its political system was. I am totally loyal and enormously grateful to my new host country, Britain. But that does not interfere with my natural affinity with Israel. Neither does that affinity affect my other loyalties including that to my former long-time and very good employer, the BBC.

I am too sceptical to be religious, though I hesitate whether this complex universe of ours could exist without some superior force. Does that make me an agnostic? When someone asked Bertrand Russell, who was an atheist: 'Mr Russell, supposing after you die, you find there is another world and you meet God – what will you say to him?' Russell replied: 'I would say – why on earth didn't you give better evidence of your existence?' I would call myself a secular Jew but I feel a deep affection for Jewish traditions though, by dint of circumstance, I don't practise them. I respect and in a way envy observant, Orthodox Jews; they seem to draw so much strength, confidence and joy from their belief. And I envy their need for the continuous study of the Talmud, that Judaic encyclopaedia of 'divine knowledge', which not only sharpens their wits but – in the words of the Jewish historian Cecil Roth – 'brought him [the Jew] another world, vivid, calm, and peaceful, after the continuous humiliation of ordinary existence'.

However, I despair of fanaticism and of the misuse of religion for personal gain, privilege or political ends. Alas, in this respect, I believe the experience in Israel to have been rather deplorable. Rabbi René Samuel Sirat, the president of the Conference of European Rabbis and former Chief Rabbi of France, speaking to an inter-faith conference in Jerusalem, boycotted by leading Israeli rabbis, criticized religious leaders, including the leaders of Israel's religious parties who seemed to prefer political power to religious values. He said: 'What is achieved in political gains is lost in spiritual values.'[5] And the former British Chief Rabbi, Lord Jakobovits, maintained that the Israeli rabbinate should be disestablished so that the forces of 'sane Judaism' can combine 'to curb the wave of neo-Khomeinistic fanaticism which threatens to engulf the Jewish world'.[6]

Lord Jakobovits wrote the above long before that most tragic manifestation of right-wing religious fanaticism – the assassination of Prime Minister Rabin, which resulted mainly from the seditious opposition to the peace process with the Palestinians, incited by 'rabbis who cloak a message of hatred in the words of the Torah'.[7]

In connection with the faltering peace process and the pressures on the new Netanyahu government not to redeploy its forces from Hebron, I was not surprised at what the celebrated Israeli writer, Amos Oz, had to say in his article of 26 October 1996 published in *The Times*:

For 30 years, fundamentalist elements within the hawkish side of the Israeli spectrum have been reducing all of Judaism into a rite of Holy Places. A choir of fiery rabbis who have never bothered to utter a single note of Jewish morality about society's starving and homeless, its battered women, its justice or injustice, its compassion – these rabbis have condensed all of Jewishness into the holy tombs of the Patriarchs. They may well be responsible for alienating an entire generation of Israelis from their own Jewishness.

As the neurologist and writer, Professor Oliver Sacks, has said: 'I like the idea of a quiet religion – if that is not a contradiction in terms – which makes people behave decently and gives them a real psychological centre in their lives, whether based on an illusion or not.'[8]

Though I have now been out of Poland for more than 25 years I continue to speak Polish with my family, including those in Israel, with my Polish friends and former colleagues, and still feel the need to follow developments in Poland. At the same time I have a deep nostalgic interest in Jewish and particularly Israeli affairs. My wife and I have visited Israel on a number of occasions since 1974, particularly after my mother moved there from Paris in 1980.

My Family

I have been blessed with a loyal, sensible and conscientious wife who is a devoted and doting mother to our son. She has been a tremendous help to me in my endeavours. Our son Stefan, a graduate of Manchester University, with an upper-second class honours degree in psychology, now a computer specialist in London, married at 40 and now at long last we have the great joy of our first grandchild.

My close friend, the multi-lingual, erudite and very sociable Janek Gelbart emigrated from Poland with his wife Barbara (Basia) soon after we did. They settled in Stockholm where ever since he has been teaching mathematics in which he graduated in Romania. Throughout all these years we have remained in constant touch.

My brother Naftali had Hebraized his surname, along with some other members of the family, to Shimrat. The first to do so was Mendel's son Moshe, whose wife was a Bible scholar and found the name among the long list of names in Deuteronomy. Mendel himself and his brother Itzhak retained the name Sieradzki. Moshe, a mathematician, left Israel for the United States and Canada and became dean of the

Mathematics Department of the University of Michigan at Ann Arbor and professor at York University in Toronto.

After his return from Venezuela, my brother at first joined a large management consultancy firm, then established his own firm which collapsed during the 1973 Yom Kippur War when he rejoined the army for several months. One of the most exciting and dangerous assignments he ever had was as liaison officer at the ceasefire site in Sinai when he established close relations with the leaders of Egyptian and UN forces at the site, among them General Gamazi, later Egyptian minister of defence. Michael Binyon of *The Times*, reporting from the ceasefire site on 14 November 1973, wrote about Captain Naftali Shimrat: 'Bronzed, good-looking with long silver hair, he swaggered around like a John Wayne figure, clearly in control of the whole scene. He posed for cameramen, told the United Nations when to allow lorries through and came over with a smile to talk to journalists.' And the *Bangkok World* reported from Cairo on 24 November:

> 'The Israelis are often accused of not fitting into the Middle East, of being too 'Western', Captain Naftali Shimrat, the Israeli liaison officer at 101, a burly, attractive character who performed his early morning yoga exercises on the road itself, has done much to correct that image.
>
> Shimrat's Egyptian counterpart, Colonel Yusuf Mekki, an equally robust-looking figure whose spiritual nourishment was limited to nightly prayer in the privacy of his bunker, was hard-pressed to match him. The tussle soon became three-sided as the UN, increasingly tough-minded with the Secretary-General's personal backing, entered the fray.

After the war my brother re-established his business and developed a new field he calls business and social architecture, a specialized branch of management consultancy in which he is very successful.

First married in 1952, he was divorced four years later. His second wife and two children from that marriage did not return with him from Venezuela to Israel, although they were meant to join him there at the end of the school year. They now live in the United States. My brother lives in Tel Aviv with his third wife Philippa, hailing from Leeds in England, and their three teenage children.

Mother, after she moved to Israel, lived for several years in Ramat Hasharon in a flat she and the late Zineman had bought. She kept up a lively interest in world and specifically Jewish affairs by reading Yiddish and Polish-language newspapers and periodicals. She never learned Hebrew but got by with her Yiddish, Polish and often Russian. I remember her anger when in Israeli museums, including one devoted to the Holocaust, she found no facilities or explanations for Yiddish speakers. She was still happy to receive and accommodate guests, especially relatives from abroad. After she slipped in her flat and broke her hip, she needed full-time care and moved to an old people's home. She died in a Tel Aviv hospital in 1989, aged 90. On her tombstone we also engraved the details of Father's death.

November 1995

Notes

1 Leo Rosten, *Hooray for Yiddish!* (London: Elm Tree Books/Hamish Hamilton, 1983), p. 362.
2 *Jewish Chronicle*, 17 September 1993.
3 *Observer*, 15 January 1978.
4 *Jewish Chronicle*, 5 March 1993.
5 *Jewish Chronicle*, 4 February 1994.
6 Quoted in *Jewish Chronicle*, 18 August 1995, from Jeffrey M. Cohen (ed.), *Dear Chief Rabbi: From the Correspondence of Chief Rabbi Immanuel Jakobovits on Matters of Jewish Law, Ethics and Contemporary Issues, 1980–1990* (Ktav Publishing House).
7 *Jewish Chronicle*, 10 November 1995.
8 Interview in *Jewish Chronicle*, 10 February 1995.